THE REVELS PLAYS

Former general editors
Clifford Leech
F. David Hoeniger
E. A. J. Honigmann
J. R. Mulryne
Eugene M. Waith

General editors
David Bevington, Richard Dutton, Alison Findlay,
Helen Ostovich, and Martin White

THE FAMILY OF LOVE

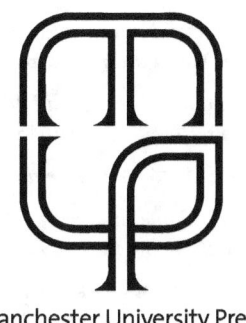

Manchester University Press

THE REVELS PLAYS

ANON *Thomas of Woodstock
or King Richard the Second, Part One*

BEAUMONT *The Knight of the Burning Pestle*

BEAUMONT AND FLETCHER *A King and No King
The Maid's Tragedy   Philaster, or Love Lies a-Bleeding*

CHAPMAN *All Fools*

CHAPMAN *Bussy d'Ambois   An Humorous Day's Mirth*

CHAPMAN, JONSON, MARSTON *Eastward Ho*

DEKKER *The Shoemaker's Holiday   Old Fortunatus*

FORD *Love's Sacrifice   The Lady's Trial*

HEYWOOD *The First and Second Parts of King Edward IV*

JONSON *The Alchemist   The Devil Is an Ass
Epicene, or The Silent Woman   Every Man In His Humour
Every Man Out of His Humour   The Magnetic Lady
The New Inn   Poetaster   Sejanus: His Fall
The Staple of News   Volpone*

LYLY *Campaspe* and *Sappho and Phao   Endymion
Galatea* and *Midas   Love's Metamorphosis
Mother Bombie   The Woman in the Moon*

MARLOWE *Doctor Faustus   Edward the Second
The Jew of Malta   Tamburlaine the Great*

MARSTON *Antonio and Mellida
Antonio's Revenge   The Malcontent*

MASSINGER *The Roman Actor*

MIDDLETON *A Game at Chess   Michaelmas Term
A Trick to Catch the Old One*

MIDDLETON AND DEKKER *The Roaring Girl*

MUNDAY AND OTHERS *Sir Thomas More*

PEELE *The Troublesome Reign of John, King of England
David and Bathsheba*

WEBSTER *The Duchess of Malfi*

Contents

LIST OF ILLUSTRATIONS	viii
GENERAL EDITORS' PREFACE	ix
ACKNOWLEDGEMENTS	xii
ABBREVIATIONS AND REFERENCES	xiv
INTRODUCTION	1
The text	1
Lording Barry: playwright, pirate, gentleman	9
The 'moment' of *The Family of Love*, 1605–06	13
The authorship debate	19
Sources and intertexts	23
Staging and stagecraft	29
The play	33
THE FAMILY OF LOVE	57
APPENDICES	
1 Marginal annotations in *The Familie of Love*	212
2 'Marstonian?' features of *The Family of Love* identified by Charles Cathcart	214
3 Representations of the Family of Love in *Basilicon Doron* and *The Displaying of an Horrible Sect*	215
INDEX	221

Illustrations

1. Sig. Av of *The Familie of Love* (1608), showing casting-copy method.   4
2. Woodcut of London porters accompanying 'A New Ballad, composed in commendation of the society, or company of the Porters' (1605).   16
3. Title page of *The Familie of Love* (1608), EEBO (The Huntington Library, San Marino, California).   58

General Editors' Preface

Clifford Leech conceived of the Revels Plays as a series in the mid-1950s, modelling the project on the New Arden Shakespeare. The aim, as he wrote in 1958, was 'to apply to Shakespeare's predecessors, contemporaries, and successors the methods that are now used in Shakespeare's editing'. The plays chosen were to include well-known works from the early Tudor period to about 1700, as well as others less familiar but of literary and theatrical merit. 'The plays included', Leech wrote, 'should be such as to deserve and indeed demand performance'. We owe it to Clifford Leech that the idea became reality. He set the high standards of the series, ensuring that editors of individual volumes produced work of lasting merit, equally useful for teachers and students, theatre directors and actors. Clifford Leech remained General Editor until 1971, and was succeeded by F. David Hoeniger, who retired in 1985.

Ever since then, the Revels Plays have been under the direction of four or five general editors: initially David Bevington, E.A.J. Honigmann, J.R. Mulryne, and E.M. Waith. E.A.J. Honigmann retired in 2000 and was succeeded by Richard Dutton. E.M. Waith retired in 2003 and was succeeded by Alison Findlay and Helen Ostovich. J.R. Mulryne retired in 2010. Published originally by Methuen, the series is now published by the Manchester University Press, embodying essentially the same format, scholarly character, and high editorial standards of the series as first conceived. The series now concentrates on plays from the period 1558–1642. Some slight changes have been made: for example, starting in 1996 each index lists proper names and topics in the introduction and commentary, whereas earlier indexes focused only on words and phrases for which the commentary provided a gloss. Notes to the introduction are now placed together at the end, not at the foot of, the page. Collation and commentary notes continue, however, to appear on the relevant pages.

The introduction to each Revels play undertakes to offer, among other matters, a critical appraisal of the play's significant themes and images, its poetic and verbal fascinations, its historical context, its characteristics as a piece for the theatre, and its uses of the stage for which it was designed. Stage history is an important part of the story. In addition, the introduction presents as lucidly as possible the criteria for choice of copy-text and the editorial methods employed in presenting the play to a modern reader. The introduction also considers the play's date and, where relevant, its sources, together with its place in the work of the author and in the theatre of its time. If the play is by an author not previously represented in the series, a brief biography is provided.

The text of each Revels play, in accordance with established practice in the series, is edited afresh from the original text of best authority (in a few instances, texts), in modern spelling and punctuation and with speech headings that are consistent throughout. Elisions in the original are also silently regularised, except where metre would be affected by the change. Emendations, as distinguished from modernized spellings and punctuation, are introduced only in instances where error is patent or at least very probable, and where the corrected reading is persuasive. Act divisions are given only if they appear in the original, or if the structure of the play clearly points to them. Those act and scene divisions not in the original are provided in small type. Square brackets are also used for any other additions to, or changes in, the stage directions of the original.

Rather than provide a comprehensive and historical variorum collation, Revels Plays editions focus on those variants which require the critical attention of serious textual students. All departures of substance from the copy-text are listed, including any significant relineation and those changes in punctuation which involve to any degree a decision between alternative interpretations. The collation notes do not include such accidentals as turned letters or changes in the font. Additions to stage directions are not noted in the collations, since those additions are already made clear by the use of brackets. On the other hand, press corrections in the copy-text are duly collated, as based on a careful consultation of as many copies of the original edition or editions as are needed to ensure that the printing history of those originals is accurately reported. Of later emendations of the text by subsequent editors, only those are reported which still deserve attention as alternative readings.

One of the hallmarks of the Revels Plays is the thoroughness of their annotations. Besides explaining the meanings of difficult words and passages, the annotations provide commentary on customs or usage, on the text, on stage business – indeed, on anything that can be pertinent and helpful. On occasion, when long notes are required and are too lengthy to fit comfortably at the foot of the page below the text, they are printed at the end of the complete text.

Appendices are used to present any commendatory poems on the dramatist and play in question, documents about the play's reception and contemporary history, classical sources, casting analyses, music, and any other relevant material.

Each volume contains an index to the commentary, in which particular attention is drawn to meanings for words not listed in the OED, and (starting in 1996, as indicated above) an indexing of proper names and topics in the introduction and commentary.

Our hope is that plays edited in this fashion will promote further scholarly and theatrical investigation of one of the richest periods in theatrical history.

DAVID BEVINGTON
RICHARD DUTTON
ALISON FINDLAY
HELEN OSTOVICH
MARTIN WHITE

Acknowledgements

I would not have tackled this prickly play without the encouragement and support of Helen Ostovich, whose knowledge and love of editing, and enthusiasm for early modern drama have been an inspiring example. At the outset I was blessed with two superb research assistants, Sally Hoare and Anya Banerjee, both of whom swiftly grasped what was interesting about *The Family of Love* and, through their efforts, helped me to realise it.

I offer heartfelt thanks to Michael Wright who gave unstintingly of his time and expertise in things technical, dialectical, linguistic and literary. Stephanie Hollis give moral support and uplift with delicious lunches. My thanks to friends and colleagues who answered queries, provided references, read drafts, and lent ongoing support to the project: Hannah August, Lisa Bailey, Tom Bishop, Alecia Bland, Rob Conkie, John Davidson, Murray Edmond, Elaine Hobby, Peter Holland, Mark Houlahan, Mac Jackson, Claudia Marquis, Michael Neill, Roger Nicholson, Sarah Ross, Jonathan Scott, and Sarah Shieff. Ruth Barton generously read and commented on the Introduction at a crucial stage. I am grateful to participants in two meetings of the Shakespeare Association of America where I presented work in progress, especially Kurt Daw and Doug King in a workshop on 'Editing for Performance' in New Orleans in 2016, and Martin Butler and M. J. Kidnie in the seminar on 'John Marston: New Directions', in Atlanta in 2018. Brett Greatley-Hirsch, of Digital Renaissance Editions, deserves special thanks for his 'Keep Calm and Lording Barry On' postcard.

I am indebted to librarians at the University of Auckland General Library for their kindness and professionalism, especially to Elizabeth Evans, Mark Hangartner, for supporting a subscription to the invaluable *Lexicons of Early Modern English* database, Annette Keogh, and Jo Birks in Special Collections. During a period working at the Huntington Library in Pasadena I had the good fortune to receive the expert assistance of Sue Hodson, Stephen Tabor, and Mary Robertson.

I am grateful to colleagues who have generously shared their unpublished work on Lording Barry: Darren Freebury-Jones,

ACKNOWLEDGEMENTS

Marina Tarlinskaja, and Marcus Dahl, Mac Jackson, and Sarah Scott. I would also like to express my thanks to Malcom Campbell, Head of the School of Humanities at the University of Auckland, for his understanding and support, and to the University of Auckland for granting me two periods of sabbatical leave during the time I was working on the play.

Thanks are due to the Revels Plays production team, especially my copy-editor Andrew Kirk and Lianne Slavin. I greatly appreciate Matthew Frost's enduring support for the edition.

Lastly to Peter Haynes and Felix, our son. They have been part of this project from its inception, at home and *in utero*. Peter has played manifold parts: research assistant, genealogist, biographer, spouse, and father, with admirable good grace. *Vi ringrazio con tutto il mio cuore.*

Abbreviations and References

ABBREVIATIONS

ch	chapter
EEBO	*Early English Books Online*
Epil	Epilogue
Ind	Induction
n	note (follows line number)
Q	Quarto
Qc	corrected copies of Q
Qu	uncorrected copies of Q
Prol	Prologue
perf	performed
pub	published
SD	stage direction
SH	speech heading
subst	substantially

Quotations and line references from Shakespeare's plays and poems are cited from *The Norton Shakespeare*, gen. ed. Stephen Greenblatt (New York: W.W. Norton, 2016); titles are abbreviated according to the usual Revels conventions. Quotations and references from Jonson's works are cited from the *Cambridge Edition of the Works of Ben Jonson*, ed. David Bevington, Martin Butler, and Ian Donaldson (Cambridge: Cambridge University Press, 2012) and are abbreviated according to the conventions used therein. Unless otherwise noted, information relating to the dates and auspices of plays derives from the six-volume *British Drama 1533–1642: A Catalogue* (Oxford: Oxford University Press, 2012–15). References are to volume and page number. References to Classical texts derive from the online edition of the Loeb Classical Library, unless otherwise noted.

JOURNALS

ANQ	*A Quarterly Journal of Short Articles, Notes, and Reviews*
ET	*Early Theatre*

JBS Journal of British Studies
JEGP Journal of English and German Philology
JMRS Journal of Medieval and Renaissance Studies
MaRDiE Medieval and Renaissance Drama in England
MLN Modern Language Notes
MLR Modern Language Review
PBSA Publications of the Bibliographical Society of America
PLL Papers on Language and Literature
PQ Philological Quarterly
N&Q Notes and Queries, new series
RD Renaissance Drama
RES Review of English Studies
RQ Renaissance Quarterly
SB Shakespeare Bulletin
SP Studies in Philology
SQ Shakespeare Quarterly
TAPS Transactions of the American Philosophical Society
TJ Theatre Journal

EDITIONS OF *THE FAMILY OF LOVE* COLLATED

Q (H1) Henry E. Huntington Library, California, 62604 (STC 17879)
Q (H2) Henry E. Huntington Library, California, KD292 (STC 17879a)
Q (SHL) Senate House Library, London
Q (HRC1) Wrenn Wh M584 / 608fa / WRE, Harry Ransom Humanities Research Center, University of Texas at Austin
Q (HRC2) Pforzheimer Collection, PFORZ 694, Harry Ransom Humanities Research Center, University of Texas at Austin
Q (Bod.) Bodleian Library, Oxford University
Bullen *The Family of Love*, in *The Works of Thomas Middleton*, ed. A.H. Bullen, 8 vols (London: John C. Nimmo, 1885–86), 3.1120
Cleary Thomas Dekker, with Thomas Middleton, *The Family of Love, 1603–1607*, ed. Chris Cleary, *Works of Thomas Dekker, Luminarium: Anthology of English Literature*, 1995; http://www.tech.org/~cleary/famil.html

	ABBREVIATIONS AND REFERENCES
Dillon	'Thomas Middleton, *The Family of Love*, a Critical, Old-Spelling Edition', ed. Andrew Dillon, PhD dissertation, New York University, 1968
Dyce	*The Family of Love* in *The Works of Thomas Middleton*, ed. Alexander Dyce, 5 vols (London: Edward Lumley, 1840), 2.1209
Shepherd	*The Family of Love*, attrib. Thomas Middleton, ed. Simon Shepherd (Nottingham: Nottingham University Press, 1979)

PRIMARY TEXTS

Arber	Edward Arber (ed.), *A Transcript of the Registers of the Company of Stationers of London, 1554–1640* (1876) (New York, repr. 1950)
Beaumont, *KBP*	Francis Beaumont, *The Knight of the Burning Pestle*, ed. Sheldon P. Zitner (1984) (Manchester: Manchester University Press, rev. edn, 2004)
Bible	*The Geneva Bible: A Facsimile of the 1560 Edition* (Madison, WI: University of Wisconsin Press, 1969)
Bowers, *B&F*	Francis Beaumont and John Fletcher, *Dramatic Works in the Beaumont and Fletcher Canon*, ed. Fredson Bowers, 10 vols (Cambridge: Cambridge University Press, 1966–96)
Chaucer	*The Riverside Chaucer*, 3rd edn, gen. ed. Larry Benson (Oxford: Oxford University Press, 1987)
Corbin and Sedge	Lording Barry, *Ram Alley, or Merry Tricks*, ed. Peter Corbin and Douglas Sedge (Nottingham: Nottingham University Press, 1981)
Davies	*The Poems of Sir John Davies*, ed. Robert Krueger (Oxford: Clarendon Press, 1975)
Dekker, *Blurt*	*A Critical Old-Spelling Edition of Thomas Dekker's Blurt, Master Constable (1602)*, ed. Thomas L. Berger (Salzburg: Institute for

	English and American Studies, University of Salzburg, 1979)
De Lorris	Guillaume de Lorris and Jean de Meun, *The Romance of the Rose*, trans. Harry W. Robbins (New York: E.P. Dutton, 1962)
Displaying	J.[ohn] R.[ogers], *The Displaying of an Horrible Sect of Gross and Wicked Heretics, naming themselves the Family of Love*, 1578 (1579 edn)
Donne, *Poems*	*The Poems of John Donne*, ed. Robin Robbins, vol. 1 (Harlow: Longman, 2008)
Dutton, *Epicene*	Ben Jonson, *Epicene, or The Silent Woman*, ed. Richard Dutton (Manchester: Manchester University Press, 2003)
Fraser, '*Ram Alley*'	Robert Duncan Fraser, '*Ram Alley, or Merry Tricks* (Lording Barry, 1611): A Critical Edition', DPhil thesis, University of Sussex, 2013
Fuller	Thomas Fuller, *The History of the University of Cambridge*, in Fuller, *The Church History of Britain* (London, 1655)
Kyd, *SpT*	Thomas Kyd, *The Spanish Tragedy*, ed. Philip Edwards (Manchester: Manchester University Press, 1959)
Lyly	John Lyly, *Gallathea*, ed. G.K. Hunter (Manchester: Manchester University Press, 2000)
Marlowe, *Plays*	Christopher Marlowe, *Doctor Faustus and Other Plays*, ed. David Bevington and Eric Rasmussen (Oxford: Oxford University Press, 1995)
Marlowe, *Poems*	Christopher Marlowe, *Collected Poems*, ed. Patrick Cheney and Brian J. Striar (Oxford: Oxford University Press, 2006)
Marston, *Dutch C*	John Marston, *The Dutch Courtesan*, ed. Karen Britland (London: Bloomsbury, 2018)
Marston, *Faun*	John Marston, *Parasitaster, or The Faun*, ed. David A. Blostein (Manchester: Manchester University Press, 1978)

Marston, *JDE*	John Marston, *Jack Drum's Entertainment*, ed. John S. Farmer (1912) (New York: AMS Press, 1970)
Marston, *Poems*	*Poems of John Marston*, ed. Arnold Davenport (Liverpool: Liverpool University Press, 1961)
May Day	George Chapman, *May Day*, ed. Robert F. Welsh, in *The Plays of George Chapman: The Comedies*, ed. Allan Holaday (Urbana, IL: University of Illinois Press, 1970)
Middleton, *Collected*	*Thomas Middleton: The Collected Works*, gen. eds Gary Taylor and John Lavagnino (Oxford: Oxford University Press, 2007)
Middleton, *Trick*	Thomas Middleton, *A Trick to Catch the Old One*, ed. Paul A. Mulholland (Manchester: Manchester University Press, 2013)
Moore Smith	*Club Law: A Comedy*, ed. G.C. Moore Smith (Cambridge: Cambridge University Press, 1907)
NHo!	Thomas Dekker and John Webster, *Northward Ho!*, in *The Dramatic Works of Thomas Dekker*, ed. Fredson Bowers, 4 vols (Cambridge: Cambridge University Press, 1953–61)
Niclaes, *Prophecy*	N.[iclaes], H.[endrik], *The Prophecy of the Spirit of Love. Set forth by H.N: And by him perused anew and more distinctly declared. Translated out of base-almayne into English* (Cologne, c. 1574)
Ostovich	Ben Jonson, *Every Man Out of His Humour*, ed. Helen Ostovich (Manchester: Manchester University Press, 2001)
Overbury	Thomas Overbury (and Others), *Characters*, ed. Donald Beecher (Ottawa, Ont.: Dovehouse, 2003)
Ovid	Ovid, *Metamorphoses*, trans. Frank Justus Miller, 2 vols (1916) (London: Heinemann, 1951)
SM	John Marston, *The Selected Plays of John Marston*, ed. MacD. P. Jackson and Michael

	Neill (Cambridge: Cambridge University Press, 1986)
Stubbes	Philip Stubbes, *The Anatomie of Abuses*, ed. M.J. Kidnie (Tempe, AZ: Renaissance English Text Society, 2002)
WHo!	Thomas Dekker and John Webster, *Westward Ho!*, in *The Dramatic Works of Thomas Dekker*, ed. Fredson Bowers, 4 vols (Cambridge: Cambridge University Press, 1953–61)

SECONDARY WORKS

Abbott	E.A. Abbott, *A Shakespearian Grammar*, 3rd edn (1870) (New York: Dover Publications, 1966)
Adams	J.Q. Adams, *Shakespearean Playhouses* (Gloucester, MA: P. Smith, 1960)
Altieri	Joanne Altieri, 'Pregnant Puns and Sectarian Rhetoric: Middleton's *Family of Love*', *Mosaic* 23 (1989), 45–57
Bald, 'Chronology'	R.C. Bald, 'The Chronology of Middleton's Plays', *MLR* 32 (1937), 33–43
Bald, 'Sources'	R.C. Bald, 'The Sources of Middleton's City Comedies', *JEGP* 33 (1934), 373–87
BD	Martin Wiggins and Catherine Richardson, *British Drama 1533–1642: A Catalogue*, 6 vols (Oxford: Oxford University Press, 2012–15)
Bentley	G.E. Bentley, *The Profession of Dramatist in Shakespeare's Time 1590–1642* (Princeton, NJ: Princeton University Press, 1971)
Bly	Mary Bly, *Queer Virgins and Virgin Queans on the Early Modern Stage* (Oxford: Oxford University Press, 2000)
Boose	Lynda E. Boose, 'Scolding Brides and Bridling Scolds: Taming the Woman's Unruly Member', *SQ* 42 (1991), 179–213
Brooks	Douglas A. Brooks, *From Playhouse to Printing House: Drama and Authorship in Early Modern England* (Cambridge: Cambridge University Press, 2000)

Bullough	Geoffrey Bullough, *Narrative and Dramatic Sources of Shakespeare*, vol. 8 (London: Routledge and Kegan Paul, 1975)
Cathcart, '*Club Law*'	Charles Cathcart, '*Club Law*, The Family of Love and the Familist Sect', *N&Q* 50 (2003), 658
Cathcart, *Marston*	Charles Cathcart, *Marston, Rivalry, Rapprochement, and Jonson* (Aldershot: Ashgate, 2008)
CCM	*Thomas Middleton and Early Modern Textual Culture: A Companion to the Collected Works*, ed. Gary Taylor and John Lavagnino (Oxford: Oxford University Press, 2007)
Chakravorty	Swapan Chakravorty, *Society and Politics in the Plays of Thomas Middleton* (Oxford: Clarendon Press, 1996)
Chalfant	Fran C. Chalfant, *Ben Jonson's London: A Jacobean Placename Dictionary* (Athens, GA: University of Georgia Press, 1978)
Chambers	E.K. Chambers, *The Elizabethan Stage*, 4 vols (Oxford: Oxford University Press, 1923)
Clubb	Louise George Clubb, *Giambattista Della Porta, Dramatist* (Princeton, NJ: Princeton University Press, 1965)
Davidson	Clifford Davidson, 'Middleton and the Family of Love', *English Miscellany* 20 (1969), 81–92
Dent	R. W. Dent, *Proverbial Language in English Drama Excluding Shakespeare, 1495–1616: An Index* (Berkeley, CA: University of California Press, 1984)
DSD	Alan C. Dessen and Leslie Thomson, *A Dictionary of Stage Directions in English Drama, 1580–1642* (Cambridge: Cambridge University Press, 1999)
Duncan	Helga L. Duncan, '"The Hole in the Wall": Sacred Space and "Third Space" in *The Family of Love*', *ET* 15 (2012), 167–79
Dutton, 'Birth'	Richard Dutton, 'The Birth of the Author', in Cedric C. Brown and Arthur F. Marotti

	(eds), *Texts and Cultural Change in Early Modern England* (Basingstoke: Macmillan, 1997), 153–78
Dutton, *Mastering*	Richard Dutton, *Mastering the Revels: The Regulation and Censorship of English Renaissance Drama* (Iowa City, IA: University of Iowa Press, 1991)
EPT	*English Professional Theatre, 1530–1660*, ed. G. Wickham, H. Berry and W. Ingram (Cambridge: Cambridge University Press, 2000)
Ewen	C.L'Estrange Ewen, *Lording Barry: Poet and Pirate* (privately printed, 1938)
Ewing	Elizabeth Ewing, *Dress and Undress: A History of Women's Underwear* (1978) (London: Batsford, repr. 1981)
Fisher	Margery Fisher, 'Notes on the Sources of Some Incidents in Middleton's London Plays', *RES* 15 (1939), 283–93
Fraser, 'Lording Barry'	Duncan Fraser, 'Lording Barry: Dramatist, Pirate — and Dramatis Persona?', *ANQ* 28 (2015), 74–8
Freebury-Jones, Tarlinskaja, and Dahl	Darren Freebury-Jones, Marina Tarlinskaja, and Marcus Dahl, 'The Boundaries of John Marston's Dramatic Canon', *MaRDiE* 31 (2018), 43–77
George	David George, 'Thomas Middleton's Sources: A Survey', *N&Q* 18 (1971), 17–24
Greg	W.W. Greg, *A Bibliography of the English Printed Drama to the Restoration*, 4 vols (London: Bibliographical Society at the University Press, Oxford, 1939–59)
Gurr	Andrew Gurr, *The Shakespearian Playing Companies* (Oxford: Clarendon Press, 1996)
Heinemann	Margot Heinemann, *Puritanism and Theatre: Thomas Middleton and Opposition Drama under the Early Stuarts* (Cambridge: Cambridge University Press, 1980)
Hillebrand	H.N. Hillebrand, *The Child Actors: A Chapter in Elizabethan Stage History* (1926) (New York: Russell and Russell, repr. 1964)

Hope	Jonathan Hope, *Shakespeare's Grammar* (London: Arden Shakespeare, 2003)
Ingram	William Ingram, 'The Playhouse as an Investment, 1607–1614: Thomas Woodford and Whitefriars', *MaRDiE* 2 (1985), 209–30
Kinney	Arthur F. Kinney (ed.), *A Companion to Renaissance Drama* (Malden, MA: Blackwell, 2002)
Lake	David J. Lake, *The Canon of Thomas Middleton's Plays: Internal Evidence for the Major Problems of Authorship* (Cambridge: Cambridge University Press, 1975)
Lawrence	W.J. Lawrence, *Pre-Restoration Stage Studies* (Cambridge, MA: Harvard University Press, 1927)
Leggatt	Alexander Leggatt, *Citizen Comedy in the Age of Shakespeare* (Toronto: University of Toronto Press, 1973)
Leinwand	Theodore B. Leinwand, *The City Staged: Jacobean Comedy, 1603–1613* (Madison, WI: University of Wisconsin Press, 1986)
LEME	*Lexicons of Early Modern English*, ed. Ian Lancashire (Toronto: University of Toronto Press, 2018–), https://leme.library.utoronto.ca
Levin	Richard Levin, *The Multiple Plot in English Renaissance Drama* (Chicago: University of Chicago Press, 1971)
Linthicum	M. Channing Linthicum, *Costume in the Drama of Shakespeare and his Contemporaries* (1936) (New York: Hacker Art Books, rev. edn, 1972)
Loewenstein	David Loewenstein, *Treacherous Faith: The Specter of Heresy in Early Modern English Literature and Culture* (Oxford: Oxford University Press, 2013)
Lopez, *Convention*	Jeremy Lopez, *Theatrical Convention and Audience Response in Early Modern Drama* (Cambridge: Cambridge University Press, 2003)

Lopez, 'Whitefriars'	Jeremy Lopez, 'Success the Whitefriars Way: *Ram Alley* and the Negative Force of Acting', *RD* 38 (2010), 199–224
Love	Harold Love, *Attributing Authorship: An Introduction* (Cambridge: Cambridge University Press, 2002)
MacIntyre	Jean MacIntyre, 'Production Resources at the Whitefriars Playhouse, 1609–1612', *EMLS* 2.3 (1996), #1–35
Marotti	Arthur F. Marotti, 'The Purgations of Middleton's *The Family of Love*', *PLL* 7 (1971), 80–4
Marsh, *FLES*	Christopher W. Marsh, *The Family of Love in English Society, 1550–1630* (Cambridge: Cambridge University Press, 1994)
Marsh, 'Heresy'	Christopher Marsh, '"Godlie Matrons" and "Loose-bodied Dames": Heresy and Gender in the Family of Love', in David Loewenstein and John Marshall (eds), *Heresy, Literature and Politics in Early Modern English Culture* (Cambridge: Cambridge University Press, 2007), 59–81
Martin	J.W. Martin, 'Elizabethan Familists and English Separatism', *JBS* 20 (1980), 53–73
Maxwell, 'Date'	Baldwin Maxwell, 'A Note on the Date of Middleton's *The Family of Love*', in E.J. West (ed.), *Elizabethan Studies and Other Essays in Honor of George F. Reynolds* (Boulder, CO: Colorado University Press, 1945), 195–200
Maxwell, 'Twenty Good-Nights'	Baldwin Maxwell, '"Twenty Good-Nights": *The Knight of the Burning Pestle* and Middleton's *Family of Love*', *MLN* 63 (1948), 23–37
McKerrow	Ronald B. McKerrow, *Printers and Publishers' Devices in England and Scotland 1485–1640* (1913) (London: Bibliographical Society, repr. 1949)
Miola	Robert S. Miola, 'Seven Types of Intertextuality', in Michèle Marrapodi (ed.), *Shakespeare, Italy, and Intertextuality*

	(Manchester: Manchester University Press, 2004), 13–25
Moss, 'English Critics'	Jean D. Moss, '*The Family of Love* and English Critics', *Sixteenth Century Journal* 6 (1975), 35–52
Moss, 'Godded with God'	Jean D. Moss, '"Godded with God": Hendrik Niclaes and His Family of Love', *TAPS* 71 (1981), 1–89
Munro, 'Printed Comedy'	Lucy Munro, 'Reading Printed Comedy: Edward Sharpham's *The Fleer*', in Marta Straznicky (ed.), *The Book of the Play: Playwrights, Stationers, and Readers in Early Modern England* (Amherst, MA: University of Massachusetts Press, 2006), 39–58
Munro, 'Whitefriars'	Lucy Munro, 'The Whitefriars Theatre and the Children's Companies', in Julie Sanders (ed.), *Ben Jonson in Context* (Cambridge: Cambridge University Press, 2010), 116–23
OCD	*Oxford Classical Dictionary*, gen. eds Simon Hornblower and Anthony Spawforth, 4th edn (Oxford: Oxford University Press, 2012)
ODNB	*Oxford Dictionary of National Biography* (Oxford: Oxford University Press, 2020–)
Olive	W.J. Olive, 'Imitation of Shakespeare in Middleton's *The Family of Love*', *PQ* 29 (1950), 758
Partridge	Eric Partridge, *Shakespeare's Bawdy* (London: Routledge, new edn, 2001)
Paster, 'Humor'	Gail Kern Paster, 'The Humor of It: Bodies, Fluids, and Social Discipline in Shakespearean Comedy', in Richard C. Dutton and Jean E. Howard (eds), *A Companion to Shakespeare's Works*, vol. 3, *The Comedies* (Malden, MA: Blackwell, 2003), 47–66
Paster, 'Purgation'	Gail Kern Paster, 'Purgation as the Allure of Mastery: Early Modern Medicine and the Technology of the Self', in Lena Cowen Orlin (ed.), *Material London, ca. 1600*

	(Philadelphia: University of Pennsylvania Press, 2000), 193–205
Poole	Kristen Poole, *Radical Religion from Shakespeare to Milton: Figures of Nonconformity in Early Modern England* (Cambridge: Cambridge University Press, 2000)
Rubright	Marjorie Rubright, *Doppelgänger Dilemmas: Anglo-Dutch Relations in Early Modern English Literature and Culture* (Philadelphia: University of Pennsylvania Press, 2014)
Schmidt	A. Schmidt, *Shakespeare Lexicon and Quotation Dictionary*, 2 vols, rev. G. Sarrazin (New York: Dover Publications, 1971)
Scott	Sarah K. Scott, '"Modern for the times": Lording Barry, Christopher Marlowe, and Ovid', *SEL* 60 (2020), 347–64
Shapiro	Michael Shapiro, *Children of the Revels: The Boy Companies of Shakespeare's Time and Their Plays* (New York: Columbia University Press, 1977)
Shepherd, *Amazons*	Simon Shepherd, *Amazons and Warrior Women: Varieties of Feminism in Seventeenth-Century Drama* (Brighton: Harvester Press, 1981)
Smith	Nigel Smith, *Perfection Proclaimed: Language and Literature in English Radical Religion, 1640–1660* (Oxford: Clarendon Press, 1989)
Spufford	Margaret Spufford, *Small Books and Pleasant Histories: Popular Fiction and its Readership in Seventeenth-Century England* (London: Methuen, 1981)
Stern	Tiffany Stern, *Documents of Performance in Early Modern England* (Cambridge: Cambridge University Press, 2009)
Sugden	E.H. Sugden, *Topographical Dictionary to the Works of Shakespeare and his Fellow Dramatists* (Manchester: University Press of Manchester, 1925)

Taylor, Mulholland, and Jackson	Gary Taylor, Paul Mulholland, and MacD. P. Jackson, 'Thomas Middleton, Lording Barry, and *The Family of Love*', *PBSA* 93 (1999), 213–41
Tilley	M.P. Tilley, *A Dictionary of the Proverbs in England in the Sixteenth and Seventeenth Centuries* (Ann Arbor, MI: University of Michigan Press, 1950)
Tomlinson, 'Actress'	Sophie Tomlinson, 'The Actress and Baroque Aesthetic Effects in Renaissance Drama', *SB* 33 (2015), 67–82
Tomlinson, 'Jacobean'	Sophie Tomlinson, 'A Jacobean Dramatic Usage of "Actress"', *N&Q* 253 (2008), 282–3
Tylus	Jane Tylus, 'Women at the Windows: Commedia dell'arte and Theatrical Practice in Early Modern Italy', *TJ* 49 (1997), 323–42
Wickham	Glynne Wickham, *Early English Stages, 1300–1660*, vol. 2, *1576–1660* (London: Routledge and Kegan Paul, 1972)
Williams, *Dictionary*	Gordon Williams, *A Dictionary of Sexual Language and Imagery in Shakespearean and Stuart Literature*, 3 vols (New Jersey: Athlone Press, 1994). References are to volume number and page
Williams, *Glossary*	Gordon Williams, *A Glossary of Shakespeare's Sexual Language* (New Jersey: Athlone Press, 1997)

Introduction

THE TEXT

The Family of Love (*FoL*) was published anonymously in a single quarto edition in 1608 (Q). The entry in the Stationers' Register for 1607 reads:

> 12 October
>
> John Browne John Helme / Entered for their copy under the hands of Sir George Buck and the wardens a play called *The Family of Love as it hath been lately acted by the Children of his Majesty's Revels.* vj d.[1]

Unlike Barry's other play, *Ram Alley*, *FoL* was not available again in printed form until the nineteenth century.[2] Following the editions of Dyce and Bullen, the play was published in the Mermaid Series, edited by Havelock Ellis with an introduction by Algernon Swinburne (1887), in the Nottingham Drama Texts series, edited by Simon Shepherd (1979), and on the Luminarium website as part of the collaborative works of Thomas Dekker, edited by Chris Cleary (1995). The only full scholarly edition of *FoL* is an unpublished, critical, old-spelling edition by Andrew Dillon, which presents it as an early play by Middleton (1968). Dillon collated the seventeen extant copies of Q, including one in private ownership. For this edition, I examined six copies of Q: two at the Huntington Library, two in the collection of the Harry Ransom Center at the University of Texas at Austin, the copy in the Senate House Library, London, and the copy in the Bodleian Library, Oxford. As one would expect, Dillon found a larger number of variants, yet none of the variants discovered in copies examined solely by Dillon is substantive. My copy-text is the Huntington copy of Q owned by the actor John Philip Kemble. With the exception of the Prologue, the last line of which is illegible due to insufficient inking, this is the more complete of the Huntington Library's two copies, although it has cropped running titles and several holes.[3] While I draw on Dillon's analysis of the printing of Q, however, the reattribution of *FoL* to Barry, developments in textual scholarship and theatre history over the last fifty years, together with my own findings, require a reconsideration of the play as a material text.

Through his bibliographic analysis of the quarto, Dillon deduced that *The Family of Love* was printed by Richard Bradock. Bradock printed only two other plays, both of them in 1607–08: John Day's *Humour Out of Breath*, also performed by the King's Revels Children, and Middleton's *A Yorkshire Tragedy*, attributed on the title page to 'W. Shakspeare'. Dillon grouped *FoL* with five Middleton comedies 'that were thrown on the market in 1607 and in 1608 as a consequence of the troubles from which the children's companies suffered around the years 1606–8'.[4] Yet *FoL* is distinguished from the Middleton plays by virtue of its being 'the work of a printing house that did not usually print plays'.[5] While *FoL* is not by Middleton, it shares in common with that group of plays the likelihood, put forward by Mary Bly, that the Whitefriars management's 'turn[ing] *The Family of Love* over to the Stationers' Register [was] a move ... influenced by financial duress'.[6]

Dillon found three reasons for assigning the play to Bradock: 'the use of a printer's device on the title page, the appearance of a headpiece on sig. A2r, and the appearance of a badly bent letter [JJ]'.[7] A fourth factor not noted by Dillon is Bradock's use of Latin act and scene divisions, and Latin designations of the ends of acts in both the *FoL* and the *Humour Out of Breath* quartos. While the quarto of *Humour Out of Breath* uses Latin consistently to mark act divisions, the *FoL* quarto is less methodical. Act 3 marks only the first and fourth scenes, and only the first three acts terminate with '*Finis Actus*'.[8] The culminating scene is headed '*Act.5. Scoena ultima*', as if in recognition of the play's virtuoso finale. No such heading appears in *Humour Out of Breath*.

Bradock's quarto of *FoL* comprises eighteen unnumbered leaves, collating A–I3. The title page names no author, but credits the performance to the Children of the King's Revels, a company of boy actors that flourished for a period of about twelve months between 1607 and 1608.[9] On my copy-text's title page, two scribal annotations attribute the play to Middleton. The Latin epigraph 'To the Reader' ('*Lectori*') derives from Eclogue 5 of *Adulescentia* [*Youth*], by Baptista Mantuanus, entitled 'The treatment of poets by rich men'. 'Mantuan' (1447–1516), as he was known in English, was an Italian Carmelite reformer whose eclogues attacking the papal Curia were a popular teaching text in Protestant England and on the Continent. In Eclogue 5, Candidus, an impoverished poet, pleads with a rich shepherd, Silvanus, for patronage. The cited verses run: '*Sidera iungamus, facito mihi Iuppiter adsit,* / *Et tibi Mercurius noster dabit omnia faxo*' (Let us unite our stars then; make Jupiter be favourable to me and I will cause [our] Mercury to grant you all his gifts). Mercury, god of eloquence (and thieves), stands for the playwright and actors.[10] The title page names the play's printer as John Helmes, even while the material evidence points to the text as Bradock's work. The Stationers' Register assigns *FoL* to Helme and John Browne, both of whom had shops in St Dunstans. Rights to the play were transferred to one W. Washington by Anne Helms, John's widow, in 1627, but the play was not reprinted until Dyce's edition of 1840.

The printer's device showing an eagle carrying an eaglet was used by Bradock from 1600 to 1615; it also appears on the title page of *A Yorkshire Tragedy* (1608). Ronald McKerrow suggests that the eagle is forcing the eaglet 'to gaze at the sun as a test whether it is worthy to be reared', a potential analogue for Barry's first foray into print. The scrollwork at the bottom of the device bears the phrase '*Sic crede*' ('so believe').[11]

On the verso of the title page the printer has squeezed the two-column '*Actorum Nomina*' between 'To the Reader' and '*PROLOGUS*' (figure 1). This extreme economising on space, together with the misplacement of the name 'Mistress Glister' beside rather than underneath the rubric '*Weomen*', provides evidence of the compositors having used the casting-copy method in setting the type. The appearance of the second song sung by the gallant, Lipsalve, on B2v supports this hypothesis. Whereas Lipsalve's first song is printed in italics, indented, and lineated correctly (A3v), his second, longer song is printed in roman, with two lines of song to one line of type, rendering it more like prose (B2v). Dillon notes that 'The advantage of [the casting-copy] method is that the play can be printed more quickly.'[12] This significant point favours Bly's conjecture that the play's publication was influenced by the financial troubles of the fledgling company.

The Prologue printed on Av contains only 15 lines, but is written in the standard rhyming couplets. Thus its opening four lines are metrically unorthodox, rhyming ABBC. One might deduce that the Prologue's first line is missing from all copies of Q, as do W.W. Greg and Dillon; alternatively Barry may have been struggling, or experimenting, with literary form.[13] The rhyming of 'merits / spirits' in lines 4–5 is inverted as 'spirits / merits' in lines 8–9. The end word

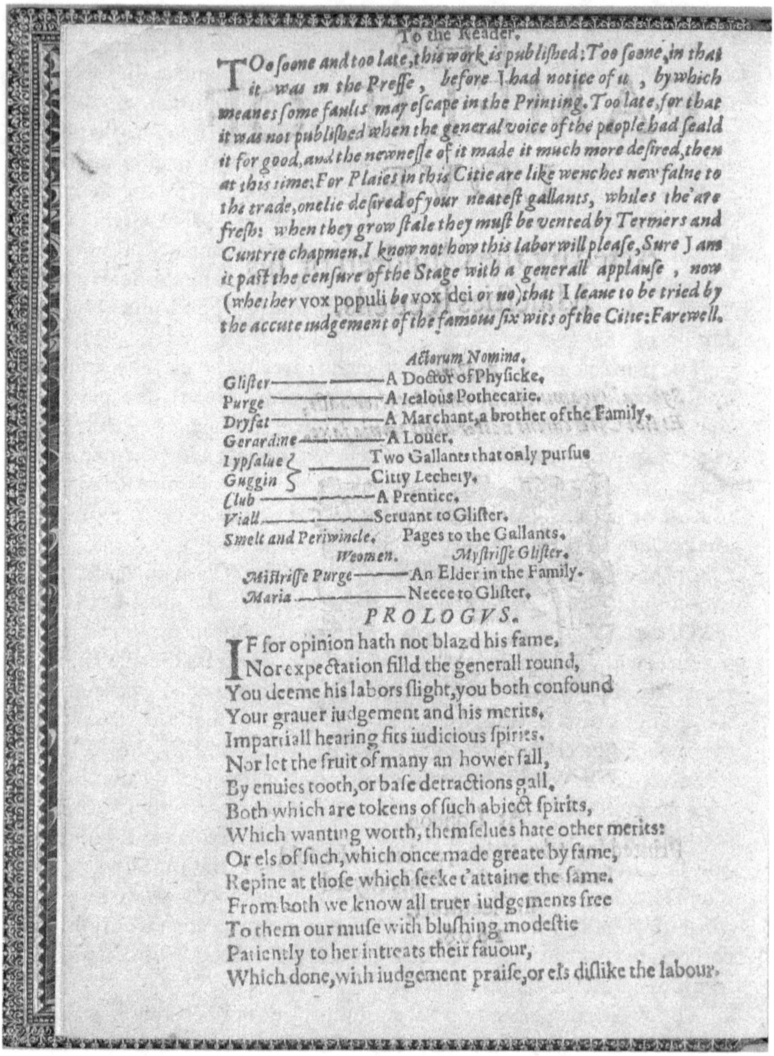

To the Reader.

Too soone and too late, this work is published: Too soone, in that it was in the Presse, before I had notice of it, by which meanes some faults may escape in the Printing. Too late, for that it was not published when the generall voice of the people had seald it for good, and the newnesse of it made it much more desired, then at this time. For Plaies in this Citie are like wenches new falne to the trade, onelie desired of your neatest gallants, whiles the'are fresh: when they grow stale they must be vented by Termers and Cuntrie chapmen. I know not how this labor will please, Sure I am it past the censure of the Stage with a generall applause, now (whether vox populi be vox dei or no) that I leaue to be tried by the accute iudgement of the famous six wits of the Citie: Farewell.

Actorum Nomina.

Glister ———— A Doctor of Physicke.
Purge ———— A Iealous Pothecarie.
Dryfat ———— A Marchant, a brother of the Family.
Gerardine ———— A Louer.
Lypsalue ⎱ ———— Two Gallants that onely pursue
Guggin ⎰ ———— City Lechery.
Club ———— A Prentice.
Viall ———— Seruant to Glister.
Smelt and Periwincle, Pages to the Gallants.

Weomen. Mystrisse Glister.

Mistrisse Purge ———— An Elder in the Family.
Maria ———— Neece to Glister.

PROLOGVS.

IF for opinion hath not blazd his fame,
Nor expectation filld the generall round,
You deeme his labors slight, you both confound
Your grauer iudgement and his merits,
Impartiall hearing fits iudicious spirits.
Nor let the fruit of many an hower fall,
By enuies tooth, or base detractions gall,
Both which are tokens of such abiect spirits,
Which wanting worth, themselues hate other merits:
Or els of such, which once made greate by fame,
Repine at those which seeke t'attaine the same.
From both we know all truer iudgements free
To them our muse with blushing modestie
Patiently to her intreats their fauour,
Which done, with iudgement praise, or els dislike the labour.

Figure 1 Sig. Av of *The Familie of Love* (1608), call mark 62604, The Huntington Library, San Marino, California. Sig. Av suggests that the compositors used the casting-copy method of setting type.

INTRODUCTION 5

'fame' from line 1 is repeated in line 10 and rhymed with 'same' in the following line. Repetition of words in close proximity and reiteration of words in proximal forms are Barryisms visible throughout *FoL*.[14] In one striking case the reading of Q diverges from this stylistic trend. In his speech at the start of 4.4, Lipsalve tells Gudgeon how a stranger pre-empted his attempt to seduce Mistress Purge at the Familist meeting. His self-description as 'ready to have feared th'expected prize' (4.4.6) was emended by Dyce and subsequent editors to 'have *seized* th'expected prize'. As 'seized' occurs six lines later, one could argue on the grounds of authorial uninventiveness that 'seized' is more likely to have been the word written. Dillon postulates that a compositor took the 'z' of 'seiz'd' for an 'r' and the long 's' for an 'f'.[15] However, the act of 'fearing' or inspiring with terror a woman perceived as a 'prize' by Lipsalve is redolent of the libertine ethos critiqued by the hero Gerardine at 1.2.14–15. A printer's error is evident in Q's stage direction at 3.2.91 (Ev). The instruction 'Let in' is printed in roman, but the words are preceded by a long dash like the one setting off the stage direction '*Within*' that precedes the anonymously voiced question 'Who's there?' (90). Arguably the compositor was confused as to the status of the words.

In the main, Q is a well-printed play text. The comprehensively marked entrances and exits of major and minor characters, the care with which stage directions are positioned in relation to dialogue, and the minimal nature of those directions led Dillon to conjecture that the text of the play was printed from 'prompter's copy' or 'playhouse-copy'.[16] Dillon asserts that 'no sheet was so carefully reconsidered as to have three states', but in the course of my collation I found one such variant.[17] In editing Q I have, with Dyce, substituted 'than' for 'then' in the numerous instances where the flexibility of early modern spelling led Q to print 'then' for our modern 'than'. I have also changed 'And' to 'An' on the several occasions where the context makes clear that the conjunction means 'if'. Q uses question marks for terminal exclamation marks, both at the ends of sentences, mid-sentence and, on one occasion on G3, after the penultimate word in a sentence (collation, 5.1.7–8n). I have altered this pointing to conform with modern usage.

Many of the cruxes faced by an editor of *FoL* derive from what Dillon interprets as 'an unusual combination of carelessness and diligence' in the work of the two compositors responsible for setting the text.[18] A challenging crux is Q's 'large cousenst Lawyer Fees' (Gv) which occurs during backchat between the pages. A compositor's eye-skipping to 'honest' in the next line (potentially as much a product of tiredness as carelessness) may have produced this scrambled epithet. Dyce emended the phrase, plausibly, to 'large-conscienced lawyer fees'. This edition's emendation, 'large cozening-lawyer fees' (4.4.77n), emphasises that Periwinkle's master Gudgeon digests more disgraces than he does exorbitant legal charges during a Michaelmas term. Elsewhere, Dyce's instinct for Jacobethan idiom produces an apt emendation; witness his choice of the comprehensively insulting 'limb-lifter' for a word which the compositor saw as 'Timelifter' (5.3.375n).

Particular diligence is evident in the printing of sheets D, G, and H, which received multiple press corrections.[19] H2v of sheet H is critical for the question raised by Martin Wiggins of whether the texts of *The Family of Love* were censored during printing. He proposes that the text was censored owing to the consonance between the name 'Poppin' assumed by the merchant Dryfat in the culminating mock trial scene (5.3) and that of the Lord Chief Justice, Sir John Popham, who died in June 1607:

> The name of Dryfat's alter-ego in the final scene changes from moment to moment in a way that is not suggestive of a division between multiple authors. The likeliest explanation is that the copy was marked up to indicate a change of name, but that the job was not done consistently. This could have been in response to censorship.[20]

This hypothesis makes sense of the changing of 'Poppin' to 'Exigent' in eleven out of the seventeen extant copies of Q. Alternatively, Wiggins suggests, 'Poppin' might have been changed because, following Popham's death, the allusion was no longer relevant. From his analysis of the corrected sheets of Q, Dillon deduces that 'Exigent' is the name regarded as correct by the proofreader, and that it was the playwright's final decision. But when our data set involves only seventeen copies of Q from a larger print run, it is surely impossible to regard the figures as conclusive. On the other hand, as Maxwell observes, it is hard to imagine an author jettisoning the alliterative 'Poppin the Proctor' for the pedestrian 'Exigent the Proctor'.[21] Dillon remarks that the name 'Exigent', in the senses both of 'urgent, pressing' and 'exacting', fits Dryfat's task as proctor, though he notes that 'Poppin' 'has the virtue of alliteration'.[22] The

INTRODUCTION   7

sheer delightfulness of the name 'Poppin' does not weigh with
Wiggins: it is apt for the disguised Dryfat in the sense of 'puppet',
for, above all, he is playing a part in Gerardine's play. In support of
his case for censorship, Wiggins asserts that Dryfat 'is posing as, in
effect, a judge', but as *OED* tells us, a proctor's role in a court of
law was equivalent to an attorney or solicitor: the character who acts
as judge or arbiter in the mock trial is Gerardine, in his final disguise
as Doctor Stickler.[23] It is impossible to prove whether or not the
text of *FoL* was censored.[24] Wiggins's useful raising of the question
is one further factor which makes this once obscure comedy seem
more central than peripheral in the canon of early modern drama.

Although Dyce's edition of *The Family of Love* included in his
Works of Thomas Middleton made the text of the play more acces-
sible, it consolidated an erroneous attribution that has persisted for
over three centuries, and was shaped by Victorian chauvinism and
decorum. Witness his handling of an exchange between Master
Purge, Gerardine, and the gallant Lipsalve in the scene of Gerardine's
parting feast at the house of his cousin. Purge addresses Gerardine:

> *Purge.* Cousin Gerardine, shall the will be read before supper?
> *Gerardine.* Before supper, I beseech you.
> *Lipsalve.* Ay, ay, before supper, for when these women's bellies be full their bones will be soon at rest. (1.3.114–17)

Dyce split Lipsalve's lines between a rejoinder to the two men and
a misogynist aside:

> *Lipsalve.* Ay, ay, before supper, [*Aside*] — for when these women's bellies be full, their *tongues* will be soon at rest. (my emphasis)

Concern for feminine decorum may have led Dyce to bowdlerise
Maria's assertion to her aunt that her sex was 'made, [for] / Society
in nuptial beds' (2.4.31–2n). He emended her frank reference to
lovemaking as 'Society in nuptials', conjecturing the word 'nuptials'
to be the author's substitution in the manuscript, and 'beds' redun-
dant. This edition preserves the sometimes erratic grammar of Q,
such as when Gerardine apostrophises Maria as a woman 'whose
dishevelled locks, / Like gems against the repercussive sun, / *Gives*
light and splendour' (4.2.88–90). And when Gerardine, in the
supper-party scene, tells Mistress Glister, *sotto voce*, 'I have thought
it a point of charity to reveal the wrongs you *sustained* by your husband's looseness' (1.3.161–2, my emphasis), I have resisted the

temptation, to which Dyce and Dillon succumbed, to fiddle with the tense.[25] To his credit, Dyce thought hard and carefully about issues of staging. Nevertheless, as Cleary observes, a number of Dyce's and Bullen's emendations, together with Dyce's comments on locations 'involve a modern bias toward realism that the staging of [Barry's] time did not have'.[26] In compiling the commentary, and in many other aspects of this edition, I have drawn on Shepherd's edition of *FoL* which achieves a miraculous amount in an economical format.

In the course of collating the two copies of Q in the Huntington Library collection, I discovered some scribal annotations in my copy-text, in two different hands. These annotations are described in full in Appendix 1. What is striking about the annotations is their departure from the 'analogical habit of reading' that characterises the majority of scribal marginalia discovered in early modern playbooks.[27] Instead, the bulk of the annotations supplement or correct minor deficiencies of the printed text, anticipated in Barry's address 'To the Reader' as 'faults [which] may escape in the printing' (3). I conclude here by discussing the most intriguing annotation, which we may term 'post-theatrical'.[28]

This annotation occurs in 4.1, where Rebecca Purge instructs Lipsalve and Gudgeon, disguised as Familists in 'demure habit' (4.1.11–12), on how they should behave themselves, in general, and at meetings of the Family. Mid-edification, Master Purge enters, unobserved by his wife and (perhaps) the gallants. To the right of the stage direction, '*Enter Mayster Purge*', there is a faint annotation that reads (when viewed under ultra-violet light) '*And ever he was there*'. The phrase '*And ever he was there*' may bear witness to the scene's theatrical impact. Is this, in fact, a stage description that allows us to watch and laugh with the dead? The words accurately comment on the action, for the jealous Purge remains onstage throughout the conversation between his wife and the disguised gallants; subsequently he gains access to the meeting by overhearing the correct password spoken by Rebecca. We should not underestimate the extent to which what we regard as a conventional stage technique – eavesdropping – might have intrigued or captivated a Jacobean spectator. And there is no arbour or box hedge for Purge to hide in. He remains onstage, tantalisingly close to his wife and the men who want to seduce her, for the rest of the scene. In this instance, the handwritten annotation in the Huntington quarto allows us to experience the dramatic moment as at once riveting *and* comic: the annotation's effect is like the boy at the pantomime who cries, 'Look out! There's a lion behind you!'[29]

LORDING BARRY: PLAYWRIGHT, PIRATE, GENTLEMAN

Lording Barry was the fifth of eleven children born to Nicholas Barry and his second wife Anne Lording, both originally from Hertfordshire. His family lived in the parish of St Lawrence Pountney in London, and Barry was baptised in the church there on 17 April 1580. A freeman of the Company of Fishmongers, Nicholas Barry was probably a small businessman with upwardly mobile aspirations. His marriage to Anne, daughter of George Lording, citizen and merchant taylor, enabled the education of at least two of his sons at Cambridge, the eldest, George, who became a minister, and John, who attended the renowned Merchant Taylors' School in London, followed by a BA and MA.[30] No record survives of younger son Lording's education, but the dramatic texture of his two plays suggests a writer who had attended both grammar school and university, or one of the Inns of Court. Possibly, like umpteen young men whose destiny was neither academia nor the Church, Barry was in residence at Cambridge and the Inns of Court for a couple of years each without proceeding to a degree.

In a manner exemplary of a Jacobean Londoner, Barry's life was marked by a series of attempts to improve his wealth and social standing. He was an adventurer who took sizeable risks. In the summer and autumn of 1607, a few months after receiving a small legacy from his father, he embarked on a spree of borrowing, engaging himself in loans approximating the hefty sum of £120. The fact that six of these loans were transacted in just twelve days suggests the intensity of the enterprise. Joined by several co-investors, including the poet Michael Drayton, the 27-year-old Barry needed money to finance what Jeremy Lopez calls 'an upstart boy-company theater in a bad part of town'.[31]

The company was the brainchild of a syndicate led by Barry and Drayton.[32] The latter, an established poet-playwright, negotiated a share of the new lease of the old Whitefriars precinct in Fleet Street from the financier Thomas Woodford in July 1607, after which, in August, Barry bought out Woodford.[33] The performance space for the new children's company was the former refectory of the monastery, repurposed as a small hall theatre. Drayton had secured a patent from King James to name the company 'The Children of his

Majesty's Revels'; in this, the syndicate emulated, and was perhaps hoping to rival, the Children of his Majesty's Revels at the Blackfriars.[34] Envisaged as a professional troupe that would tour the provinces when plague prevented them from playing in London, this group lacked the religious and educational affiliation of boys' troupes such as the second Children of Paul's and the Blackfriars Boys, who evolved from the earlier Children of the Chapel. The company operated for at most a year from an uncertain date in spring or summer 1607 to April 1608, during which time they performed nine plays, including Barry's recognised comedy *Ram Alley*, as well as his *Family of Love*.[35]

The Children of the King's Revels, however, struggled to survive, their success hampered by the closure of the playhouse due to plague in the autumn of 1607, and a prolonged ban on playing imposed by King James in April 1608.[36] When the various loans of summer 1607 became due, Barry and his partners were 'forced to default, resulting in a string of lawsuits' and the ultimate demise of the company. In all, during the first half of 1608, bills were filed claiming over £200 in liabilities from Barry, who 'had been living in a style inspiring confidence in tradesmen'.[37] Consigned to the Marshalsea prison, Barry somehow persuaded two of his creditors to stand bail for him, whereupon he disappeared from London, leaving the two men to settle his debts, and 'took to the high seas as a pirate'.[38]

If we accept the argument that *The Family of Love* was written between mid-May 1605 and 1606, then Barry was not merely 'a prospective playwright' nor a 'novice' when the shareholders in the Whitefriars playhouse were launching their venture in the competitive world of London theatre.[39] Rather, he was an investor-dramatist whose first comedy, set loosely in London, satirised the Family of Love, a subject of great topical interest following King James's attack on Familists as 'Puritans' in 1603. We do not know in what professional context Barry devised and wrote *FoL*, nor whence he derived what his twentieth-century biographer, Cecil L'Estrange Ewen, terms 'his dramatic instincts'.[40] Robert Fraser, who suggests that Thomas Middleton represented Barry as a character, speculates that Barry may have worked in the theatre 'as an actor as well as a writer' prior to the formation of the King's Revels Children.[41] No evidence of Barry as a player, however, exists beyond an isolated reference almost a decade after the Whitefriars enterprise to 'Captain Barrow ... who was a player in England'.[42] While he moved in the same city as Middleton, and absorbed a great deal from the more seasoned dramatist, we should be chary of constructing a backstory for Barry, such as Fraser suggests, which has him 'learning the craft of writing' in close proximity to Middleton.[43] This feeds too easily into the view of *FoL* as a collaborative work, an argument this edition calls into question.

Barry was not just a bold, ambitious entrepreneur. His activities as a pirate off the south coasts of England and Ireland and, briefly, in the Mediterranean prove that he was willing to risk death for a lucrative livelihood. In August 1608 he took part in the capture of two Flemish ships, in the course of which a crew member was shot dead and thrown overboard. Subsequently, the 'financially troubled' Barry became part of a powerful 'piratical fleet' operating out of Baltimore, County Cork, and extending as far as the Barbary ports.[44] Raids on French ships by a pink boat that formed part of this fleet were halted when Sir William St John, captain of an English navy ship concealed near Crooke's Castle, arrested all the men on board. Barry was among 'the poorer sort and such as were newly come' whom St John turned ashore.[45] Twenty-four of the captured men were indicted for piracy in a sensational trial at the General Sessions in Southwark in December 1609. Nineteen were hanged, including a London poulterer, Roger Notting, and his brother-in-law, Richard Baker, both innocent men whom Barry had lured aboard ship in Cork with a promise of paying Notting money Barry owed him for a horse.[46]

Barry escaped the gallows. Ewen and Lopez conjecture that he played on the coincidence of his name with that of an Admiralty commissioner in piracy in Munster, Lord Barry, Viscount Buttevant.[47] Lopez pictures 'the spirit of Barry's life' in this instance as representing 'the evil genius of theater itself'. More plausibly, he focuses our attention on Richard Baker's striking description of Barry as 'one Lodowick Barry, a poet as he understandeth'.[48] As Lopez observes, this characterisation of Barry suggests that the entrepreneur turned seaman 'imagined playwriting as his vocation ... thought of himself as poet, and ... insisted upon that identification even in the most remote of contexts'.[49] Only we later moderns have had difficulty accepting Barry's self-image as a poet. In a bill of complaint reporting transactions for the lease of the Whitefriars playhouse that took place ten years earlier, the joint lessees Drayton and Barry are designated 'the ... Masters of the Children of the Kings Revels'.[50] The playwright-shareholder-impresario had achieved the status and regard due to a gentleman and 'master'. Clearly, to invoke the Prologue to his first play, Lording Barry was no 'abject spirit' (8), miserably overthrown by circumstances. And when he participated in Sir Walter Raleigh's unsuccessful goldmining expedition to Guiana in 1617, he was the captain of *The Confidence*.[51]

The second half of Barry's life was less eventful than the first. At some point after his father's death he became free of the Fishmongers' Company by patrimony; the quarterage book records payments to the company 'from about 1611 to 1622'.[52] There is no record of his ever having married. Following his return to England at an unknown date after the Guiana venture, Barry engaged in legitimate trading out of London until his death there in 1629. In his will he calls himself 'Lording Barry, captain and part-owner of the good ship called the Edward of London'.[53] Lopez notes the 'remarkable fact' that in 1627 the *Edward* was 'granted a letter of mark by the Duke of Buckingham to take pirates and enemy ships'; moreover, 'Barry's association with the ship's principal owner, Edward Bennett, would have meant a close involvement in the regulation of legitimate international trade'.[54]

Thus, by the time Barry died, the family of Nicholas, citizen-fishmonger, had moved up in the world. Lording's niece by his sister Alice married Captain Edmund Scarborough, a graduate of Caius College, Cambridge, who in 1621 emigrated to Virginia. Edmund's son, Colonel Edward Scarborough, was a prominent early settler and member of the Virginia House of Burgesses. Barry left money for a gold ring to each of his great nephews, the second of whom, Sir Charles Scarborough, was a founding member of the Royal Society and physician successively to Charles II and James II.

We are over-familiar with Hamlet's labelling of Polonius a 'fishmonger' (2.2.172) – evoking the stench of corruption – and forget his follow-up remark that he wishes Polonius 'were so honest a man' (2.2.174). Whether he was 'honest' or not (in all senses of that word), Nicholas Barry's trading in fish left its mark on his dramatist son, who named page characters in *FoL* 'Periwinkle', 'Shrimp' and (possibly) 'Smelt' (see 'Names of the Characters', 9n). Perhaps, Robert Fraser has offered, Barry's association with his father's business can be seen in the fishily named 'Lamprey' in Middleton's *Trick to Catch the Old One*. Lording Barry's turning to a life at sea seems appropriate for a poet and proto-capitalist. In relation to his engagement in piracy, including his involvement in the deaths 'of at least three men he encountered', it is tempting to wonder whether, like Chaucer's shipman, 'Of nyce conscience took he no keep'.⁵⁵ Yet that would be a presumptuous judgement of a writer who was familiar with *Hamlet* and *The Spanish Tragedy*, and who has a page in *FoL* quip that many men 'have neither law nor conscience' (2.3.23–4). Just how Lording Barry dealt with his own conscience we cannot tell.

THE 'MOMENT' OF *THE FAMILY OF LOVE*, 1605–06

The Family of Love remains an obscure Jacobean comedy. Unattributed on the title page, it was played by a short-lived children's company, the Children of the King's Revels. Suggested dates for its composition range from 1602 to 1607. I endorse the argument put forward by distinguished textual scholars Gary Taylor, Paul Mulholland, and MacDonald P. Jackson that the play was written by Barry between mid-May 1605 and late 1606, but only published several years later in 1608.

It would be hard to better *The Family of Love* as an attention-grabbing play title in the early years of the seventeenth century. The Family of Love was a sect widely but unjustly accused of libertinism and hypocrisy. The group had been singled out by King James I in the new preface to his revised *Basilicon Doron* (1603) as a particularly 'vile sect amongst the Anabaptists'. James was drawing back from the original treatise's (1598) apparent wholesale attack on all Puritans. The Family of Love, he wrote, 'think themselves only pure, and in a manner, without sin, the only true Church, and only worthy to be participant of the sacraments'.⁵⁶ As Christopher Marsh notes, the king's reference to the Family of Love was 'misplaced'; it showed his ignorance of 'the long-established antipathy' between Puritans and members of the Family.⁵⁷ By scapegoating Familists, James ensured that the Family of Love, outlawed by Queen Elizabeth I in 1580, once again became a 'talking point ... within government and reformist circles'.⁵⁸

Variously known as the *Familia caritatis*, or the House of Love, Familism was established in Germany in the 1540s by Hendrik Niclaes, a 'Messianic merchant with ... an assured command of the printing press'.⁵⁹ The movement was transplanted to England three decades later through the translations of Christopher Vittels, a charismatic spiritual teacher. In common with other religious separatist groups before and after, Familist thought challenged predestinarian theology through its emphasis on religion as an inward, personal experience. Niclaes decried the 'false hearts of the scripture-learned' and exhorted his followers 'to love the virtues of the lovely being of the love'.[60] His writings personify love so that it becomes, in Nigel Smith's words, 'a female image of love and truth', enveloping and protecting the man or woman who, by spiritually imitating Christ's sufferings, would attain the mystical state of being 'godded with God'.[61]

As Smith points out, 'the *idea* of the Family of Love exercised a considerable hold over the [English] popular and literary imagination for most of the [seventeenth] century'.[62] Historians of English Familism have shown how members of the sect, concentrated in the eastern and south-eastern counties, were recognised as upright, sober individuals rather than ungodly extremists. Indeed, Familists served in the royal households of both Queen Elizabeth I and King James I.[63] Middleton gives the image of Familist sobriety an amusing twist in *A Mad World, My Masters* (1606). The citizen Harebrain admires the courtesan whom he believes is persuading his wife to greater piety, when the courtesan is actually instructing his wife in the art of dissembling so she can pursue an illicit affair: 'How earnestly she labours her, like a good wholesome sister of the Family' (1.2.73–4). In reality a non-dogmatic group, Familists preferred outward conformity to proselytising or martyrdom. Through the attacks of the Family's 'clerical antagonists' under Elizabeth I, however, a stereotype of the Familist emerged as licentious, subversive and hypocritical. Barry's *FoL* builds on these accusations. This sensationalised view of the Family flourished, as Kristen Poole points out, in inverse proportion to the group's decreasing cultural visibility as the seventeenth century wore on.[64]

Six other plays from the period 1602–07 allude to the Family of Love, only one of which preceded *Basilicon Doron*, and then only in performance.[65] Among these, *The Dutch Courtesan* by John Marston is particularly important, as it has been juxtaposed with *FoL* in discussions both of dating and authorship.[66] Contemporary condemnations of Familists, together with proliferating references to them in drama, led older critics to date Barry's play as early as 1602–04.[67] More recently, on the basis of internal evidence, critics have determined May 1605 as the earliest possible date and, on the basis of external evidence, the end of 1606 as the latest possible date of composition of *FoL*.

The description of *FoL* in the Stationers' Register entry for 12 October 1607 as 'lately acted by the Children of his Majesty's Revels' implies performance some months, at least, earlier.[68] Moreover, Barry, in his epistle 'To the Reader', tells us that it was published 'Too soon and too late' (1). He amplifies the contention of lateness by asserting that the play 'was not published when the general voice of the people had sealed it for good, and the newness of it made it much more desired than at this time' (4–6). This interesting statement by an early modern playwright allows for the audience's *desire* both to see and read his play.

Often an interval of years elapsed between first performance and publication of a play. As Wiggins observes, 'The context for the epistle may be a tendency for the interval between stage and page to grow shorter.'[69] For example, George Wilkins's *The Miseries of Enforced Marriage*, performed in 1606 and printed in 1607, advertises on the title page, 'As it is *now* played by his Majesty's servants' (my emphasis). When Middleton's *A Yorkshire Tragedy* was printed in 1608, three years after its performance at the Globe, the title page carried the catchphrase, 'not so new as lamentable and true'.[70]

Playhouse owners protected their investments by postponing printing. The Articles of Agreement between the Whitefriars shareholders drawn up in March 1608 stipulated that no company member should 'at any time hereafter put into print, or cause to be put in print any manner of play book now in use'; this measure was designed to keep the plays as company property in communal ownership.[71] Nevertheless, a tangible note of regret resounds in Barry's statement that *FoL* was *not* printed 'when the newness of it made it ... desired' by the audience, when the play's *newsiness*, we could infer, was at its height, and might have persuaded the coterie playgoers who frequented the Whitefriars theatre to purchase a printed copy. Based on the above two examples, we could allow anything from a few months to a few years between performance and publication.

One internal allusion gives the earliest possible date of composition as mid-May 1605. In 4.3, the disguised Gerardine affiliates himself to the 'spick-and-span new-set-up company of Porters' (4.3.45–6; see 1.3.107–8n). Baldwin Maxwell first noted the play's references to the London Company of Porters, which was newly incorporated in 1605. A ballad published in June of that year documented this event (figure 2). Maxwell writes that, on the evidence

Figure 2 Woodcut of London porters accompanying 'A New Ballad, composed in commendation of the society, or company of the Porters', published in 1605. The captions read: 'At the first went we, as here you see'; 'But since our corporation, on this fashion'; 'And to our hall, thus we go all'. Reproduced by permission of the Pepys Library, Magdalene College, Cambridge.

of the ballad, 'some London porters were obviously organizing or reorganizing early in James's reign – probably in the spring of 1605'. Spring 1605 thus provides the *terminus a quo* of mid-May 1605 proposed for *FoL*'s composition by Taylor, Jackson, and Mulholland.[72]

Allusions made to other contemporary events allow, but do not require, earlier dates, 1603 or 1604, and reinforce the sense that the play is set in the middle of the first decade of the seventeenth century. Mistress Purge refers in the mock trial with which the play concludes to 'subscriptions ... raised in England ... for the defense of the besieged city of Geneva'.[73] Geneva had endured a blockade for more than six months in 1602–03 by the Catholic Duke Charles Emmanuel of Savoy (see 5.3.268n), and on 8 October 1603, and again on 25 March 1604, James I had requested his archbishops and bishops to initiate collections of funds in parish churches. The play might be alluding to either of these collections.

Again, in 3.1, Maria asks Gerardine how he is tolerating 'thy little-ease, thy trunk', from which he has emerged for the second time (3.1.9). Taylor et al. show that *FoL*'s use of 'little-ease' was almost certainly prompted by the scandal attending the renewed use of the cramped and foul prison in the Tower of London that went by that name. On 11 May 1604 the *Journals of the House of Commons* record the committal of John Trench, Warden of the Fleet, to Little Ease for refusing to honour a writ for the release of Sir Thomas Sherley. The neglected state of the prison moved the House of Commons to consider imposing a hefty fine on the Lieutenant of the Tower for failing to prepare the prison for Trench. None of these earlier allusions counters the earliest dating of mid-May 1605 argued above on the basis of the reference to the Company of Porters.

A later date has recently been proposed. Wiggins makes two suggestions supporting a date of composition of 1607 for *FoL*. The first is a parody of the trunk sequence (by which Gerardine is conveyed into Glister's house) by Beaumont in *The Knight of the Burning Pestle* (1607). Whereas Barry uses a trunk, Beaumont uses a coffin as a device for the apprentice, Jasper, presumed dead, to steal into the Merchant's house and gain access to his love. In the final scene, Jasper appears to his father, Old Merrythought, and '*heaves up*' the coffin so his lover Luce can scramble out.[74] There is no reason, however, why Beaumont could not have been echoing a play performed in the previous two years. In his estimate of 1607, Wiggins is clearly influenced by his belief that 'the text has been censored'. He suggests that Dryfat's sobriquet 'Poppin' allowed a connection to be made with Sir John Popham, the Lord Chief Justice, who died on 10 June 1607.[75] But Barry's complaint regarding the time lag between the play's performance and its publication makes a date of 1607 unlikely. Even if the text was censored when it was printed, that possibility need not determine the actual date of composition, which is plausibly sited closer in time to the play's most straightforward topical allusion, the incorporation of the London Company of Porters. The date of composition for *FoL* is best placed between mid-May 1605 and late 1606, with performance following in 1606 or sometime in 1607.

Both satirical and sexual mileage had been made from the Family of Love in Marston's *The Dutch Courtesan*, performed in close proximity to *FoL*'s composition, probably early in 1605.[76] It is possible that Marston's interest in the Family of Love might have suggested a play with that title to Barry. Certainly, it makes sense to view the two plays as written in dialogue. The fact that both Barry and Marston make dramatic use of the Family of Love is one element that leads Charles Cathcart to propose Marston as a co-author of Barry's play. However, to assert, as Cathcart does, that the two plays have in common 'a structural deployment of the sect' overstates the centrality of the Family of Love to *The Dutch Courtesan*'s plot.[77] The Family of Love is more central to Barry's plot, more incidental to Marston's. Marston invokes the Family of Love in the context of the bawd Mary Faugh's brothel (for which 'family of love' is a euphemism), and the Familist household of the vintner Mulligrub and his wife. His characters use the full name, 'the Family of Love', as if signalling to the audience each of the three times the scandalous group is invoked. This usage differs from the casual, pervasive reference to 'the Family', 'Familists' and their meetings in Barry's play. *FoL* involves two Familist meetings attended by three characters and infiltrated by three others. Differing accounts of what transpired in the meetings are crucial to the play's dénouement.

As the Children of the King's Revels, established with the new monarch's patent, Barry's company might have regarded themselves as royally privileged to take the Family of Love as its target.[78] Nonetheless, Barry's choice of title for his first play was politically contentious. In his recent discussion of heresy and gender in the Familist movement and in Barry's play, Marsh argues that *FoL*'s 'reported success ... owed a great deal to the thoroughly knowledgeable nature of both the playwright and the playgoers'.[79] Indeed, read in tandem with *Ram Alley*'s passing references to 'the Brownist' and

INTRODUCTION 19

'a new sect' (1.2.125, 124), *FoL* suggests a lively engagement with religious separatism among Barry's coterie audience. The play's title was also risqué. In England, communal ownership of property and ease of divorce and remarriage were understood to form part of Familist practice and belief. The English popular imagination misunderstood Niclaes's idea of 'communialtie' as a prescription for sexual promiscuity. Thus, as Sarah Scott reminds us, '"Family of love" was a euphemism for libertinism'.[80] We may assume, therefore, that the title aroused expectations of both satire and salaciousness among London playgoers hungry for novelty. This edition of *FoL* brings together discussion of the play from a literary and historical perspective with the often complex analysis underpinning investigations of its authorship.

THE AUTHORSHIP DEBATE

Why, Sir, I think every man whatever has a peculiar style, which may be discovered by nice examination and comparison with others: but a man must write a great deal to make his style obviously discernible. (Samuel Johnson)[81]

Will the real author of *The Family of Love* please stand up? Four candidates have been put forward for whole or part-authorship of *FoL*: Thomas Middleton, Thomas Dekker, Lording Barry, and John Marston. Wiggins summarises modern scholarship: 'Current consensus holds that the play is of single authorship.'[82] I follow Middleton scholars Taylor, Mulholland, and Jackson, who in 1999 argued powerfully for the sole authorship of *FoL* by Barry. I consider *FoL* as the first comedy of Barry, documented author of the ribald, hilarious *Ram Alley, or Merry Tricks* (1608, pub. 1611), also performed by the Children of the King's Revels.

Forty years after its only early modern edition, *FoL* was attributed to Middleton in the bookseller Edward Archer's so-called 'Exact and Perfect Catalogue of all the Plays that were ever Printed' (1656).[83] In the twentieth century, Archer's catalogue was demonstrated by W.W. Greg and subsequent investigators to be 'remarkably unreliable'.[84] The ascription of *FoL* to Middleton was canonised in the Victorian multi-volume editions of Middleton's *Works* produced by Alexander Dyce (1840) and Arthur H. Bullen (1885–86). These editions, and contemporary responses to them, entrenched a view of *FoL* as Middleton's worst play, a view that endured for over three centuries.

The view of *FoL* as a collaboration between Middleton and Dekker was first advanced by Gerald Eberle in 1948. However, in his monograph on Dekker, George R. Price concluded that the play belonged to neither author, and the Cambridge edition of Dekker's *Dramatic Works* (1953–61) excluded *FoL*.[85] Nevertheless, the possibility that he was a contributing author was reiterated as recently as 2008, and persists in the edition of *FoL* as a collaboration between Dekker and Middleton available on the Luminarium website.[86] The new textual scholarship that flourished in the 1970s under the influence of Fredson Bowers produced two key studies of Middleton's canon. The first and most influential was David Lake's *The Canon of Thomas Middleton's Plays* (1975); the second, MacDonald P. Jackson's *Studies in Attribution: Middleton and Shakespeare* (1979). Although Lake found 'gross discrepancies of linguistic style between *The Family* and the undoubted [Middleton] canon', he constructed an elaborate theory that placed *FoL* early in Middleton's career, with subsequent revision first by Dekker, and then by Barry.[87] The strongest evidence isolated by Lake *against* Middleton's authorship is the high frequency in *FoL* of the colloquial '′a' meaning 'he' (41 instances), and oaths, both declared and quoted, that Middleton never uses, such as 'Gog's nowns! Gog's blood!' (3.3.44). Middleton uses '′a' for 'he' not at all in ten of his plays, and never above five times in a single play. In his independent study, Jackson argued that linguistically, metrically, and in several other respects, *FoL* 'is completely unlike Middleton's comedies of the same period, and unlike his plays in general', concluding, as had Price, that the play 'is not Middleton's at all'.[88] The unanimity with which Lake's theory was accepted in subsequent work on the play belies the tentativeness with which it was offered, for he admitted that the theory was 'one about which I am not confident in detail'.[89] Yet the fact that Lake's book was published by a higher profile press and was distributed more widely than Jackson's meant that his account of *FoL*'s composition was accepted by Marsh in his history of the Family of Love in England (1994), and cited in 2015 by Kristen Poole in her literary-critical monograph *Radical Religion*.[90]

The development in criticism exploring collaborative authorship of early modern drama may have contributed towards the longevity of the multiple-author theory regarding *FoL*, as well as the tendency of dramaturges, directors, and actors to 'revise' plays to this day. In his edition of the play for the Nottingham Drama Texts series in 1979, Simon Shepherd described the Jacobean play text, with some validity, as a 'corporate entity', acknowledging the input of revisers, scribes, and actors to the final printed text.[91] Shepherd's edition ascribes *FoL* to Middleton while acknowledging Lake's hypothesis of double revision by Dekker and Barry. Even while stating the shift towards a theory of single authorship, Wiggins worries over several details that might suggest multiple hands.[92]

The pendulum swung back to single authorship in 1999 when Taylor, Mulholland, and Jackson argued for Barry's sole authorship of *FoL*; their argument was reinforced by the play's omission from the magisterial *Thomas Middleton: The Collected Works* published in the new millennium (2007). These scholars' investigation of *FoL*'s authorship marries appraisal of external evidence provided by the 1608 quarto with stylometrical analysis of the play's linguistic texture, using the *Literature OnLine* database of early modern drama. For instance, the Prologue to *FoL* refers to the author in the third person three times, indicating a single writer without an established reputation: 'opinion hath not blazed his fame' (1). Middleton does not fit this image of a novice playwright, for he was well established as a publishing author and dramatist by 1604-05: opinion *had* blazed his fame.[93] In addition, reinforcing the findings of Jackson and Lake, the linguistic texture and deployment of oaths in *FoL* differs strikingly from Middleton's drama. On the other hand, Barry's obscurity in the years preceding 1607-08 bears out the Prologue's claims about the author; moreover, the phrases 'the relief of the distressed Geneva' (5.3.268) and *pauca sapienti* (5.3.126), the frequency of the interjection 'tut' and the colloquial "a' are paralleled only by the text of Barry's *Ram Alley* in the entire database of English drama for the period 1580–1640.[94] Further close stylometrical analysis shows strong relationships between *FoL* and Barry's recognised comedy *Ram Alley*. In research commissioned by the general editors of the *Oxford Marston*, the '21 unique verbal links' the authors found between *FoL* and *Ram Alley* 'suggest a single author's word associations'.[95]

The copious imitation of other dramatists in *FoL* has proved a sticking point for acceptance of the theory of sole authorship by attribution scholars. Lake, for example, identified in the text of *FoL* three verbal parallels with Middleton's plays: the Latin word *subaudi* (3.1.90); the adjective 'suspectless' for 'without suspicion' (3.1.119); and reference to Chaucer as a 'sexually frank' poet. The third feature occurs in 3.1, where *FoL*'s hero Gerardine 'exemplifies' the Latin word *amore* for his lover, Maria, rounding off with a sexy flourish: 'Lastly, take *o*, in *re* stands all my rest, / Which I in Chaucer style do term a jest' (3.1.54–5n). For comparison, Lake cites references to Chaucer's 'broad' style in *No Wit* and *More Dissemblers*.[96] Commenting on the coincidence of these 'unique features' appearing in *FoL*, Lake observes: 'one uncommon parallel may be due to imitation, two possibly to imitation coupled with a rare coincidence, but three is really too much'.[97] Too much, that is, not to believe that this cluster of Middletonisms proves Middleton's authorship of *FoL*.

A similar inclination governs Charles Cathcart's novel hypothesis that John Marston was an 'original composer' of *FoL*. His theory is put forward in two chapters of his study reappraising Marston's role in the 'war of the theatres', in particular the relationship between Marston and Jonson.[98] Cathcart's argument for a close relationship between *FoL* and Marston's drama is buttressed by Mary Bly's study of the Whitefriars' repertory in terms of 'queer collaboration'.[99] Against the arguments of Taylor et al. for Barry as sole author, Cathcart postulates a Marstonian first draft of *FoL*, with later revisions by Barry, possibly Dekker, and possibly 'one or more additional writers'. But rather than indicating an authorial role for Marston, the parallels Cathcart cites between *FoL* and Marston's work show that (as he himself entertains) 'the play's author ... [was] highly influenced by Marston's own writings'.[100]

As Jackson has written à propos of Middleton,

> There is a sense ... in which a play is the expression of a *Zeitgeist*, a recipient of the current ideologies, a fabrication of the available language, a product of intertextual transactions ... But as well as a 'tradition' that encompasses everything from theatre practice to the prevailing cosmology there is the 'individual talent'.[101]

Problematically, the key marker of Barry's authorial style that critics have identified over time is his penchant for pastiche, parody, or quotation from other dramatists' work. Richard Barker characterises *FoL* as 'a pastiche of Marston and Shakespeare', while Shepherd suggests that the poetry of the lovers 'is careful parody, rather in the manner of Marston's *Antonio* plays'.[102] In his scholarly edition of *FoL*, Andrew Dillon comments on the author's 'youthful enthusiasm, still excited by the language of Marlowe and Shakespeare'.[103] In considering author attribution of early modern drama, it is vital to distinguish authorship from influence and imitation. Darren

Freebury-Jones, Marina Tarlinskaja, and Marcus Dahl propose that 'Barry was an inveterate borrower who knew Marston's works intimately and was able to weave Marston's phraseology into his own passages'. Thus the striking number of verbal links between *FoL* and Marston's dramatic corpus could be 'indicative of imitation'.[104]

Crucial to Cathcart's case for Marston's involvement in *FoL* is the poet's authorship of *The Dutch Courtesan*, which he describes as 'the only other play to offer an extended treatment of the religious group, the Family of Love'.[105] But I question whether either comedy can faithfully be described as 'an extended treatment' of English Familists or Familism. Suffice it here to note the close proximity in date between *The Dutch Courtesan* and *FoL*, which explains in some measure their many resemblances. *The Dutch Courtesan* was probably performed in early 1605, while *FoL* was completed between mid-May 1605 and the end of 1606, and may have been performed in the summer of 1607. Barry need not have been an actor to have engaged in the prolific sampling of Elizabethan and Jacobean drama evinced by *FoL* and *Ram Alley*.

Responding to Johnson's dictum (in my epigraph for this section), Harold Love remarks that 'individuality [in writing] will always betray its authorship to a skilled enough investigator with sufficient data to work from'.[106] But what constitute 'sufficient data'? Lording Barry wrote comparatively little, yet as Taylor and his co-authors wrote in 1999, the attribution to Barry of *FoL* 'doubles the size of the Barry canon'. I argue that while it is not easy 'to prove, to everyone's satisfaction, that Barry *did* write' *The Family of Love*, it is a risk well worth taking precisely because of the greater scope the attribution allows us to discern and discuss Barry's 'peculiar style' (pace Johnson) and his distinctive dramaturgy.[107]

SOURCES AND INTERTEXTS

The plot drivers in the '"three-level" drama' of *The Family of Love* have their origins in a mixture of tales from Boccaccio's *Decameron*, Italian Renaissance *commedia erudita*, and a popular tradition of jests and trickery that formed a staple of English comedy.[108] The ruse by which Gerardine purports to travel to sea while bequeathing his material assets to Maria in a trunk in which he has smuggled himself borrows from the wager story of the *Decameron* (1349–51), where the villain accesses a middleclass wife's bedchamber in a chest while she is sleeping, steals personal items, and observes a mole beneath the woman's breast in an attempt to convince her husband that she has been unfaithful. This is the source Shakespeare employed in a more menacing key in *Cymbeline* (1610), several years after *FoL*'s publication.[109] In *FoL* the trunk as prop is allied with the twin comic concepts of 'opportunity' and the 'scope' of Gerardine's stratagem, bent as he is on rescuing Maria from Glister's clutches.[110] The sex between the couple that results in Maria becoming pregnant forms a crucial element in the intrigue. Once a child is in the offing, Gerardine sets about orchestrating the mock trial that will bring his and Maria's hopes to fruition.

In engineering the trial Gerardine employs fraudulent summonses delivered in his persona of 'Placket the paritor' to Mistress Purge and Glister. Dillon suggests Chaucer's 'Friar's Tale' as an analogue for Gerardine's persona of Placket initiated in 4.4 and 'for the coney-catching nature of the summons to an ecclesiastical court'.[111] Gerardine's use of so-called 'Chaucer style' in making love to Maria (3.1.55), and his reference to 'Phitonissa's power' (3.4.5), recalling the disguised devil's mention of 'the Phitonissa' in 'The Friar's Tale' (lines 1509–10), indicate Chaucer's presence in the world of stories, both aural and textual, that inspired Barry's play. But Dillon posits too direct a correlation between Chaucer's Summoner and the role played by Gerardine in the final intrigue.

That stories travel, that they are retold, adapted, and become the stuff of news and myth, is pointed out by Gerardine to the merchant Dryfat as he enlists the latter in his scheme: 'as I play the paritor, so wouldst thou but assume the shape of a proctor, I should have the wench, thou the credit, and the whole City occasion of discourse this nine days' (4.2.44–7). Gerardine's boast glances at the pamphlet *Kempe's Nine Day's Wonder* (1600), published to capitalise on the comedian Will Kemp's stunt of morris dancing all the way from London to Norwich. This reference reminds us of the rich pamphlet literature of Jacobethan London which provided Barry with a 'multiplicity of stories' on which he might draw for the play's action.[112]

R.C. Bald and Margery Fisher survey a number of cony-catching tales that could have supplied Barry with the kernel of Gerardine's fictitious summonses. Henry Chettle's *Kind-Heart's Dream* (1593) provides a good instance:

> How say ye by some jugglers that can serve writs without any original, and make poor men dwelling far off, compound with them for they know not what: I tell you there be such ... who troubling threescore or fourscore men without cause, get of some a crown, of others a noble, of diverse a pound ... to put off their appearance, when no such thing was toward.[113]

Fisher points out that Gerardine uses the imposture described here 'as a step towards winning Maria', rather than a money-making enterprise *per se*. Gerardine as summoner 'is not bought off but the affair is actually taken to a (mock) court and is there compounded'.[114] From a wider perspective, Gerardine does indeed use the feigned writ to obtain money; he tells Glister he will marry the pregnant Maria (whom he has accused Glister of impregnating in an act of incest) if Glister yields Maria to him with her portion, plus an extra thousand pounds, an exorbitant amount.

The farcical subplot comprising the punishments visited upon the libertine gallants by Glister has been linked by David George to the last tale of Robert Armin's *Tarleton's News out of Purgatory* (1591).[115] The connection is tenuous, the story featuring an 'old doctor', Mutio, and two illicit lovers of Pisa, Lionello and Margaret, who are pictured being whipped in purgatory with nettles. The whipping, the doctor character, and the atmosphere of transgressive desire can be linked to the action in which Glister gulls Lipsalve and Gudgeon into whipping each other (but not with nettles) for lusting after Mistress Purge. Swapan Chakravorty locates an alternative source for this plot in the anonymous jestbook *Jack of Dover, his Quest of Inquiry, or his Privy Search for the Veriest Fool in England* (1604).[116] The story entitled 'The Fool of Berkshire' concerns the revenge taken on a 'lewd' doctor of physic by a merry 'mealman' (or miller) from Reading, whose wife the doctor is in love with. The mealman inveigles the doctor to come to his house by counterfeiting madness; once there, the doctor is subjected to physical punishment that involves flaying, being soaked overnight in a tub of brine, and having his testicles removed the next morning by a surgeon. In *FoL*, Glister and Lipsalve take a course of physic at Glister's house, hoping thereby to seduce his wife (5.1), while in the jestbook the hapless doctor himself is lured to the miller's house where the latter, aided by his wife and their neighbours, executes his blackly comic revenge.

Louise Clubb has located an Italian source for the action in which Glister administers an overdose of laxatives to the gallants while they are resident in his home. Clubb likens this *burla* to the 'misadventure' suffered by the braggart captain Basilisco in 4.5 of *La Furiosa* ('The Madwoman') by Neapolitan playwright and polymath Giambattista Della Porta (*c.* 1535–1615). While it was not published in Italy until 1609, Clubb suggests that *La Furiosa* was composed by 1600, and she cites evidence of the play's circulation soon after this date.[117] This potential source is particularly suggestive when viewed in the context of the popularity of Della Porta's drama with Cambridge playwrights, one of whom, George Ruggle, has been linked to the Cambridge comedy *Club Law* (discussed below), which Barry certainly knew. On the suggestion of Foiana, the frustrated wife of an impotent doctor who specialises in madness, Basilisco counterfeits insanity in order to be admitted to the doctor's house as a patient. Mistaken for the distracted young lover, Ardelio, Basilisco 'is beaten for resisting his keepers, and is locked in the cellar for refusing to eat'.[118] Discovering the error, Foiana's maid Nespila releases Basilisco from the cellar, and he and Foiana have sex. Although the doctor discovers Foiana and Basilisco *in flagrante delicto*, the clever Nespila substitutes his patient Vittoria (Ardelio's mad lover) for Basilisco while the doctor is fetching witnesses. The doctor has to apologise to Foiana, for Nespila's trick discredits his accusation of adultery. Nespila describes her substitution of a woman for a man in 4.9 and 5.2; the play does not enact it.

The commonality between Della Porta's and Barry's plots is grounded in the male lovers disguising themselves as patients to procure access to the doctor's wife.[119] Both plays feature doctors, but in keeping with the tragicomic sensibility of *La Furiosa*, Della Porta's '*medico*' is 'serious and high-minded', prior to his humiliation as a cuckold. In contrast, Doctor Glister is Gerardine's 'mighty opposite': his avarice and lust propel the plot.[120] Moreover, Glister defeats the gallants through his cunning: first he orchestrates their mutual whipping in revenge for their designs on Rebecca Purge, his mistress; later he administers the laxative 'pill' (5.1.135) that ensures the men are in no fit state to bed Mistress Glister as they intend.

Clubb notes that the trick by which Foiana deceives her husband – suggesting that Basilisco impersonate a madman to gain access to the house – is modelled on the *Decameron*, Book 7, Tale 8, and it is found in several other *commedie erudite*.[121] Barry might well have read the story or heard it recounted. Four of Della Porta's comedies were adapted by Cambridge playwrights between 1603 and 1615, while Middleton's *No Wit/Help* (1611) drew for its incest plot on Della Porta's *La Sorella*.[122]

Barry's borrowing of a motif traceable to an Italian comedy is especially interesting in relation to his play's representation of gender. Remarkably, the pregnant, unwed Maria, while experiencing 'shame and guilt' (5.2.3) at her sexual transgression, is invited by Gerardine, at the end of the scene where she dwells in troubled fashion on her plight, to be 'an actress in the comedy' (5.2.36).

Barry may be nodding here at the tradition of the *commedia dell'arte*, in which women were prominent performers.[123] In *Ram Alley*, the cross-dressed Constantia entertains the man she secretly loves with a tale of a 'city dame' who, naked in bed while her maid is warming her smock, gets her leg stuck behind her head while 'practis[ing]' the tricks of the baboons she went to see the previous day (1.2.42, 49). Barry's use of the word 'tumbles' to describe the plight of the woman who, 'trussed up like a football', falls on to the floor is evocative of early modern acrobats or 'tumblers' (1.2.54, 57). In the late sixteenth century, report was made of 'the unchaste … and unnatural tumbling of the Italian women' who performed in London, doubtless more dexterously than Constantia's city wife.[124] Thus, the self-reflexivity of Barry's plays for the King's Revels Children accommodates the comic representation of female performance. *Ram Alley*'s cameo of a female citizen exposing her vulva to her husband and neighbours is both lewd and satirical; in contrast, Gerardine's use of the term 'actress' is more neutral. Yet the critical reception of Maria's and Gerardine's sexual relationship in *FoL* highlights the problematic aspect of Maria's premarital pregnancy.[125]

In my discussion of the authorship debate surrounding *FoL* I have pointed to Barry's predilection for pastiche, what Freebury-Jones and his co-authors term his operation as a 'literary pirate'.[126] Most of the 'seven types of intertextuality' identified by Robert Miola are at work in *FoL*, but predominantly quotation, the 'source proximate' and the 'source remote'.[127] An Elizabethan attack on a 'pre-Familist' group by John Rogers warrants consideration as a 'paralogue', a text 'that illuminate[s] the intellectual, social, theological, or political meanings' of another text.[128] Dryfat's remark about almsgiving in 3.2, and the password for entry to the Familist meeting bungled by the jealous Purge in the same scene, form part of a penumbra of Familist practices described and enacted in the play that derive from a 'confession' of 1561 excerpted in Rogers's *The Displaying of an Horrible Sect of Gross and Wicked Heretics* (1578). Barry subordinates these details to his comic purpose as he was engaged 'not by the reliability of the text but by its extravagance with the truth'.[129]

FoL contains parallels to a second intertext with Familist resonances, the anonymous, unpublished Cambridge play *Club Law* (1600). This 'merry (but abusive)' comedy was performed at Clare Hall, as part of 'a long-standing feud between the University and the town of Cambridge, which at the close of the sixteenth century had become specially acute'.[130] Composed, according to the seventeenth-century Church historian Thomas Fuller, by unidentified 'young scholars', *Club Law* was performed before an academic audience among whom were interspersed the mayor of Cambridge with members of the town corporation and their wives. The townsfolk had been invited expressly to see themselves lampooned, and in Fuller's account fifty-five years later, 'Sit still they could not for chafing, go out they could not for crowding, but impatiently patient were fain to attend till dismissed at the end of the comedy.'[131] In the mock trial that concludes *FoL*, Gerardine and his associates bounce the term 'club-law' around in a manner that suggests Barry's familiarity with the Cambridge play. Furthermore, the alias 'Nicholas Nebulo' assumed by Gerardine (4.3.52) forms an 'obvious and precise' parallel with the name 'Nicholas Nifle' belonging to the new mayor elected in the course of *Club Law*. Both names pointedly allude to Familism's founder, Hendrik Niclaes, whose surname Jonson englished in *The Alchemist* as 'Harry Nicholas' (5.5.117).[132]

In his overview of intertextual relationships, Miola posits a mode of imitation that he calls 'the source coincident', where an 'earlier text exists as a whole in dynamic tension with [a] later one, a part of its identity'.[133] Two literary sources manifest themselves within *FoL* in this manner: Marlowe's erotic epyllion *Hero and Leander* and Shakespeare's *Romeo and Juliet*.[134] Barry's 'adaptive impulse' contributes especially to his exposition of Maria's character.[135] In the opening scene she proclaims love's unstoppable force to her uncle and aunt in lines that echo the celebrated passage from Marlowe's poem beginning, 'It lies not in our power to love or hate' (1.1.13–16n). Later, Maria mocks Lipsalve's efforts to woo her in Gerardine's persona by channelling Hero from her bedroom window:

> *Maria.* Whom do I see? Oh, how my senses wander!
>   Am not I Hero? Art not thou Leander?
> *Gerardine.* Th'art in the right, sweet wench, more of that vein. (3.1.98–100)

Gerardine's 'more of that *vein*' points to the tone of burlesque that pervades the scene. While the register here enhances the audience's view of Maria as a comic agent, the window sequence of 1.2, informed both by the balcony scene of *Romeo and Juliet* and Marston's 'unmistakably comic' reminiscence of it in *Jack Drum's Entertainment*, sets up an instability of representation surrounding the heroine.[136] Barry's use of his sources produces at its best this kind of dialectical dramaturgy that keeps us questioning our responses to the characters.

STAGING AND STAGECRAFT

Like the district foregrounded in Thomas Shadwell's *The Squire of Alsatia* (1688), the liberty of Whitefriars, where Barry and Drayton's indoor playhouse was located, afforded sanctuary to 'fugitives, debtors, and prostitutes' and as a result had earned a reputation as a shady part of London.[137] In Jonson's *Volpone* (1606), Lady Would-Be mistakes the youth Peregrine for a cross-dressed Venetian courtesan, believing s/he hails from 'your Whitefriars nation!' (4.2.51). In her passionate dressing-down of the 'hermaphrodite', Lady Would-Be mingles accusations of sexual and religious dissidence with threatened punishment for the former:

> for your carnival concupiscence,
> Who here is fled for liberty of conscience
> From furious persecution of the marshal,
> Her will I disple [discipline]. (4.2.60–3)

Lady Would-Be's association of 'liberty of conscience' with the area of Whitefriars suggests an appropriateness of fit between *FoL*'s venue and its notional subject, a consonance further demonstrated in Jonson's Whitefriars comedy *Epicene* (1610), with its Ladies Collegiate who advocate for women's freedom to commit adultery with impunity.

Two companies successively occupied the Whitefriars playhouse: the shortlived Children of the King's Revels, followed by the Children of the Whitefriars from 1609 to 1614. Their audiences were diverse. Jonson wrote *Epicene* for the latter troupe, envisaging his comic repast in the Prologue as containing some elements 'fit for ladies: some for lords, knights, squires, / Some for your waiting-wench and city-wires, / Some for your men and daughters of Whitefriars' (22–4). To Jonson's census of the Whitefriars audience we must add a good number of lawyers and law students from the Inns of Court, with one of which the precinct of Whitefriars shared a gate (see *FoL*, 2.4.3–4n).

The playhouse that was built in the old 'great hall' of the former monastery appears to have been a good deal longer and narrower than the private playhouse at the Blackfriars, and both Barry and

Jonson after him exploited its smaller stage and reduced upper playing area.[138] In the opening scene of *FoL* Glister tells Maria that her zone of movement will be restricted to 'this gallery and your upper chamber' (1.1.31), his words mapping a dichotomy between main stage and upper stage around which the action unfolds. Three scenes take place at and below Maria's window: in each Barry maintains a dual audience focus on characters below and those above (1.2, 3.1, 5.2), ringing changes on the interplay of observer(s) and observed. He varies this stage dynamic in a further scene where Glister views the 'barriers' he has engineered between the gallants Lipsalve and Gudgeon from an elevated 'standing' or vantage point (3.3.26).[139]

In her discussion of the expedients used by playwrights in response to the particularly confined playing space of the Whitefriars, Jean MacIntyre notes the 'interior realism' created by 'large pieces of furniture set up in the discovery space ... as well as numerous smaller pieces carried onto the main stage by servant characters'.[140] The trunk bequeathed by Gerardine to Maria in his will is one such piece of furniture, providing realism, diversion, and topical interest. Carried on to the stage by Glister's apprentice Club and a helper in 2.4, it was probably placed in the discovery space. The scene shifts to the heroine's bedroom, where the trunk becomes the target of Maria's 'moan' lamenting 'th'unequal scale / Of avarice' (2.5.8, 7) which caused Glister to reject Gerardine for his lack of material 'substance' (2.4.54). The melodrama intensifies as Gerardine, *'rising out of the trunk'*, alarms Maria, who *'seems fearful and flies'* (2.5.14.1). Only when Gerardine assures his lover that he is 'the firm substance of [her] truest friend' does she relax (2.5.21). Gerardine's re-entry into the trunk and his appearance out of it on two more occasions gives Barry the opportunity to maximise reference to the noisome, cramped, and claustrophobic prison dubbed 'Little Ease' to which the Warden of Fleet prison had recently been committed (3.1.9n). Following the couple's stolen consummation, implied as occurring between 3.1 and 3.4, there is no dramatic purpose for the trunk. The focus of the main plot shifts to Gerardine's 'intercourse amongst [his] friends' in various guises (3.4.34) as he engineers the mock trial that culminates in the lovers' marriage.

The spectacle of Gerardine emerging from an opened trunk, perhaps from within the recessed discovery space between the two stage doors, brings to mind the remark of the Renaissance architect

Leon Battista Alberti that 'theatres are made entirely of openings ... particularly of windows and doors'.[141] The four window or balcony scenes reinforce this impression, shifting tones between romance, parody, and farce. The moments when 'the bawdy intricacies of comedy' are most tantalisingly evoked occur in the two scenes where characters enter – or attempt to enter – the religious zone of the Familist meeting (3.2, 4.1).[142] In both scenes the activities transacted within the meeting provide an absent centre around which the action spirals; that space, synonymous with the discovery space in the theatre, is represented only by an anonymous voice that answers '*within*' (3.2.90 SH). Having been refused entry in the first of these scenes for want of the password, Master Purge overhears his wife and the gallants gain entry to the meeting with the correct password. Speaking the password, he is admitted with the delicious words of the voice within, 'Enter, and welcome' (4.1.125).

One city locale associated with the Family of Love in the play is the Hole in the Wall, where, according to Purge, its members 'assemble together *in the daytime*' (5.3.96, my emphasis). 'The Hole in the Wall' was a traditional name for a pub. However, as they were alleged to do in an Elizabethan attack on the group, in the play the Family holds its meetings by night; in 3.2 Dryfat specifically queries why Mistress Purge and Club, her linkbearer, are heading to a meeting 'by night' (3.2.18). Thus, contrary to the argument developed by Helga Duncan in her exploration of notions of space in *FoL*, the Hole in the Wall is unlikely to be the venue of the Familist meeting that is integral to the plot.[143] Instead, Familist 'exercise' takes place in a literal hole in the tiring-house wall – an indeterminate space that Barry leaves deliberately unspecified. As a consequence, what the Family *does*, the activities its members engage in, remains tantalisingly off limits.

The origin of the 'young men [and] lads' who comprised the Children of the King's Revels is unknown, nor, with one exception, do we know what happened to them when the enterprise folded.[144] Bly estimates that the Whitefriars actors 'were probably between 14 and 17 years of age'. Other scholars suggest an extended upper age limit of the early twenties for so-called 'boy' players; what is key is that Jacobean companies comprised wholly of youths presented an image of 'sexually liminal adolescent perform[ance]'.[145] The first company at the Whitefriars would have had actors to perform the spectrum of *FoL*'s characters, with the older, more physically mature youths taking the roles of Glister, Purge, Dryfat, Club, Gerardine, and the two gallants, and younger, smaller 'lads' assuming the three female roles and those of the pages Periwinkle and Shrimp.

Unlike many other children's company plays, *FoL* contains no directions for entr'acte music, even though 'music' (meaning musicians) is listed as one of the 'charges of the house' in the Articles of Agreement between the shareholders and Martin Slater. Nevertheless, as consort music was a special feature of the indoor playhouses, such music may have been provided. The two songs that appear so casually tossed off by Lipsalve in 1.2. and 1.3 may also have had musical accompaniment. One scene arguably demands musical performance of a more arresting kind. In 1.2 Maria enters '*at the window*', unaware of Gerardine and the gallants below. Following an emotive soliloquy that is undercut by the libertines' asides, Barry allows Maria a moment of reflection and fantasy, scripting words that clearly call for a prop.

> Maria. [*Taking her lute*] Come thou, my best companion, thou art sensible
>   And canst my wrongs reiterate. Thou and I
>   Will make some mirth, in spite of tyranny.
>   [*She plays.*] (1.2.84–6.1)

No editor has discussed the object Maria addresses as her 'best companion', with which she envisages 'mak[ing] ... mirth'. The obvious action for the actor playing Maria is to take up a lute (or other instrument) to musically resound her woes, affording her both solace and mirth. Deanne Williams remarks that in the early modern period, 'lute instruction constitut[ed] a form of serious play, a girl's rehearsal or imaginative preparation for love and marriage'.[146] In this vein, playing the lute would be preparatory to Maria's meditation on love and lovers, in tones replete with erotic yearning (1.2.87–94). In performance, the scene could be rendered effective by the boy-actor either playing a lute, or miming to a lutenist concealed on one side of the upper stage area. The coterie audience would have appreciated a musical interlude, similar to Francheschina's singing and lute-playing in Marston's *Dutch Courtesan*.

Peter Corbin and Douglas Sedge have identified in Barry's *Ram Alley* 'a quality of conscious and comparatively sophisticated theatricality suggesting a relaxed and knowing contract with its audience'.[147] Barry's rapport with his audience and his dramaturgical responsiveness to the spatial dynamics of the Whitefriars are evident throughout *FoL*, from the small talk before supper in which Lipsalve describes Samson bearing the town gates 'from the lower to the upper stage' to the play's evocation of hidden spaces and its sympathetic staging of its *innamorata*. Although Dutton doubts that the company reached a sufficiently high standard to perform at court, the author's testimony that the comedy won 'a general applause' ('To the Reader', 11), together with other playwrights' imitation of aspects of its staging, make the play's contemporary success a plausible idea.[148] The fact that *FoL* was not revived or reprinted in the seventeenth century is less likely a result of its original reception than of the changing theatrical and political climate which would have found Barry's rumbustious comedy offensive.[149] To date there have been no modern productions of *FoL*. In Marsh's study of the sect published in 1994, he noted that the Royal Shakespeare Company had 'failed to respond to [his] suggestion that it consider staging *The Family of Love* in the Swan Theatre'.[150] Twenty-five years on, additional performance venues suggest themselves, especially the intimate space of the London Globe's Wanamaker Playhouse. It is my hope that this edition will provoke and enable modern productions that afford Barry's comedy a fresh hearing.

THE PLAY

It is remarkable how interest in *The Family of Love* among literary scholars and historians has developed independently of critical discussion of the play's authorship. Superseding Swinburne's influential dismissal of it as 'unquestionably ... the worst of Middleton's plays', formalist and historicist critics publishing since the 1960s have found *FoL* worthy of notice for its multiple plots, its handling of tropes of pregnancy, purgation and sacred space, and its refreshingly tolerant, even celebratory, depiction of the religious sect it mocks.[151] Investigations of the play as authored by Barry are currently few, but this edition may provoke an increase in such discussions.[152] While his comedies lack the satirical urgency of Marston's and Middleton's ironic social nuance, Barry was an effective writer who exploited the farcical, flexible possibilities of action and character offered by drama tailored for youthful players. As London's cosmopolitan culture enabled Shakespeare to imagine a heroine who pleads eloquently as a lawyer in *The Merchant of Venice*, so its religious melting pot allowed Barry to script a citizen, Rebecca Purge, who is an 'elder' in the Family of Love. Moreover, the comedy arguably celebrates its heroine, Maria, as an 'actress'. In these respects and others, Barry's play warrants the epithet 'experimental'. *FoL* culminates in a richly detailed pastiche of a Church court hearing, where Doctor Glister appears on charges of fornication and incest with his niece. Maria appears at the court session pregnant and unmarried. Following an elaborate hoax perpetrated against Glister by Gerardine and his friends, Maria is given to Gerardine in marriage. The anticipated condemnation of the roving Mistress Purge, charged with concupiscence, does not eventuate. Instead, Rebecca Purge is reclaimed within the marital fold, although she declares that her love 'must be free still to God's creatures' (5.3.412–13).

In 1986 Mistress Purge's proviso drew this response from a critic of city comedy: 'If Mistress Purge's love "must be free still to God's creatures" … then we have no reason to imagine that a new, purged, comic society will emerge from the fifth-act trial.'[153] But we do not watch or read comedy solely for the promise of social and moral reform. The world Barry represents in *FoL* commands and repays our interest partly for the unusual features already mentioned, partly for its palpable stageability, and again because of its pungent, vital comedic texture.

Genre

Humours play; dramatic satire; citizen comedy; scatological farce: *The Family of Love* shares in all these modes. As Mulholland notes, the terms 'city comedy' and 'citizen comedy' 'are more or less interchangeable, but signify different focuses of attention or emphases'. A 'citizen comedy' involves 'a fluid social group … [and] dramatize[s] broad social issues that do not depend on class only'. Such comedy deals with 'everything from lightweight farce to pieces that verge on domestic drama'.[154] The domesticity of *FoL* inheres in its focus on marriage and its infringement through adultery, fornication, and alleged incest, and in the array of domestic phenomena to which we are exposed: a trunk, close-stools, a standing cup, brown sugar candy, eggs, and 'taps-droppings' (a Barry neologism for ale). While its action takes place in London, the comedy is oddly delocalised, lacking the topographical reference that characterises plays such as Barry's *Ram Alley*, Middleton's *Michaelmas Term* and *Chaste Maid in Cheapside*, the collaborative *Eastward Ho!*, and Jonson's *Epicene* and *The Alchemist*. In his first play, Barry does not attempt 'a verisimilar London setting'.[155] Instead, the focus is at once international (Brussels, Geneva) and urban, with fleeting references to Holborn Bridge (4.1.121), Pissing Alley and Do Little Lane (5.3.355, 356), the latter addresses invoked by Dryfat as residences of back-street female abortionists. The city environment is brought to life by references to lawyers, porters, citizens, playgoers, indeed, to 'youths' like those who enacted Barry's play at the Whitefriars. The dialogue bristles with the language of merchants, of clothing such as ruffs, standing collars and 'dirty startups' (4.3.60), the panoply of 'observed life' that distinguished the new mode of London comedy at which Barry was trying his hand.[156]

Commentators have differed over the degree of satirical punch landed by *FoL*. The descriptor 'sectarian bigotry' used by Taylor, Mulholland, and Jackson is overstated, for the mystical fellowship indicated in the title forms only part of the comedy's wider concerns with love and marriage.[157] Barry's multiple plot juxtaposes the romantic natural love of Gerardine and Maria; the marriages of the citizen couples, the Glisters and the Purges (with the satire focusing on the men's conduct, rather than the women's); and the libertine pleasure-seeking of Lipsalve and Gudgeon.[158] The action is pitched strongly against Glister's credo, 'Wealth commands all' (3.1.173). Yet at the same time, this doctor wields considerable power by overseeing the punishments visited upon two younger men whose cynicism about women and sexual relationships mirrors his own. While Barry saves Glister's demise for the final scene, the character of Purge forms a focus of satirical humour throughout. In his first soliloquy Purge strikes a note of complacent inclusiveness as he determines to 'wink at small faults' (2.1.22–3), rationalising his exploitation of his wife's attractiveness as good for his business:

> I smile to myself to hear our knights and gallants say how they gull us citizens, when indeed we gull them, or rather, they gull themselves. Here they come in term time, hire chambers, and perhaps kiss our wives — well, what lose I by that? God's blessing on's heart ... that makes much of my wife; for they were very hard-favoured that none could find in's heart to love but ourselves. (2.1.12–19)

Although prostitution and capitalism (commodification) are frequently linked in city comedies, Purge here trades on his wife's physical attractions, but not explicitly her sexual favours. Mistress Purge is the magnet that draws customers inside the shop. Likewise, Glister and Purge are bound by a desire for mutual profit: 'Drugs would be dog cheap', continues the apothecary, 'but for my private, well-practised doctor, and such customers' (19–21). By prescribing pills to his female patients, Glister inflates the price of drugs;

furthermore, he keeps his sexual intimacies with patients such as Mistress Purge close to his chest. While Middleton's Allwit in *A Chaste Maid in Cheapside* (1613) makes no bones of the fact that the aristocratic Sir Walter Whorehound 'keeps' his wife and family (1.2.17), Purge's 'wink at small faults' is ambiguous, concealing from the audience whether he is ignorant of his wife's affair with Glister.

When we next see Purge in 3.2, his jealousy of his wife has gained the better of him; hence, he intercepts her on her way to the Family, but bungling the password, fails to gain entry to the meeting. His soliloquy at this point drives home his fundamental misogyny and disrespect for Mistress Purge:

> For my part I like not this Family, nor indeed some kind of private lecturing that women use; look to't, you that have such gadders to your wives; self-willed they are as children, and i'faith capable of not much more than they, peevish by custom, naturally fools. (3.2.104-8)

Barry expands the inclusive pronouns of Purge's earlier soliloquy ('our', 'us') to direct audience address: 'look to't, you'. This technique whereby Purge takes the audience into his confidence sets him up to fail. His uncertainty about becoming a cuckold is illustrated by his show of bravado at the end of the scene: 'What wise men bear is not for me to scorn; / 'Tis a horner-able thing to wear the horn' (3.2.128-9). The self-betraying pun, 'horner-able', plays on honour as a gentry trait and being 'horned' as a cuckold. The couplet captures Purge's anxiety about his social status; he would join the ranks of the 'honourable' knights he boasts of gulling, yet his slip reveals that 'wear[ing] the horn' is merely 'horner-able'.

Purge's inherent meanness is brought home by his tactics after he gains entry to the second Familist meeting that occurs offstage (4.1.125 SD). Afterwards, he laments that he has made himself 'a plain cuckold' (4.4.44). He is overheard by the gallants, who themselves attended the meeting disguised as Familists, hoping thereby to seduce Mistress Purge. Failing in their intent, and having witnessed Purge's quandary, the libertines tell Purge they are willing to testify against his wife in court. Purge's narrative pivots on the ring he took from his wife's finger as a symbol of sexual intimacy:

> This is my wedding ring. 'Tis it, I know it by the posy. This I took from her finger in the dark, and she was therewith very well pleased. Were not this, trow, a sufficient testimony? She knows not that it was myself got so near her. (4.4.50-4)

Once again, in the phrase 'trow' ('don't you think?'), the audience becomes privy to Purge's obsessive jealousy. That the gallants readily support his urge to have his wife publicly exposed and condemned points to the masculine bias underpinning the city's social hierarchy. The same bias explains the merchant Dryfat's willingness to play a prominent role in Gerardine's plot, and these two men's ability to co-opt Club, the Purges' apprentice, into the legal masquerade that subjects his master's marriage to close scrutiny.

Glister alludes to Mistress Purge as his 'vessel of ease' (2.4.143), insinuating both that she is his mistress, and that he uses her for his sexual recreation. Even though the audience is aware of this fact, the charge of adultery brought against Rebecca by her husband in the concluding mock trial is discounted by Gerardine in his guise as the legal Doctor Stickler: 'Go to, thou hast a good wife', he tells Purge (5.3.416). This is a verdict not so much on Mistress Purge's morality, which is certainly flawed, as on her quick wit, illustrated by her terming her missing wedding ring an 'unnecessary thing' in comparison to 'the poor [who] begs at [her] gate', a point she drives home with reference to the moral axioms she 'learned last lecture' (5.3.255-7).

Initially Club and subsequently Dryfat put forward the satirical view of the Family of Love as an immoral sect. Chatting with Mistress Glister after delivering to her house the trunk in which Gerardine is concealed, Club informs her that Familists 'love their neighbours better than themselves'; he offers this admiringly as one instance of their 'perfection' (2.4.71-2, 68). When Mistress Glister demurs, 'Not than themselves, Club', he responds, 'Yes, better than themselves, for they love them better than their husbands, and husband and wife are all one; therefore, better than themselves' (2.4.74-6). Club narrows his terms of reference specifically to female Familists, representing them across the board as adulterers. Dryfat describes the threat of female Familist promiscuity in the mock-court scene in Act 5. He performs in this scene as Gerardine's accomplice, disguised as Poppin the proctor, an attorney acting for Masters Glister and Purge. He acts not just as proctor, but as prosecutor in characterising Familist gatherings, and Familists' sexual mores, to those assembled at the trial. Poppin indicts the group as

> a crew of narrow-ruffed, strait-laced, yet loose-bodied dames, with a rout of *omnium gatherums*, assembled by the title of the Family of Love

... if they be not punished and suppressed by our club-law, each man's copyhold will become freehold, specialities will turn to generalities; and so from unity to parity, from parity to plurality, and from plurality to universality: their wives ... will be made common. (5.3.185–95)

This articulation of the threat posed by sexually independent female Familists is comically melodramatic, but informed by authentic anxiety conveyed in scaremongering words such as 'crew', 'rout', 'punished and suppressed'.[159] Here, as elsewhere, it is difficult to determine where Dryfat stands. At this point, he ventriloquises for Purge as the fellowship's 'accuser' (5.3.184). Does he draw on the impression formed when, apparently innocently, but possibly underhandedly, he 'popped in' to the Familist meeting with Mistress Purge in 3.2? Shepherd states that Dryfat 'becomes a Familist, apparently for sexual reasons', but the most we can say is that Dryfat's motivation is undeveloped.[160] His questions to Mistress Purge about the fellowship's beliefs and practices in 3.2 could be interpreted as a respectable ploy masking lewd intentions; at the same time, the discussion allows Mistress Purge to expatiate on what Familists do in their meetings. Following his attendance at the meeting, Dryfat avers to Gerardine, 'I hope to see you a Familist before I die' (4.2.67–8). Rather than an articulation of religious belief, this surely constitutes bantering encouragement to the younger man to persist in his relationship with Maria through to marriage and the birth of children. Marsh notes astutely that 'Much of [*FoL*'s] appeal lies in the inconsistency of its judgements'.[161] Whether we regard Dryfat as a Familist or not is one of the play's awkward conundrums.

The point to stress here is that, like both Maria and Club, Dryfat provides Gerardine with crucial assistance in obtaining what the latter wants, namely the girl and the money. Critics have stressed Gerardine's origins in Roman New Comedy, calling him, for example, 'a[n] ... actor of Ovidian pretensions and intent'.[162] Gerardine is certainly a Protean trickster, whose flamboyant disguises bear a relationship both to Cocledemoy in *The Dutch Courtesan* and Jonson's Volpone. His clever device of the trunk as a false bequest and means to smuggle himself into Glister's house sets the intrigue plot in motion. Yet, in contrast to Marston and Jonson, the author of *FoL* 'controls his people in the same way that baroque musicians subordinated the individual to give fullness and harmony to the piece as a whole'.[163] In Barry's first comedy (unlike

Ram Alley), no one character has sufficient flair to dominate over the others.

'I hope my body has no organs': language and style
Two words in a seventeenth-century hand on the title page of my copy-text sum up a long-standing response to *FoL*: 'sorry comedy' (figure 3). Denoting something judged of inferior value, the epithet 'sorry' also suggests an earlier reader's recoil from the play's scabrous elements. Expressions such as Gudgeon's 'I could never yet open the close-stool of my mind to [Mistress Purge]' (3.3.16–17) form part of the play's exploration of the bodily grotesque. The cynical libertines receive a full measure of audience contempt via such language. This contempt is fully unleashed in Lipsalve's and Gudgeon's sufferings at the hands of Doctor Glister, and publicly marked in the proctor Poppin's mocking invitation to them to 'Cast about this way, and bewray what you can concerning Mistress Purge' (5.3.228–9), where the verbs 'cast' and 'bewray' pun respectively on vomiting and defecating. The 'dung-hill' humour is shared by the male characters, young and old: a choice example is Club's account of Glister's entrance to his neighbour Purge's shop: 'comes Master Doctor Glister, as his manner is, squirting in suddenly' (4.1.59–61n). Glister 'squirts' in as liquid would squirt from a syringe with which this punningly named doctor might administer a 'clyster', or even as liquid faeces 'squirts' from an anus. One imagines the company of adolescent actors taking a riotous pleasure in these lines, and in whatever action accompanies an exuberant speech uttered by Gerardine, as the porter Nicholas Nebulo, delivering a fraudulent letter to the Glister household. When Mistress Glister exclaims 'you would be bummed [walloped] for your roguery if you were well served', Nicholas may slap his well-padded porter's behind before offering it to her to kiss, retorting, 'I am bummed well enough already, mistress. Look here else ... sir-reverence in your worship, master doctor's lips are not made of better stuff' (4.3.81–6). The outwardly respectful address, 'sir-reverence in your worship', cloaks a delight in toilet humour, for 'sir-reverence' was a catchphrase uttered when one came across a lump of human excrement in the street. Writing about the 'small, merry books' of late Stuart England, Margaret Spufford notes that 'jokes about defecation and urination' appear to have been universally relished; women as well as men in the Whitefriars audience might have laughed at the above jests.[164] Significantly the character most disturbed by the play's

seamy humour is the houseproud Mistress Glister. Gerardine's impersonation of the boorish porter (whose name chimes with the surname of Hendrik 'Niclaes') causes her acute physical discomfort; she reviles him, and expresses the fear that 'he will spew or do worse before [her]' (4.3.92–3n). 'Do worse' suggests that Mistress Glister is anxious that the 'filthy' Nicholas might defecate on her clean floor (4.3.60).

In pointed contrast to the crude language employed by the citizen characters and the lustful gallants, Barry employs a metaphysical diction for his young lovers that shows how they are swept away by the experience of being in love. Maria's defence of married sexual relations to her aunt is a case in point:

> Disgrace not that for which our sex was made,
> Society in nuptial beds. Above these joys
> Which lovers taste, when their conjoinèd lips
> Suck forth each other's souls, the earth, the air,
> Yea, gods themselves know none. Elysium's sweet,
> Ay, all that bliss which poets' pens describe,
> Are only known when soft and amorous folds
> Entwine the corps of two united lovers,
> Where what they wish they have, yet still desire,
> And sweets are known without satiety. (2.4.31–40)

The diction is Latinate ('conjoinèd', 'Elysium', 'corps', 'satiety'), yet the speech gains momentum and flow from the high number of run-on lines, a feature of Barry's verse generally. While one sees Trollope's point in describing the verse of *FoL* as 'more prosaic than the prose', Maria's rhapsody does not qualify for that putdown; indeed, when she celebrates lovers' 'conjoinèd lips / Suck[ing] forth each other's souls', the line has a positive erotic inflection that startlingly re-pitches it from its source in Marlowe's *Faustus*.[165] Critics have used words such as 'strained' or 'frigid' to describe Maria's and Gerardine's speech, but arguably 'juvenile' would be more apt, bearing in mind the ages of the 'young men and lads' who enacted the play. The tutelary tone of Gerardine's discourse with Maria at the start of Act 3 sounds like an experienced actor instructing a neophyte (3.1.1–59). As Scott proposes, in the language of Maria, with its echoes of Marlowe's Ovidian epyllion, 'the playwright strongly hints that [*Hero and Leander*'s] more romantic, earnest, and honest view of love and relationships is a preferable alternative to the cynical masculine Ovidian perspective ... advanced by the Mercurial libertinism of Lipsalve, the cynicism of Glister, and the misogyny that their lines promulgate almost unconsciously'.[166]

In contrast to Barry's classically inflected verse, his colloquial prose seethes with energy derived from its obsessive punning and bodily biases. This trait especially invigorates the female voices that are heard in the play, like that of the wet nurse Thomasine Tweedles, alleged author of a begging letter fabricated by Gerardine but addressed to Doctor Glister:

> *The cause of my writing ... is to let you understand that your little son is turned a ragged colt, a very stripling, for being now stripped of all his clothing, his backside wants a tail-piece, commends itself to your fatherly consideration. Woe worth the time that ever I gave suck to a child that came in at the window, God knows how!* (5.3.316–21)

Read aloud in full at the trial by Dryfat, the letter has already been cited, in soundbites, by an increasingly enraged Mistress Glister after Gerardine delivers it to her in 4.3, disguised as Nicholas Nebulo. Watching the housewife read aloud the words he has concocted, Gerardine comments aside, 'She begins to nibble; 'twill take, i'faith' (4.3.99), before quietly disclosing his identity to the bystanding Maria. He thus alerts the audience to the pleasure of witnessing the deception, while the aggrieved response of Mistress Glister on discovering evidence of her husband's 'knavery' allows a virtuoso performance opportunity to the actor playing her role:

> 'Tis so. Rats-bane! I ha' t, it racks on, it torments me! Here 'tis: — *Woe worth the time that ever I gave suck to a child that came in at the window, God knows how!* — villainous lecher! —. *'Yet if thou did but see how like the pert little red-headed knave is to his father'* — damnable doctor! — A bastard in the country, and another towards here. I am out of doubt this is his work. [*To Maria*] You are an arrant strumpet! — Incest, fornication, abomination in my own house! ... Oh, for long nails to scratch out his eyes! (4.3.112–21)

The impact of Mistress Glister's lines relies on the two-tone clown act, like Carlo Buffone's two-cup act in *Every Man Out of His Humour*, or Feste's two-voice act outside Malvolio's prison window.

Another striking feature of *FoL* is Barry's dependence on puns as a source of humour. Bly usefully terms such wordplay 'performative puns'.[167] This linguistic aspect of the play comes strongly to the fore in 3.2, where Dryfat engages Mistress Purge in dialogue about spiritual 'exercise' (3.2.17). Their discussion touches on genuine religious questions, even while such questions are resolved into carnal meanings.

> *Dryfat.* I think we perform those functions best when we are not thrall to the fetters of the body.
> *Mist. Purge.* The fetters of the body? What call you them?
> *Dryfat.* The organs of the body, as some term them.
> *Mist. Purge.* Organs? Fie, fie, they have a most abominable squeaking sound in mine ears; they edify not a whit, I detest 'em. I hope my body has no organs.
> *Dryfat.* To speak more familiarly, Mistress Purge, they are the senses: the sight, hearing, smelling, taste, and feeling.
> *Mist. Purge.* Ay, marry. ('Mary', said I? Lord, what a word's that in my mouth!) You speak now, Master Dryfat, but yet let me tell you where you err, too: this feeling I will prove to be neither organ nor fetter, it is a thing — a sense, did you call it?
> *Dryfat.* Ay, a sense.
> *Mist. Purge.* Why, then, a sense let it be — I say it is that we cannot be without, for, as I take it, it is a part belonging to understanding. Understanding, you know, lifteth up the mind from earth; if the mind be lift up, you know the body goes with it. Also it descends into the conscience, and there tickles us with our works and doings, so that we make singular use of feeling. (3.2.22–43)

The punning impetus in 'organ', 'thing', and 'feeling' steers this dialogue away from the interesting matter of the role of the senses in religious devotion. Yet for a moment, Dryfat's assertion of the desirability of keeping separate spirit and sense inspires Rebecca Purge to discourse on the simultaneity of feeling and spiritual understanding.

'Understanding' is a key word in Niclaes's writings: for example, in *Prophecy of the Spirit of Love* he exhorts readers to 'harken unto the upright serviceable word of the holy understanding', while an anonymous Familist manuscript, *Ordo Sacerdotis*, sets forth the stages of the priesthood of 'holy understanding'.[168] In tracing some precedents and influences on the historical Family of Love, Marsh suggests that the English versions of Niclaes's writings are better placed within a tradition of medieval English mystics than within the sectarian traditions of Lollardy and Anabaptism. Familist writings stress the idea of human perfectibility via the transformation of the individual soul; this transformation was necessary to become one of the fellowship's elders. The believer achieved this end by developing 'an extraordinary power to empathise with Christ' in his suffering and death. English antecedents for this aspect of Familist devotion can be found in the medieval mystics Thomas à Kempis and Walter Hilton; this 'sensory consciousness' also has elements in common with the writings of the continental mystic Saint Ignatius, whose *Spiritual Exercises* prescribed the systematic sensory contemplation of scenes from the New Testament.[169] Mistress Purge's disputation with Dryfat on feeling, of which she says the Family 'makes singular use', bears traces of this broader spiritual tradition.

'Efficacy in carnal mixtures' (3.2.49–50): marriage and sexuality
In his study of citizen comedy Alexander Leggatt pairs *FoL* with Middleton and Rowley's *A Fair Quarrel* as two plays 'which ... challenge the idea that an unmarried woman must be either a virgin or a whore'.[170] As a randy young woman who fancies herself a romantic heroine, Maria is arguably a relative of the 'bawdy virgins' who, as Bly points out, populate the Whitefriars repertory. Maria differs from these characters in that she does not cross-dress; moreover, her mode of eroticism is more learnedly sensuous than 'manifestly lewd'.[171] Unlike her namesake in Middleton's *Chaste Maid*, Maria masquerades as a dishonoured woman who has been impregnated by her uncle, so as to blackmail Glister into relinquishing 'her father's portion' if Gerardine adopts the alleged bastard that is in fact his own child (5.3.423–4). In this respect, Barry's comedy resembles the Italian *novelle* whose heroines Shakespeare made chaste, more than it does the chastely desiring girls and women so familiar to us from Shakespeare's drama.[172]

Scott interprets Maria's pregnancy as Barry's 'secular use of the *felix culpa* trope', an unhappy lapse that turns to good.[173] But Maria's becoming pregnant is more considered than Scott acknowledges, by both partners in the relationship. Maria refers to her 'blushing fault' with a worldly understanding of her pregnancy's role in Gerardine's plan to foil Glister: ''twas ... thine aim', she says, 'T'enforce consent in him that bars thy claim' (3.4.15–16). Maria actively participates in Gerardine's sexual stratagem in order to entrap her uncle; in doing so she *risks*, and indeed endures, the temporary opprobrium of her family, as well as public shame. If Maria is a Hero refashioned for the early seventeenth century, she differs crucially from her Marlovian avatar in not 'saving', but willingly giving her maidenhead.

The 'festal elements' of first wave boys' company plays identified by Michael Shapiro continued into the experimental repertory of the Jacobean indoor theatres.[174] An element of carnival misrule is manifest in the stage image of the sensualised woman presented by Maria in 5.3, her womb containing (as he hopes) Gerardine's 'boy' (3.4.36). Do we imagine the boy-actor playing Maria as running the affective gamut from shame to triumph? One possible posture for the actor is patient and penitent; this attitude seems likely at Maria's first entrance at 5.3.139.2. However, we need to imagine Maria's pregnancy, also, in terms of a prosthetic femininity of the kind required by the actor playing Joan Go'too't when she enters in *The Birth of Merlin*, 'great with child' (2.1.0), or the actor of Helena in *All's Well that Ends Well*, when she enters in the last scene with her pregnant belly leading the way. Maria is silent from the moment of her entrance, but her body is made to speak by Mistress Glister, intent on incriminating her lecherous husband: she addresses the court, 'what say you to his own niece *that looks big upon him*?' (5.3.362–3, my emphasis). This marvellous pun evokes Maria's physicality in the sense of her being 'big with child'; it implies further that she looks boldly at Glister, confronting her uncle with his misdeed. Maria's 'looking big' might encompass the laddish actor's delight in his role, for a youth simulating a great-bellied woman is a preposterous triumph. As the editors of a volume of essays addressing the performance of maternity in early modern England observe, 'both playwrights and actors crafted maternity as a role; as a result theatre would have reflected early modern understanding of maternity but also … it would have participated in producing that understanding'.[175] We should keep this in mind when considering the displaying of Maria's swollen belly that contributes so largely to the hyper-theatricality of *FoL*'s final scene.

Maria's silence in the final scene means that Mistress Glister and Mistress Purge take centre stage as loquacious, articulate women; they deliver some of Barry's liveliest dialogue. Few female characters can rival the élan of Mistress Purge facing down the men at her trial with a word borrowed from Falstaff: 'I had a secret operation, and I knew [Master Purge] then to be my husband e'en by very instinct' (5.3.287–8n). Yet throughout the play the wives are the butts of Barry's satire, oblivious to the insults pitched at them by Gerardine's sexually suggestive bequests: '*a fair, large standing … cup*' and '*a fair bodkin of gold, with two orient pearls*' (1.3.144–5, 148). Mistress Glister's duping by Gerardine and Maria is an unpleasant aspect of the play. Taking her aside at his farewell supper at the end of Act 1, Gerardine carefully primes her for the accusation of incest against her husband that will be critical to the outcome:

> [*While the witnesses sign the will*] Mistress Glister, I have found you always more flexible to understand the estate of a poor gentleman than your husband was willing; therefore, I have thought it a point of charity to reveal the wrongs you sustained by your husband's looseness. Let me tell you in private that the doctor cuckolds Purge oftener than he visits one of his patients; what 'a spares from you, 'a spends lavishly on her. These pothecaries are a kind of panders — look to it! If 'a keep Maria long close, it is for some lascivious end of his own. (1.3.158–67)

Posing as her confidante, Gerardine first discloses to Mistress Glister the fact of her husband's adultery with her neighbour, then, Iago-like, alerts her to the possibility of Glister's more intimate transgression. The shocked distress of Mistress Glister's response — 'She is his niece!' (1.3.168) – returns with added anger in her 'painful public complaint to her husband at his trial': 'thou liest by me like a stone, but abroad th'art like a stone-horse, you old limb-lifter!' (5.3.373–4).[176] Sexual loneliness and resentment fuel the withering insults 'stone-horse' and 'limb-lifter', indicting Glister as a rampantly promiscuous, fundamentally untrustworthy man.

The death of melancholy

The culminating mock trial of *FoL*, with its multiple disguisings and histrionic performances, is acted in what is, in one sense, a purely ludic space. In the scene prior, Gerardine tells Maria to meet him 'at Dryfat's house … *there's our scene*' (5.2.39, my emphasis). 'Dryfat's house' is the theatrical space in which Gerardine and Maria, with their supporting cast, enact the 'comedy' that effects their 'wished conjunction' (5.2.36, 34). That this is playful rather than bitter comedy is made clear in the warm-up exchange between Dryfat and Club, dressed respectively as proctor and crier. Dryfat encourages Club, 'come, there's a merry fray towards. We shall see the death of melancholy, wherein thou and I must call a grand jury of jests, and pass upon them with the club-law' (5.3.1–4). Dryfat invokes the affirmation of mirth within a framework of patriarchal judgement: those called to account before the mock 'grand jury' — Doctor Glister, Mistress Purge, and, incidentally, the gallants — will be judged and sentenced by the men's 'club-law'. Dryfat explains this as 'a law enacted … to qualify the rage of the time, to follow, to call back, and sometimes to encounter gentlemen when they run in arrearages' (5.3.8–11). Grasping the baton, Club asserts enthusiastically that club-law is 'as easily learned as the felling of wood and getting of children; all is but laying on load the downright blow' (5.3.19–21). Defined by Club, 'club-law' is masculinist and coercive, a matter of brute force. Dryfat qualifies Club's aggression when he explains that 'by way of exhortation [club-law] prints this moral sentence on their costards ... "Agree, for the law is costly"' (5.3.22–4). This tactic of moral manipulation parallels the judgements dealt to Doctor Glister and Master Purge by the quasi-legal team of Gerardine and Dryfat. The most blatant transgressor is Glister, who, in prohibiting Gerardine's and Maria's union, proved himself a 'ward / To gold opinion' (3.1.26–7). 'Doctor Stickler' mollifies the 'severe sentence' (5.3.418–19) he pronounces on Glister by inducing him to consign Maria and her portion to Gerardine, with an additional thousand pounds. Only when Glister has signed and sealed Gerardine's bond do Stickler, Poppin, and Oy the crier uncase as Gerardine, Dryfat, and Club. Glister's astonishment and ire are met by Dryfat and Club, who chorus ironically, 'You are welcome to our club-law!' (5.3.437–8).

Responding to Poole's interpretation of 5.3 as 'a triumphant celebration of the type of spiritual/sexual independence embodied in Mistress Purge', Marsh proposes that the scene 'might ... well be read as a carnivalesque reaffirmation of patriarchy, achieved by highlighting the dangers of its improper application'.[177] This reading tallies with Gerardine's handling of the Purges' troubled marriage. While Dryfat's 'audit' implicitly rebukes Mistress Glister as a 'clamorous wife' (5.3.303), in contrast, Gerardine's final words to Purge are 'thou hast a good wife, and there an end' (5.3.416). The greater fault in this domestic dispute is Purge's, whose 'jealousy and unkindness ... only made [his wife] a stranger in [his] land of Ham' (5.3.398–400). Gerardine enjoins husband and wife to renew sexual relations, in a phallic key: 're-advance your standard, give her new press-money!' (5.3.400–1). Purge's pompous pledge to receive Rebecca 'into the lists of my favour' on condition that she leaves the Family elicits her robust reply: 'Truly, husband, my love must be free still to God's creatures; yea, nevertheless preserving you still as the head of my body, I shall do as the spirit shall enable me' (5.3.412–15). Mistress Purge's shift in the trial scene from the attitude of meekly suffering victim to spirited defiance parallels the doubleness identified by Marsh as characteristic of the Familist's faith. While conservatism and restraint governed the 'outward man' or woman, the inward person 'was bolder and more ambitious', and 'scorned and threatened all who disagreed with him', or her. Mistress Purge's declaration of faith resembles this attitude; indeed, her pronouncement, 'my love must be free still to God's creatures', echoes a Familist ballad printed in 1574, which claimed that while obedience was essential, 'Yet love is free'.[178]

Who is absent from the comic community in *FoL*'s final scene? The witty pages Shrimp and Periwinkle vanish at the end of 4.1, having remarked that their masters Gudgeon and Lipsalve are a 'rare gull' and something 'not much short of a fool' (4.4.74–5, 78–9). Gerardine verbally dismisses the would-be rakes when he rejects Purge's attempt to make them testify to his wife's infidelity: 'Your witness is weak, and sir-reverence on't, without sounder proof they may depart to the close-stool whence they came, and you to your pothecary's shop' (5.3.246–9). While his speech raises our expectation of the gallants' departure, smelly and humiliated, in fact Q indicates no exit for them. Gerardine's later advice that they 'learn the ABC of better manners' and tell the court how the City has used them (5.3.393–4) shows their absorption within the community manifested in the play's conclusion.

Scott suggests that Barry's play 'should end with a marriage or a dance, preferably both'.[179] Gerardine's closing appeal to the audience supports her observation with Puckish confidence: 'Now join with me / For approbation of our Family' (5.3.440–1). This final usage of 'family' resonates expansively: it refers to the newly constituted family of Gerardine, Maria, and their unborn child, to the play *The Family of Love*, to the Family of Love as represented by the play, and possibly to the Whitefriars company of actors, shareholders, and playwrights, and even the 'family' of their audiences and supporters.

NOTES

1 Arber, 3.360.
2 *Ram Alley, or Merry Tricks* was published in two quarto editions in 1611, and was printed in a third quarto edition in 1636. See Fraser, '*Ram Alley*', 7–8.
3 STC 17879a. Dillon misnumbers this copy STC 17879; Dillon, liii.
4 Dillon, xxi.
5 Dillon, xxii.
6 Bly, 127–8.
7 Dillon, xxii.

8 After the initial 'Act 1, scene 1', *Humour Out of Breath* has no further scene divisions.
9 Gurr, 361–2.
10 Baptista Mantuanus, *Adulescentia* [*Youth*], Eclogue 5, 'The treatment of poets by rich men', 63–4, http://www.philological.bham.ac.uk/mantuanus/trans.html#5_1, trans. Lee Piepho (accessed 18 April 2021).
11 McKerrow, no. 280.
12 Dillon, xxviii.
13 Greg, 1, 396; Dillon, ii, ixxx.
14 See 1.2.55–6; 1.2.89–90; 2.4.35, 40.
15 Dillon, 4.4.6n.
16 Dillon uses the terms 'prompt-book', 'prompter's copy', and 'playhouse-copy' (xvii–xviii). Paul Werstine questions the validity of categorising the printer's copy through terms such as 'foul papers', 'fair copy', or 'playhouse-copy' in his article, 'Narratives About Printed Shakespeare Texts: "Foul" Papers and "Bad" Quartos', *SQ* 41 (1990), 65–86.
17 Dillon, xxiv. As it is not substantive, the variant does not appear in my collation notes. The catchword on E2 appears as: 'mour', (H1, SHL, HRC1, Bod.); 'mour:' (H2); 'mour' (HRC2).
18 Dillon, ixxx. Dillon summarises the evidence in favour of two compositors on pp. xxvi–xxx of his introduction.
19 See Dillon, Appendix A, 127–32.
20 *BD* 5.368.
21 Maxwell, 'Date', 196.
22 Dillon, 4.4.80n. Shepherd defines Q's 'Exigent' as an 'officer of [the] Court of Common Pleas', 5.3, 1828n. See *OED* exigenter n. hist.
23 *BD* 5.368; *OED* proctor n.1.
24 See Dutton, *Mastering*, esp. ch. 7, 'The Question of Authority II: The Boy Companies, 1604–10'. Dutton links the 'topical indiscretions' deplored by Samuel Calvert in a letter to Ralph Winwood from 1605 with the Children of the Queen's Revels, who succeeded the King's Revels Children as the Whitefriars' resident company (Dutton, *Mastering*, 190). Given the letter's date, however, Calvert's statement that 'the play[er]s do not … spar[e] either King, state, or religion' from satirical representation is suggestive in the context of possible censorship of *FoL*.
25 Dyce emends 'the wrongs you sustained' to 'the wrongs you sustain', 2.127; while Dillon renders the phrase, 'the wrongs you have sustained', 1.3.160.
26 http://www.tech.org/~cleary/famil.html#PEACE (accessed 18 April 2021).
27 Albert H. Tricomi, 'Counting Insatiate Countesses: The Seventeenth-Century Annotations to Marston's *The Insatiate Countess*', *HLQ* 64 (2001), 111. I owe this reference to Hannah August.
28 Munro, 'Printed Comedy', 40.
29 I am grateful to Murray Edmond for this insight.
30 Biographical information derives from Ewen, and David Kathman, 'Lording Barry', *ODNB*. For details of John Barry's degrees taken at Trinity College in ?1602–03, and 1606 see *Alumni Cantabrigienses*, ed. J. Venn and J. A. Venn (Cambridge: Cambridge University Press, 1922–54),

INTRODUCTION 49

http://www.archive.org/details/alumnicantabrigiptivoliuniviala (accessed 18 April 2021).
31 Lopez, 'Whitefriars', 202. For a comprehensive discussion of the Whitefriars venture, see Ingram, 209–30.
32 By March 1608, the 'Barry–Drayton syndicate' comprised seven shareholders (Ingram, 213).
33 I rely on Ingram's reconstruction of the redrawing of the Whitefriars lease, 219–20. Drayton co-authored twenty-one plays for the Admiral's Men, only one of which survives, *Sir John Oldcastle* (1599); see Jean R. Brink, 'Appendix B: Drayton's Plays', in *Michael Drayton Revisited* (Boston: Twayne, 1990), 140–1.
34 On the patent, see Adams, 311; Ingram, 209. Bly, 117, notes that Drayton's name appeared on the patent. To avoid confusion, I use 'Blackfriars Boys' for the Children of Blackfriars.
35 Bly, 126. Ingram, 209, notes, 'we still do not know ... when [the Whitefriars] began to be used as a playhouse'.
36 Ingram, 217, 212; Bly, 29, 129. On the suspension of all playing in London in April 1608 due to the satirical content of plays staged by the Blackfriars Boys, see Michael Shapiro, 'Boys Companies and Private Theaters', in Kinney, 323.
37 Kathman, 'Barry', *ODNB*; Ewen, 9.
38 Kathman, 'Barry', *ODNB*.
39 Herbert Berry, 'Playhouses', in Kinney, 157; Lopez, 'Whitefriars', 202.
40 Ewen, 6.
41 Fraser, 'Lording Barry', 74. Middleton's *A Trick to Catch the Old One*, in which Fraser spots a first allusion to Barry, was performed first by the second Paul's Boys in 1605, and several years later by the Blackfriars Boys; see Valerie Wayne (ed.), *Trick*, in Middleton, *Collected*, 373–4.
42 Deposition of Thomas Brookes of Maidstone, joiner, dated 15 June 1615, cited in Ewen, 14, 1n.
43 Fraser, 'Lording Barry', 75.
44 Ingram, 225, uses 'financially troubled' of the young Thomas Woodford; see Ewen, 11.
45 Ewen, 11.
46 For a discussion of the mass execution, see Mark Hutchings, 'Acting Pirates: Converting *A Christian Turned Turk*', in Claire Jowitt (ed.), *Pirates? The Politics of Plunder, 1550–1650* (Basingstoke: Palgrave Macmillan, 2007), 92; see also Lois Potter, 'Pirates and "Turning Turk" in Renaissance Drama', in Jean-Pierre Maquerlot and Michèle Willems (eds), *Travel and Drama in Shakespeare's Time* (Cambridge: Cambridge University Press, 1996), 124–40. On the relationship between Barry's piracy and Robert Daborne's *A Christian Turned Turk* (1612), see Potter, 'Pirates', 133–4; Bly, 135–6.
47 Ewen, 13–14; Lopez, 'Whitefriars', 218. For the historical confusion surrounding Lording Barry's name, see Lopez, 'Whitefriars', 213–18.
48 Lopez, 'Whitefriars', 218; deposition of Richard Baker of Youghall, yeoman, dated 12 August 1609, cited in Ewen, 12.
49 Lopez, 'Whitefriars', 216.
50 Bill of complaint of Thomas Woodford, 25 October 1620, cited in Ingram, 215. Critics have decried Barry as derivative, and 'a theatrical

dabbler' (Leinwand, 124). Lopez more generously calls Barry a 'would-be professional entertainer' and 'passionate theatrical amateur' ('Whitefriars', 202, 216).

51 On Barry's maritime activities during 1614–16, see Ewen, 14–15. For an account of an earlier 'gentleman pirate', Henry Strangwish, that resonates with Barry's biography, see Claire Jowitt, *The Culture of Piracy, 1580–1630: English Literature and Seaborne Crime* (Farnham: Ashgate, 2010), 199–201.

52 Kathman, 'Barry', *ODNB*, and David Kathman, 'Grocers, Goldsmiths, and Drapers: Freemen and Apprentices in the Elizabethan Theater', *SQ* 55 (2004), 18–19.

53 Will of Lording Barry, 18 July, 1625, cited in Ewen, 16. Fraser estimates that Barry returned to England in 1620 or 1621, after amassing sufficient money off the coast of North America to buy his share of the *Edward* ('Lording Barry', 76).

54 Lopez, 'Whitefriars', 219.

55 Lopez, 'Whitefriars', 217; Chaucer, 'General Prologue to the Canterbury Tales', line 389.

56 King James I, *Basilicon Doron. Or His Majesty's Instructions to his Dearest Son, Henry the Prince* (1603); see Appendix 3 of this edition, lines 17–19.

57 Marsh, *FLES*, 205; Marsh, 'Heresy', 70.

58 Marsh, *FLES*, 201.

59 Marsh, *FLES*, 17.

60 Niclaes, *Prophecy*, D6, A8.

61 Smith, 164, 173; Moss, 'Godded with God', 1–89; Martin, 60.

62 Smith, 147 (my emphasis).

63 Marsh, 'Heresy', 70–1; Marsh, *FLES*, 116–22.

64 'Clerical antagonists' derives from Martin, 56, 8n; Poole, 76.

65 The six plays are Chapman, *Sir Giles Goosecap* (1602, pub. 1606); Marston, *The Dutch Courtesan* (1605); Chapman, Jonson, and Marston, *Eastward Ho!* (1605); Day, *Isle of Gulls* (1606); Middleton, *A Mad World, My Masters* (1606); Lewis Machin (attrib.), *Every Woman in Her Humour* (1607). Although performed in 1602, the first edition of *Sir Giles Goosecap* 'had been subjected to revision as a result of objections by an ecclesiastical licenser', Taylor, Mulholland, and Jackson, 219.

66 For discussions of the two plays see Sophie Tomlinson, 'Sensuality, Spirit, and Society in *The Dutch Courtesan* and Lording Barry's *The Family of Love* (1608)', *ET* 23 (2020), 67–83; and Andrew Fleck, 'Proximity and the Pox: Pathologizing Infidelity in Marston's *Dutch Courtesan*', *ET* 23 (2020), 98–9.

67 F. G. Fleay, *A Biographical Chronicle of the English Drama* (London: Reeves and Turner, 1891), 2.94; Bald, 'Chronology'. Following Fleay, Hillebrand, Shapiro, Gurr, and Bly view *FoL* as performed initially by the second Children of Paul's, whose last performance was in July 1606, and subsequently by the Children of the King's Revels. See Hillebrand, 234–5; Shapiro, 263, 266; Gurr, 345, 362, 365; and Bly, 147, 12n, 178, 4n.

68 Arber, 3.360.

69 *BD* 5.369. *BD*'s assertion that the title page to *FoL* describes the play as 'lately acted' is an error.

70 Middleton, *Collected*, 452.
71 Articles of Agreement between Martin Slater and the Whitefriars shareholders, cited in Hillebrand, 224. On the 'constraints of corporate bonding' articulated in the Whitefriars contract, see Dutton, 'Birth', 160–1. For accounts of play publication in the period, see Bentley, ch. 10; Brooks, ch. 1.
72 Maxwell, 'Date', 198; Taylor, Mulholland, and Jackson, 224.
73 Dillon, 5.3.251n.
74 Beaumont, *KBP* 5.197.1. The full stage direction in Zitner's edition reads, '*Heaves up the coffin* [and LUCE, *up-ended, scrambles out*].' With Beaumont's use of the coffin in Acts 4 and 5 of *KBP*, compare *FoL* 2.5.14.1–2n, 2.5.15–21n.
75 *BD* 5.368. The *BD* entry for *FoL* spells the pseudonym 'Popin': this spelling occurs once in the 1608 quarto, on Gv. The name is spelled 'Poppin' on H2v (in 6 out of 17 copies), H3v, and H4.
76 MacD. P. Jackson and Michael Neill place the performance of *The Dutch Courtesan* in late 1604/early 1605 (*SM*, 292), Wiggins in summer 1604 (*BD* 5.120). I accept Karen Britland's estimate, 'in the early months of 1605' (Marston, *Dutch C.*, 62).
77 Cathcart, *Marston*, 104.
78 I am indebted to Jonathan Scott for this point.
79 Marsh, 'Heresy', 70.
80 Scott, 349. For hostile English views of Familists, see Moss, 'English Critics', 37, 40; William C. Johnson, 'The Family of Love in Stuart Literature: A Chronology of Name-Crossed Lovers', *JMRS* 7 (1977), 95–112. On Niclaes's concept of 'communialtie', see Martin, 62. For the reputed easiness of divorce in Familist congregations, see J.[ohn] R.[ogers], *The Displaying of an Horrible Sect of Gross and Wicked Heretics, naming themselves the Family of Love*, 1578 (1579 edn), Appendix 3 of this edition, lines 70–3; for communal ownership of goods among Familists, see Appendix 3, lines 9–16.
81 *Boswell's Life of Johnson* (1791), cited in Love, 7.
82 *BD* 5.369.
83 Appended to *The Old Law* (1656), by Middleton, Massinger and Rowley; repr. in Greg, 3.1332.
84 Taylor, Mulholland, and Jackson, 213.
85 Gerald J. Eberle, 'Dekker's Part in *The Familie of Love*', in James G. McManaway (ed.), *Joseph Quincy Adams: Memorial Studies* (Washington, DC: Folger Shakespeare Library, 1948), 723–38; George R. Price, *Thomas Dekker* (New York: Twayne, 1969), 177–8.
86 Chris Cleary (ed.), *The Family of Love*, http://www.tech.org/~cleary/famil.html (accessed 18 April 2021). Cleary's edition was published under the imprint 'Stage Door' in 2016, without attribution to an editor.
87 Lake, 94.
88 MacD. P. Jackson, *Studies in Attribution: Middleton and Shakespeare* (Salzburg: Institute for English and American Studies, University of Salzburg, 1979), 107.
89 Lake, 107.
90 Marsh, *FLES*; Poole, 215–16, 58n. In his essay 'Heresy', Marsh accepts the arguments of Taylor et al. for Barry's authorship.

91 Shepherd, iv. On the critical focus on collaborative authorship see Gary Taylor, 'Collaboration 2016', in Dympna Callaghan and Suzanne Gossett (eds), *Shakespeare in Our Time* (Bloomsbury: Arden Shakespeare, 2016), 141–9.
92 See *BD* 5.369: 'the reference to Bocardo in 1.3 points to an author with an Oxford background, but the links with *Club Law* … are unambiguously Cantabrigian'. However, a writer familiar with Philip Stubbes's *Anatomy of Abuses* (1583) would have known of Bocardo (see 1.3.8n), so this does not undermine the case for Barry's authorship. Stubbes's work was published in two parts in 1583 and reprinted in 1584, 1585 and 1595.
93 Taylor, Mulholland, and Jackson, 225, my emphasis.
94 Taylor, Mulholland, and Jackson, 226–30.
95 Freebury-Jones, Tarlinskaja, and Dahl, 62. This research has been published in two versions. For the shorter report, see Darren Freebury-Jones, Marcus Dahl, and Marina Tarlinskaja, 'Attributing John Marston's Marginal Plays', *Studia Metrica et Poetica* 5 (2018), 28–51, http://ojs.utlib.ee/index.php/smp/article/view/smp.2018.5.1.02 (accessed 18 April 2021). For confirmation of Barry's authorship of *FoL*, see MacD. P. Jackson, 'Lording Barry, Trigrams, and *The Family of Love*', *N&Q* 66 (2019), 49–52.
96 Lake, 97. In the first instance, the passage from *No Wit* invokes 'Chaucer's days' as a time when 'honest words' allowed only one meaning, although as John Jowett notes, the reference is 'equivocal because Chaucer … was seen as a bawdy poet' (*No Wit/Help*, scene 4, 79–80n, in Middleton, *Collected*).
97 Lake, 96.
98 Cathcart, *Marston*, 79.
99 Bly, ch. 5, passim.
100 Cathcart, *Marston*, 139, 89. Cathcart does not 'exclude … altogether' the possibility that *FoL* was written by 'a follower of Marston' (*Marston*, 140). I address Cathcart's arguments in Appendix 2.
101 MacD. P. Jackson, 'Early Modern Authorship: Canons and Chronologies', in *CCM*, 80, invoking T. S. Eliot, 'Tradition and the Individual Talent' (1919).
102 Richard Barker, *Thomas Middleton* (New York: Columbia University Press, 1958) 31; Shepherd, iii. For similar observations made of *Ram Alley*, see Brian Gibbons, *Jacobean City Comedy*, 2nd edn (London: Methuen, 1980), 115–16.
103 Dillon, xiv.
104 Freebury-Jones, Tarlinskaja, and Dahl, 62. See also Darren Freebury-Jones, 'Kyd and Shakespeare: Authorship versus Influence', *Authorship* 6.1 (2017), https://doi.org/10.21825/aj.v6i1.4833.
105 Cathcart, *Marston*, 88.
106 Love, 7.
107 Taylor, Mulholland, and Jackson, 239, 236.
108 Levin, 55.
109 *Decameron*, Day 2, Tale 9, in Bullough, 13–63. The earliest English translation of Boccaccio's *Decameron* was published in 1620, so like Shakespeare, Barry may have come across this plot motif in other

INTRODUCTION   53

forms. Three cinquecento Italian comedies anticipate the device of a lover infiltrating his lady's room in a chest: Bibbiena's *La Calandria* (perf. 1513), Ariosto's *Il Negromante* (1520–30), and Cecchi's *Lo Spirito* (1549); R. Warwick Bond, *Early Plays from the Italian* (New York: Benjamin Blom, 1911); Bald, 'Sources', 385–6.

110 Melissa Walter explores the trunk as a device in the 'novellesque spaces' that feature in narrative and dramatic material informing Jacobean drama; Walter, 'Dramatic Bodies and Novellesque Spaces in Jacobean Tragedy and Tragicomedy', in Robert Henke and Eric Nicholson (eds), *Transnational Exchange in Early Modern Theater* (Aldershot: Ashgate, 2008), 63–77.

111 Dillon, 4.4.106n.

112 Fisher, 283.

113 Henry Chettle, *Kind-Heart's Dream* (1593), F4v. Cited in Fisher, 287. Bald identified a parallel for the summonses delivered to Glister and Mistress Purge in Robert Greene's *Notable Discovery of Cozenage*, 1591 (1592 edn), C4v (Bald, 'Sources', 379–80). Fisher adds a further parallel in Samuel Rowlands's *Greene's Ghost-Haunting Coney-Catchers* (1602), Br–v (Fisher, 287, 5n).

114 Fisher, 287; *BD* 5.370–1.

115 George, 18; *Tarlton's News out of Purgatory*, in *The Collected Works of Robert Armin*, intr. J. P. Feather, vol. 1 (New York: Johnson Reprint, 1972), 42–53. Bald notes a precedent for Glister's playing Lipsalve and Gudgeon off against each other in Ariosto's *Il Negromante*, where three characters go to the same astrologer for advice (Bald, 'Sources', 386).

116 Chakravorty, 30, 49n. The jest begins on C2v of *Jack of Dover*, and continues on Erv.

117 Clubb, 293; Appendix A, 'Dating the Plays', 300; 66, 31n. *La Furiosa* was adapted as a *commedia dell'arte* scenario (Clubb, 306, 22n). For an Italian text of *Furiosa*, see Giovan Battista Della Porta, *Teatro*, vol. 4, ed. Raffaele Sirri (Naples: Italian Scientific Editions, 2000).

118 This paragraph draws on Clubb's synopsis of *La Furiosa*; Clubb, 223–4.

119 Clubb, 293, 115n, observes that Middleton and Rowley may have drawn directly on *La Furiosa* for the subplot of *The Changeling*, rather than deriving it from *FoL*, as suggested by Bawcutt in his edition (Middleton and Rowley, *The Changeling*, ed. N. W. Bawcutt [London: Methuen, 1958], xxxviii). The punishment of laxative-induced purging dealt to a libertine figure was imitated by Massinger in his *Parliament of Love* (1626), noted by Bullen, *The Works of Thomas Middleton*, ed. A.H. Bullen, 8 vols (London: John C. Nimmo, 1885–86), 3.98–9.

120 Clubb, 226; Dillon, xl, quoting Shakespeare, *Hamlet*, 5.2.63.

121 Clubb, 224.

122 The adaptations are *Labyrinthus* (1603), a Latin verse translation of Della Porta's *Cintia*, by Walter Hawkesworth; *Melanthe* (1615), a Latin pastoral play by Samuel Brooke, modelled on Della Porta's *La Sorella*; the popular Latin prose comedy *Ignoramus* (1615) by George Ruggle, modelled on Della Porta's *La Trappolaria*, trans. 1622, adapted by Edward Ravenscroft as *The English Lawyer* (1677); *Albumazar the Astronomer*, by Thomas Tomkis, derived from Della Porta's *L'Astrologo*; and Middleton's *No Wit/Help*, which reshapes material from *La Sorella*.

The academic vogue for Della Porta's plays led to a performance of three of the Cambridge adaptations for James I at the university in 1615. A lost play, Thomas Cecil's *Aemilia*, may also have drawn on Della Porta's drama (*BD* 6.435–6; Clubb, 288–9). While *La Furiosa* was not published in Italian until 1609, its plot could have been relayed orally, or one of the 'bad' manuscript copies referred to by a contemporary of Della Porta might have travelled to Cambridge (see Clubb, 66, 31n, 274–5).

123 Tomlinson, 'Jacobean', 282–3; Tomlinson, 'Actress', 77–9.
124 Chambers, 1.282, 4.273; Thomas Norton, City Remembrancer, to the new Lord Mayor, James Hawes, 1574. A troupe of *comici* that included three actresses, led by Drusiano Martinelli of Mantua, performed in London from January 1578 until the first week of Lent. See M.A. Katritzky, 'Reading the Actress in Commedia Imagery', in Pamela Allen Brown and Peter Parolin (eds), *Women Players in England, 1500–1660* (Aldershot: Ashgate, 2006), 127–8.
125 Leggatt, 107, calls 3.1 of *FoL* 'a thoroughly improper seduction scene'; David Holmes writes of Maria's 'erotic wilfulness', in *The Art of Thomas Middleton: A Critical Study* (Oxford: Clarendon Press, 1970), 74.
126 Freebury-Jones, Tarlinskaja, and Dahl, 61.
127 Miola, 17–20.
128 Marsh, 'Heresy', 80, 64n; Miola, 23.
129 Marsh, 'Heresy', 80–1, 64n. See Appendix 3 for passages from Rogers's *Displaying* relevant to *FoL*.
130 Fuller, 4V2v; Moore Smith, xii; *BD* 4.201–5.
131 Moore Smith identified 'Nicholas Nifle' as a satire on John Yaxley, mayor of Cambridge in 1599–1600 and a vigorous opponent of the university (Moore Smith, xli–xliii); see also Cathcart, '*Club Law*', 66–7. For the attribution of *Club Law* to George Ruggle, see Moore Smith, lv–lvi. Wiggins notes, 'it is worth keeping in mind the possibility that the play might have been collaborative' (*BD* 4.202).
132 Cathcart, '*Club Law*', 67.
133 Miola, 19.
134 Scott, 347, situates *FoL* within an early modern culture of neo-Ovidianism. For Barry's debt to *Romeo and Juliet*, see David L. Frost, *The School of Shakespeare: The Influence of Shakespeare on English Drama 1600–42* (Cambridge: Cambridge University Press, 1968), 28–33; Chakravorty, 29; Olive, 75–7.
135 Cathcart, *Marston*, 118.
136 Michael C. Andrews, '*Jack Drum's Entertainment* as Burlesque', *RQ* 24 (1971), 231. I am indebted to Scott's discussion of parody in *FoL*; see also Altieri, 50–6.
137 Chalfant, 198–9.
138 The phrase 'great hall' is from the 1608 Articles, cited in Hillebrand, 223. Scholars have based their estimates of the Whitefriars theatre's specifications on an early seventeenth-century survey of the original priory, reprinted in *EPT*, 548. The dimensions of 'approximately eighty-five feet long and thirty-five feet wide' given by Wickham, 123, and MacIntyre, #3, derive from Adams, 312. Adams located what he interpreted to be the monks' former refectory (the 'great hall') as

INTRODUCTION 55

corresponding to a room named 'My Lords Cloister' on the survey. Berry calculates dimensions of 'about 90 feet by 17 feet' for the playhouse on the ground floor of the building called the hall (*EPT*, 549). Lucy Munro notes that this 'would have been a particularly odd, extreme space for performance' (Munro, 'Whitefriars', 117). The Second Blackfriars playhouse measured 66 feet north to south by 46 feet east to west, but the size and shape of its stage are unknown (*EPT*, 501).

139 Jonson appears indebted to this scene for the staging of *Epicene*'s 'non-duel' between Daw and La Foole, viewed, perhaps serially, by the Ladies Collegiate from above (4.5); see Dutton, *Epicene*, 56–7.
140 MacIntyre, #3.
141 Alberti, *De Re Aedificatoria* (1485), cited in Tylus, 332.
142 Tylus, 329.
143 Duncan, 167–79.
144 1608 Articles, cited in Hillebrand, 224. The exception is the actor William Barksted, who became a member of the Children of the Whitefriars, and retained the title 'servant of his Majesty's Revels' (Dutton, *Epicene*, 5). See also Bly, 130.
145 Bly, 127; Lucy Munro, *Children of the Queen's Revels: A Jacobean Theatre Repertory* (Cambridge: Cambridge University Press, 2005), 41, 47.
146 Deanne Williams, *Shakespeare and the Performance of Girlhood* (Basingstoke: Palgrave Macmillan, 2014), 79.
147 Corbin and Sedge, iv.
148 Dutton, *Epicene*, 3. For Jonson's possible imitation of *FoL*, see above 139n, and for Beaumont's parody of the trunk sequence in *KBP*, see commentary, 2.5.14.1–2n.
149 I am grateful to Jonathan Scott for this point. On continuities between Elizabethan Familism and English radical religion between 1620–1660, see Smith, ch. 4, passim.
150 Marsh, *FLES*, 208, 56n.
151 Algernon C. Swinburne, Introduction to *Thomas Middleton*, ed. Havelock Ellis, vol. 1 (London: Vizetelly, 1887), xiv; Davidson, 81–92; Levin, 59–66; Marotti, 80–4; Heinemann, 77–83; Shepherd, *Amazons*, 57–8, 60–2; Altieri; Paster, 'Purgation', 193–205; Poole, 93–103; Duncan; Marsh, *FLES*; Marsh, 'Heresy'.
152 See Lopez, *Convention*, 68–72; Tomlinson, 'Jacobean'; Tomlinson, 'Actress'; Scott.
153 Leinwand, 68.
154 Wayne (ed.), *Trick*, in Middleton, *Collected*, 55; Leggatt, 4.
155 Munro, 'Whitefriars', 117.
156 Dillon, xl.
157 Taylor, Mulholland, and Jackson, 240.
158 Levin, 55–66.
159 On the feminisation of the Family in the trial scene, see Poole, 218, 68n.
160 Shepherd, iii. Marsh regards Dryfat as one of the play's 'two Familist characters', *FLES*, 210. Shepherd describes Club as 'Mistress Purge's co-religionist', *Amazons*, 57.
161 Marsh, 'Heresy', 75.

162 Altieri, 50. See also Levin, 61–2; Chakravorty, 28–32.
163 Dillon, xlv.
164 Spufford, 184. For discussions of scatology in early modern drama, see Gail Kern Paster, *The Body Embarrassed: Drama and the Disciplines of Shame in Early Modern England* (Ithaca, NY: Cornell University Press, 1993), ch. 3; Bruce Boehrer, 'The Privy and Its Double: Scatology and Satire in Shakespeare's Theatre', in R. Dutton and J.E. Howard (eds), *A Companion to Shakespeare's Works*, vol. 4 (Oxford: Oxford University Press, 2003), 69–88.
165 Cited in Sara Jayne Steen (ed.), *Ambrosia in An Earthern Vessel: Three Centuries of Audience and Reader Response to the Works of Thomas Middleton* (New York: AMS Press, 1993), 125.
166 Scott, 350–1.
167 Bly, 116. Bly omits *FoL* from her study on dubious grounds (see above, 67n). See also Altieri.
168 Niclaes, *Prophecy*, B5r; *Ordo Sacerdotis*, n.d., cited in Moss, 'Godded with God', 17.
169 Marsh, *FLES*, 21; Shakespeare, *Macbeth*, ed. Nicholas Brooke (Oxford: Oxford University Press, 1999), 28.
170 Leggatt, 106.
171 Bly, 10.
172 For Shakespeare's making chaste female characters who have sex in his Italian sources, see Lorna Hutson, 'Rhetoric and the Body in *Twelfth Night*', in S. Orgel and S. Keilen (eds), *Shakespeare and Gender* (New York: Garland, 1999), 148–82.
173 Scott, 360.
174 Shapiro, 39.
175 Kathryn M. Moncrief and Kathryn R. McPherson (eds), *Performing Maternity in Early Modern England* (Aldershot: Ashgate, 2007), 6.
176 Scott, 353.
177 Poole, 218, 68n; Marsh, 'Heresy', 74.
178 Marsh, *FLES*, 48, 42–3.
179 Scott, 351.

THE FAMILY OF LOVE

Acted by the Children of his Majesty's Revels

To the Reader

Too soon and too late this work is published: too soon, in that it was in the press before I had notice of it, by which means some faults may escape in the printing; too late, for that it was not published when the general voice of the people had sealed it for good, and the newness of it made it much more 5 desired than at this time. For plays in this city are like wenches new fallen to the trade, only desired of your neatest gallants whiles they're fresh; when they grow stale they must be vented by termers and country chapmen. I know not how this labour

---

To the Reader] 1–13. Too ... Farewell] *this edn roman, in italics Q.* 8. vented] *Q;* rented *Shepherd.*

---

0. To the Reader] Perhaps an echo of the title page Latin address, *Lectori*.
1–6. *Too soon ... time*] On the play's probable date of composition and performance, indicated here as considerably earlier than the date of publication, see Introduction, 13–18.
3. *for that*] because.
4. *general*] collective (*OED* adj. 1c).
voice] (1) opinion (*OED* n. 9a); (2) vote (*OED* n. 3a).
6–8. *plays ... fresh*] This analogy between the attractiveness of new plays and novice prostitutes rings a change on the representation of untried plays as virgins. Compare Shakespeare and Fletcher, *TNK* Prol. 1: 'New plays and maidenheads are near akin.'
6–7. *wenches ... trade*] prostitutes newly entered into the sex market.
7. *neatest*] trimmest, most finely turned out (*OED* neat adj. 1b, 2a). Compare Jonson, *Epicene*, 1.1.70–1: 'Still to be neat, still to be dressed, / As you were going to a feast'.
8–9. *when ... termers*] when they (prostitutes and playbooks) are no longer current, they are sold on by legal students. Barry suggests that as well as frequenting older, more experienced prostitutes, law students were devotees of cheap, probably secondhand, books. Maureen Bell observes that 'The circulation of second-hand plays was probably widespread, but largely unidentifiable', in 'Booksellers without an author, 1627–1685', *CCM*, 281.
8. *stale*] old, out of date.
vented] sold, bartered as used goods (*OED* vent v.3).
9. *termers*] students of the Inns of Court, and others who resorted to London for business or pleasure during the four legal terms of the year.
chapmen] itinerant traders among whose goods were cheap printed items including, Barry implies, 'stale' (8) or out-of-date playbooks. For playbooks as possibly sold by 'country chapmen', I am indebted to Hannah August, 'Playbooks and their Readers in Early Modern England' (book manuscript).

will please. Sure I am it passed the censure of the stage with   10
a general applause. Now, whether *vox populi* be *vox dei* or no,
that I leave to be tried by the acute judgement of the famous
six wits of the City. Farewell.

---

11. vox populi ... vox dei] *this edn italics, in roman Q.*

---

    10. *censure*] judgement, appraisal.
    11. *general*] near universal (*OED* adj. 1a).
    Now] (1) used at the beginning of a clause, or question, with emphatic or rhetorical force (*OED* adv. 7a); (2) 'at this date', pointing up the lapse of time between performance and publication (*OED* adv. 1a).
    whether ... no] proverbial: whether the voice of the people is the voice of God or not (Dent V95).
    12. *tried*] tested, ascertained (*OED* try v. 5c).
    12–13. *famous ... City*] unidentified: (1) play on the five bodily 'wits' or senses (*OED* wit 3b), suggesting satirically that the City of London contains only six clever people; (2) possibly related to the proverbial phrase 'wise men of Gotham', who are unwise (Dillon); (3) the so-called 'university wits', a group of Oxbridge-educated poets and playwrights flourishing in the 1580s and 1590s (*OED* university C2); (4) the 'convivial societies' of wits gathering at the Mitre and Mermaid taverns in the early seventeenth century. See Michelle O'Callaghan, *The English Wits: Literature and Sociability in Early Modern England* (Cambridge: Cambridge University Press, 2007), 10.
    13. *City*] historic central part of London situated within the walls and under the jurisdiction of the Lord Mayor and City of London Corporation, characterised by trade and business (*OED* 6a 6b).

Names of the Characters

GLISTER, a doctor of physic
PURGE, a jealous pothecary
DRYFAT, a merchant, a brother of the Family

Names of the Characters] *this edn; Actorum Nomina Q; Dramatis Personae Dyce.* 2. PURGE ... *pothecary*] *Q (Pothecarie); PURGE ... apothecary Dyce; [Peter]PURGE ... pothecary Cleary.*

Names of the Characters] Q's *Actorum Nomina* is shared with Barry's *Ram Alley* (1608, pub. 1611) and the anonymous *Swetnam the Woman Hater* (1618) in the corpus of extant plays written before 1640 (Taylor, Mulholland, and Jackson, 228). The phrase appeared as 'The Names of the Actors' in Jonson's *EMO* (1600). On the evolution of the character list in early modern play texts, see Matteo Pangallo, '"I will keep and character that name": Dramatis Personae Lists in Early Modern Manuscript Plays', *ET* 18 (2015), 90–1. Q's segregation of three female characters under the rubric 'Weomen' is not reproduced here, although its hierarchical ordering of characters by gender is preserved. Taylor (*CCM*, 68–9) points to the identification table in Marston's *JDE* (1601) as the first to divide characters by gender.

1. *GLISTER*] (1) pun on the clyster, a medicine injected into the rectum to empty or cleanse the bowels; enema; sometimes, a suppository, administered with a pipe to inject enemas (*OED* clyster 1a); (2) contemptuous name for a doctor (*OED* clyster-pipe b); (3) play on the 'glister' of money, and possibly of Glister's red beard: for the latter, see 5.3.310–11.

2. *PURGE*] (1) rid a person or body of waste or harmful matter, especially through the operation of a purgative, causing vomiting or evacuation of the bowels (*OED* v. 2d); (2) in law, clear oneself of a charge or suspicion of guilt, or atone by expiation and submission (Cleary).

pothecary] apothecary. Like 'prentice' (below, 7), an aphetic form common in the early modern period that survives in regional usage.

3. *DRYFAT*] (1) from Old English, 'fat', meaning vat or vessel, hence a barrel containing dried goods sold by merchants (now 'dryvat', *OED*); (2) sweating-tub for treating venereal disease. See Dekker, *Blurt* (1602), 1.2.14–16: 'commodities which are sent out of the Low Countries (and put in vessels called Mother Cornelius dry-fats)'. This sense undermines the merchant's respectable veneer. Dryfat appears disguised as Poppin the proctor in 5.3.

brother ... Family] Q's designation of Dryfat as a Familist is misleading, and supports Maxwell's argument for the non-authorial origins of the 'Names of the Characters' ('Date', 195–6). Dryfat is essentially an interloper in the Family of Love, infiltrating a meeting with Mistress Purge in 3.2, and roundly condemning the fellowship as socially subversive in the mock-court scene (5.3.185–95).

62   THE FAMILY OF LOVE

GERARDINE, a lover
LIPSALVE ⎫ two gallants that only   5
GUDGEON, ⎭ pursue city lechery
CLUB, a prentice [to the Purges]
[Another, a prentice to the Purges]
VIAL, servant to Glister
SHRIMP and ⎫
PERIWINKLE, ⎭ pages to the gallants   10
MISTRESS GLISTER [wife to Glister]
MISTRESS PURGE, an elder in the Family
MARIA, niece to Glister [lover of Gerardine]
[Servants]

5. LIPSALVE] *Q (Lypsalue); [Laurence] LIPSALVE Cleary.* 6. GUDGEON] *Q (Guggin); [Gregory] GUDGEON Cleary.* 8. Another ... Purges] *this edn; not in Q.* 10. SHRIMP] *Dyce; Smelt Q.* 11. MISTRESS GLISTER] *Dyce; Weomen. (centred) Mystrisse Glister. (to right side of list) Q.* 14. Servants] *Dyce.*

   4. *GERARDINE*] suggesting the boy player in the feminine diminutive ending on the French Gérard; disguises himself as a porter Nicholas Nebulo in 4.2 and 4.3, as Placket the paritor in 4.4, and as Doctor Stickler, an arbiter, in 5.3.
   5. *LIPSALVE*] lip balm; hence, figuratively, flattering speech (*OED*), implying a smarmy manner; he disguises himself as Gerardine in 3.1.
   6. *GUDGEON*] (1) small bait-fish; (2) gullible person, who will bite at any bait or swallow anything (*OED* 2a fig.). Used by Marston's Cocledemoy as a comic alias (*Dutch C*. 2.1.209–10).
   city lechery] the thrill of the chase away from court, or a hint at the assailability of citizen women.
   7. *CLUB*] (1) a thick stick (*OED* 1a); (2) someone hefty and simple, appropriate for an apprentice carrying out manual service. 'Prentices and clubs' was the rallying cry of London apprentices (*OED* club 1c). He appears as Oy the crier in 5.3.
   prentice] apprentice; now mainly regional, archaic or historical (*OED*), although it survives in forms such as 'prentice work'. This edition adopts the historical usage, in phrases like 'pothecary's prentice' (1.1.47).
   8. *VIAL*] small vessel for liquids, appropriate to a doctor's servant.
   10. *SHRIMP*] diminutive person (*OED* 2a); in Q's *Actorum Nomina*, the name appears as 'Smelt', another small fish like a freshwater sardine, but 'Shrimp' throughout the play. Following Maxwell, who argued against the authorial provenance of the *Actorum Nomina*, Dillon reads the discrepancy as a printer's error (Maxwell, 'Date', 195–6; Dillon, 5).
   PERIWINKLE] a sea snail (*OED*); implying a small youth.
   12. *elder ... Family*] It is unlikely that any English women actually held the status of an 'elder' in Familist fellowships (Marsh, 'Heresy', 61). But see Dame Purecraft in *Bart.Fair*, who is an assistant deaconess (or Sister) in her sect (5.2.45).

Prologue

If, for opinion hath not blazed his fame,
Nor expectation filled the general round,
You deem his labours slight, you both confound
Your graver judgement and his merits.
Impartial hearing fits judicious spirits.   5
Nor let the fruit of many an hour fall
By envy's tooth or base detraction's gall,
Both which are tokens of such abject spirits
Which, wanting worth, themselves hate others' merits;
Or else of such which, once made great by fame,   10
Repine at those which seek t'attain the same.

Prologue] *Q (PROLOGVS)*. 9. Which,] *Dyce;* Which *Q*. worth, themselves] *Q; worth themselves Dyce.* others'] *Dyce (*other[s']*); other Q.*

1–4. *opinion ... fame*] If you prejudge the work of our playwright as mediocre because of his obscurity and the lack of audience anticipation, you betray both your better judgement and his worth. The author 'does not yet have a significant reputation' (Taylor, Mulholland, and Jackson, 215). The lack of rhyme for 'fame' suggests a line is missing, since the rest of the Prologue is in rhyming couplets.

2. *general round*] refers to the seated audience in hall playhouses. See Shapiro, 34: 'prologues and epilogues of college plays produced in rectangular halls frequently use the words "round," "ring," "orb," "circle" metaphorically to refer to the disposition of seats on three or four sides of a playing area'. For a similar usage, see Marston, *Ant. Rev.* Prol. 13.

3. *confound*] mistake (*OED* 1e).

4. *judgement*] competent criticism. Having satirised the 'acute judgement' of apocryphal 'wits' in 'To the Reader', Barry here signals the primacy of this faculty, distinguishing his desired audience as 'judicious spirits' (5). Compare Jonson, *EMO* Induction, 54: 'judicious friends'; see below, 12, 15.

7. *envy's tooth*] Envy, or 'Invidia' in Ripa's *Iconologia* (1611), is 'possessed of a sharp tooth and a sideways glance', in Lynn S. Meskill, *Ben Jonson and Envy* (Cambridge: Cambridge University Press, 2009), 18.

envy's ... detraction's gall] Compare the dedication prefacing Marston, *Scourge of Villainy* (1598), 3: 'Envy's abhorred child, Detraction'.

gall] bitterness (*OED* 1b fig. 3a).

8. *abject*] despicable, mean-minded.

9. *wanting worth*] lacking merit; compare *Ram Alley* Epil. 12: 'worth shall still itself defend'.

11. *repine*] grumble, complain.

From both we know all truer judgements free.
To them our muse, with blushing modesty
Patiently to hear, entreats their favour,
Which done, with judgement praise, or else dislike the   15
 labour.

---

14. hear] *this edn;* her *Q.*   15.] *Q; line illegible in copy-text due to insufficient ink.*

12.] The audience can distinguish themselves from the envious by exercising true judgement. Compare Marston, *Dutch C.* Prol. 13-14: 'Think, and then speak: 'tis rashness, and not wit, / To speak what is in passion, and not judgement, fit.'

13-14.] Our bashful muse entreats their favour to listen with patience.

14-15.] The 'favour' / 'labour' rhyme is repeated (in the plural) in the Epilogue. Compare *Ram Alley* Epil. 9-10.

15. *Which done*] i.e., when the truer judgements have heard patiently.

Act 1

ACT 1 SCENE 1

Enter DOCTOR GLISTER, [MISTRESS GLISTER] *his wife, and* MARIA.

Glister. Tricks and shows: protestations with men are like tears with women — forgot ere the cheek be dry. Gerardine is a gentleman. His lands be in statutes. 'A is not for thee nor thou for him. 'A is a gallant, and young thoughts be most unconstant. 5
Maria. Yet young vines yield most wine.
Mistress Glister. But old vines the best. Believe not these great-breeched gallants: they love for profit, not for affection. If 'a brings thee to a fool's paradise, 'a will forsake thee.

Act 1 Scene 1] Q *(ACTVS PRIMVS./ Actus Primus, scena prima)*. 1.1.0.1. SD MISTRESS GLISTER] *Dyce; not in* Q. 6. vines] *Dyce;* veynes Q.

---

3. *lands ... statutes*] Statutes are bonds sworn before officers of the Staple (a body of merchants) allowing the creditor to seize a debtor's land (*OED* statute 1b 5). Glister objects to Gerardine because he is in debt, his lands mortgaged, because he wastes time and money being a gallant, and is too young to select as a stable partner for life. He assumes Gerardine is after Maria's money, a normal scenario when a gentleman pursues a tradesman's daughter.

'A] He. Barry uses the colloquial 'a liberally in *FoL* and *Ram Alley*, whereas 'Middleton avoids this form almost completely' (Taylor, Mulholland, and Jackson, 229).

6-7. *young ... best*] proverbial: 'The young vine yields most but the old one yields the best' (Tilley V62). Maria asserts that she and Gerardine are marriage-ready and fertile.

7-8. *great-breeched*] A reference to *trunk-hose*, onion-shaped breeches worn immediately below the doublet from hips to thighs, and stuffed out to a huge size by the insertion of wool fleece, horse hair, cotton or tow-linen. See also 1.3.25.

9. *brings ... paradise*] seduces you, proverbial (Tilley F523); a 'fool's paradise' is enjoyment based on false hopes or anticipations (*OED*). Compare Marston, *Malc.* 5.5.101-3: 'Promise of matrimony by a young gallant, to bring a virgin lady into a fool's paradise'.

Glister. Which fortune God send my enemy! Love is a cold   10
   heat, a bitter sweet, a pleasure full of pain, a huge loss
   and no gain. Why shouldst thou love him only?
Maria. Words cannot force what destiny hath sealed.
   Who can resist the influence of his stars,
   Or give a reason why 'a loves or hates,   15
   Since our affections are not ruled by will,
   But will by our affections? 'Tis blasphemy
   'Gainst love's most sacred deity to ask
   Why we do love, since 'tis his only power
   That sways all our affections. All things which be —   20
   Beasts, birds, men, gods — pay him their fealty.
Glister. Tut, love is an idle fantasy, bred by desire, nursed by
   delight: an humour that begins his dominion in Leo the
   lion, the sign of the heart, and ends in Aries the ram, the

---

18. ask] *Dyce;* axe *Q.*

10–12. *Love ... gain*] Glister mouths Petrarchan paradoxes about love, stressing the loss of material advantage ('no gain'). The lines paraphrase Lyly, *Galatea*, 1.2.18–19.

14–17. *Who ... affections?*] See Marlowe, *Hero and Leander*, 167–8: 'It lies not in our power to love, or hate, / For will in us is overruled by fate' (*Poems*).

16. *affections*] uncontrollable feelings, especially passion, as opposed to reason (*OED* 1b).

17–18. *'Tis ... deity*] It is impious irreverence to ignore Cupid's command to love.

19–20. *'tis ... affections*] Cupid's power alone governs our feelings.

21. *fealty*] loyalty paid by a feudal tenant to his or her lord (*OED* n. 1).

22–3. *bred ... delight*] borrowed verbatim from *Galatea*, 1.2.20.

23. *humour*] temporary feeling caused by literal fluctuations of the four humours; see below, 3.4.24n. Glister sees Maria's infatuation with Gerardine as inappropriately anchored in the body and driven by powerful astrological forces. Maria's characterisation of love as a male deity ('his only power', 19) continues in Glister's use of 'his' (23) and the pun on 'prick' in 'pricks up the flesh' (25–6).

23–4. *Leo ... lion*] a constellation associated with choler, the hot and dry humour, causing ill temper, melancholy, and sexual passion.

24–5. *Aries ... head*] The ram's horns are a sign of cuckoldry, as well as aggression.

sign of the head. His power is to stir the blood, pricks up   25
the flesh, fills all the body with a libidinous humour, and
is indeed the overture of all ladies; which to prevent, I
have banished Gerardine, your dearly beloved, my house,
and as for you, since I am your guardian by my brother's
last will, I will sequester you from all other rooms in my   30
house, save this gallery and your upper chamber, till in
discretion I shall find it convenient to enlarge you.

Maria. My body you may circumscribe, confine,

---

25. *stir the blood*] incite desire, activating a sanguine humour, temperamentally 'courageous, hopeful, and amorous' (*OED* sanguine adj. 3a 4a) with physical properties of heat and moisture.

pricks up] (1) arouses, makes stand erect (*OED* 27 28a), with a pun on 'prick' meaning 'penis'; (2) selects from a list (formerly by making a small hole beside the name, *OED* prick v. 21). Compare Shakespeare, sonnet 20, 13: 'But since she [nature] pricked thee out for women's pleasure'.

26. *fills ... humour*] envelops Maria's body with lecherous desire.

libidinous] lustful.

27. *overture*] (1) overthrow, ruin; (2) opening, as in a musical composition; (3) orifice, in a bawdy sense (*OED* 8 1a).

30. *sequester*] isolate from society (*OED* v. 4e). In civil law, the 'sequester' is a person with whom the parties in a suit deposit the thing contested until the case has been decided (*OED* n. 1). Glister has already invoked law by mentioning Gerardine's ruined estate and his own role as his niece's guardian by his brother's will.

31. *this gallery*] i.e., the main stage where the action takes place. Galleries that connected different parts of a house, used for exercising in wet weather, were increasingly a feature of sixteenth- and seventeenth-century houses in Britain. They became spaces for displaying hangings and pictures, and in splendid houses might function as an alternative to the great chamber, 'used for masques, games, and music' (Mark Girouard, *Life in the English Country House* [Harmondsworth: Penguin, 1980], 102). Glister's gallery indicates his wealth and social pretensions. Compare Jonson, *Epicene*, 4.5.23 4: 'Do you observe this gallery? Or rather lobby, indeed?'

upper chamber] bedroom (theatrically, the upper stage is a windowed gallery over the main stage).

32. *enlarge*] set free (*OED* 6a). As Gerardine's plot to win Maria hangs on his accusation that Glister has made her pregnant, there may be a subliminal pun on 'enlarge' in the sense of 'to swell up' or impregnate (*OED* 4a 4b), a sense played on at 1.2.124. The innuendo in which Barry and the King's Revels Children specialised here works against Glister as the play's chief comic victim.

And keep in bounds, but my unlimited love
Extends itself beyond all circumscription. 35
Mistress Glister. Believe me, Maria, I have known the natures
of diverse of these gallants. If they possess the unlimited
love of us women in never so ample manner without the
society of the body, I know how soon their love fadeth.
Young men's love is like ivy: it must have somewhat to 40
cleave to, or it never prospers. Love is like fasting days,
but the body is like flesh days, and 'tis our English gallants' fashion to prefer a morsel of flesh before all the
fasting days in the whole year.

Enter VIAL.

Glister. The news with you, Vial? 45
Vial. An it like your worship, here's Club, Master Purge
the pothecary's prentice, come to invite you, my mistress, and Mistress Maria to supper, and to see Master
Gerardine's will sealed.
Glister. Tell Club my wife and myself will be there, but Maria 50
shall not come.

Exit VIAL.

---

39. fadeth] *this edn;* vadeth Q   46. An] *this edn;* And Q.   47. pothecary's] *this edn;* Poticaries Q.

34–5. *my unlimited ... circumscription*] my love, unlike my body, is bound-
less and therefore cannot be contained.

37. *diverse*] several different (*OED* divers 3a 3b).

39. *society ... body*] company in sex.

fadeth] passes away, vanishes; modernisation of Q's 'vadeth' (*OED* vade
3a, citing this passage).

41–4. *Love ... year*] The Christian calendar observed in early modern
England included periods of fasting, such as the forty days of Lent before
Easter, when the consumption of meat (flesh) was prohibited. Mistress
Glister agrees with her husband that young men want sex now, rather than
waiting until after the marriage ceremony.

41. *cleave*] stick fast, adhere (*OED* v. 2). Compare Ephesians 5.31: 'For
this cause [Christian love] shal a man leave father and mother, and shal
cleave to his wife.'

46. *An ... like*] If it please (*OED* if conj. and n. 8b).

48–9. *see ... sealed*] oversee the disposition of Gerardine's will.

SC 2]   THE FAMILY OF LOVE   69

    There must be your sweetheart's parting feast; now 'a
    perceives no access to my house, 'a will to sea. A good
    riddance! If 'a returns not, you, forsooth, are his heir;
    that's not much amiss. Yet there may be tricks. I will not   55
    be overreached. Come to your chamber, where till my
    return you shall be in safe custody!
Maria. [*Aside*] Oh, silly men, which seek to keep in awe
    Women's affections, which can know no law!
                                       Exeunt omnes.

            MARIA *ascends* [*and exit*].

               ACT I SCENE 2

    Enter GERARDINE [*abstracted*], LIPSALVE,
            and GUDGEON.

Lipsalve. Now by the horns of Cupid's bow, which hath been
    the bane to many a tall citizen, I think there be no finer
    fools under heaven than we men when we are lovers.
    How thou goest crying up and down with thy arms across

---

58. SD] *this edn; not in Q.*   59.2. SD] *this edn; at left margin, next line after Exeunt omnes, Q.*

Act 1 Scene 2] *this edn; Q (Scena, 2).*   1.1.0.1. SD abstracted] *this edn; not in Q.*   4. across] *Dyce; a crosse Q.*

---

   54. *forsooth*] in truth, no doubt (arch.).
   58. SD] Maria's closing couplet is more daring if spoken while the Glisters wait for her to join them.
   58–9. *to keep ... law!*] to control women's illimitable passions.
   59.2. SD] i.e., to the upper stage (Bullen). Q's stage direction has been interpreted as evidence of an 'outer and visible staircase' in Elizabethan playhouses (Lawrence, 20). If there is no external stair or ladder, Maria may show herself briefly on reaching her chamber. Maria's ascent brings home the fact of her imprisonment in Glister's house, reinforced by her appearance '*at the window*' in 1.2.70.1.

   1. *horns ... bow*] alluding to cuckoldry stimulated by Cupid, whose symbols were a bow and arrow. Cupid's bow is typically shown as a recurve bow, using animal horns in its construction.
   2. *tall*] (1) brave, bold (*OED* 3); (2) handsome (*OED* 2b).
   4. *arms across*] arms folded crosswise. Folded arms were part of the melancholy lover's (or husband's) demeanour. See below for the melancholy Purge's 'acrostic arms' (4.4.24). An anonymous portrait of John Donne painted *c.* 1595 shows the poet in a contemplative pose with 'arms across';

70   THE FAMILY OF LOVE   [ACT I

    for a wife, which, hadst thou, she'd cross both arms,   5
    head, and heart. Dost not yet know the old saying: 'A
    wife brings but two good days; that is, her wedding-day
    and death-day'?
Gudgeon. Believe him, Gerardine, 'a speaks now gospel! A
    man may take more wife with one hand than he's able to   10
    put away with ten, Gerardine. A wife is such a cross that
    all married men would most gladly be rid of.
Gerardine. And yet such a cross that all bachelors would
    gladly be creeping to.
    Profane not thus the sacred name of love!   15
    You libertines, who never knew the joys
    Nor precious thoughts of two consenting hearts —
Lipsalve. Didst ever see the true picture of a lover? I can give
    thee the hieroglyphic. And this it is: a man standing
    naked, a wench tickling him on the left side with a feather   20
    and pricking him under the right side with a needle. The

---

11. ten, Gerardine] *Dyce;* ten G *Q.*   such a] *Dyce;* such to *Q.*   14–15. creeping to. / Profane] *Dyce;* creeping:to prophane *Q.*   17. hearts] harts *Q.*

---

https://www.bl.uk/shakespeare/articles/make-me-new-the-multiple-reinventions-of-john-donne (accessed 19 April 2021).

    5. *cross*] (1) oppose, go counter to (*OED* v. 11a 14a, fig.); (2) afflict.

    7–8. *wife ... death-day*] See Tilley, 'A wife brings but two good days, her wedding day and death day' (W382). The proverb derives from an epigram by Palladas of Alexandria (fl. fourth century CE): 'women all / cause rue / but can be nice / on occasional / moments two / to be precise / in bed / & dead' (*Palladas: Poems*, trans. Tony Harrison, 2nd edn [London: Anvil Press, 1984], 33).

    11. *put away*] put an end to, i.e., kill (*OED* v. 2e).

    cross] vexation, misfortune (*OED* n. 10b).

    14. *creeping to*] sneaking up on, seducing; but alluding to the Roman Catholic penitential practice of ascending towards an outdoor cross on the knees. There is a doubleness in Gerardine's remark: he both legitimises his own desire as a bachelor, and castigates libertines such as Lipsalve and Gudgeon who are keen to find an easy or willing woman. The prostrate approach to the 'wife' suggests a desperate need for sex.

    14–15. *to. / Profane*] The compositor's misplacing of 'to' as part of an infinitive verb formed with 'Profane' may have led to the substitution of 'to' for 'a' in Q.

    16. *libertines*] amoral, promiscuous men (*OED*).

    19. *hieroglyphic*] pictorial emblem (*OED* n. 2a). Compare *RevT* 4.2.77–8, 'I have a conceit a-coming in picture upon this'.

allegory, as I take it, is this: that at the first we are so
overjoyed with obtaining a wife that we conceit no heaven
like to the first night's lodging. And that's the significa-
tion of the left side, for wives always in the night take the
left-side place. But, sir, now come to the needle on the
right side: that's the daytime wherein she commands.
Then, sir, she has a certain thing called tongue, ten times
more sharp than a needle, and that at the least displeas-
ure a man must have shot quite through him.
Gudgeon. Grammercies, Lipsalve, my neat courtier. But,
sirrah Gerardine, be thyself, sociable and free! Leave not
thy native soil for a giglot, a wench who in her wit is
proud —
Lipsalve. In her smile deceitful —
Gudgeon. In her hate revengeable —
Lipsalve. And in nothing but her death acceptable. I'll tell
thee, there's no creature more desirous of an honest name
and worse keeps it than a woman. Dost hear? Follow this

---

23. *conceit*] imagine, think (*OED* v. 5a).
24. *first ... lodging*] consummation of the marriage in sexual intercourse, using the metaphor of the wife's body as a dwelling occupied by her husband.
26. *left-side place*] i.e., of the marital bed. A misogynist twist on the Christian assumption that the left (Lat., *sinister*) is the devil's side, and the right, God's. The conceit is complicated by the hieroglyphic's linking of the left side with pleasure ('tickling ... feather', 20) and the right side with pain ('pricking ... needle', 21).
27. *the ... commands*] taps into a popular concern with female sovereignty, embodied in, for instance, Chaucer's 'Wife of Bath's Tale', and Fletcher's *Tamer Tamed* (1611).
28–30. *a certain ... him*] the woman's tongue imaged as an arrow or sharp weapon, as in Shakespeare, *MAdo* 1.1.115: 'I would my horse had the speed of your tongue'.
30. *quite*] completely, entirely (*OED* adv. 1).
31. *Grammercies*] Thank you (arch.).
neat] pithy, well-expressed (*OED* adj. 3b), referring to Lipsalve's analysis of the hieroglyphic.
33. *giglot*] lewd woman.
36. *revengeable*] vengeful, vindictive (*OED* 1). Q's less familiar adjective allows Barry's prose to echo in 'acceptable' in 33.

song and if ever thou forsake thy country for a wagtail,   40
let me be whipped to death with ladies' hairlaces.
Gerardine. Let's hear that worthy song, gentle Master Lipsalve.
Lipsalve. Observe!
[*Sings*]
>   Now if I list will I love no more,
>   Nor longer wait upon a jill,   45
>   Since every place now yields a wench,
>   If one will not, another will.
>   And if what I have heard be true,
>   Then young and old, and all will do.
>   How dost thou like this, man?
Gerardine.   No more, no more.   50

  [*Gesturing towards the upper stage*]

>   This is the chamber which confines my love;
>   This is the abstract of the spacious world.
>   Within, it holds a gem so rich, so rare,
>   That art or nature never yet could set
>   A valued price to her invalued worth.   55

43.1. SD *Sings*] *Dyce; not in* Q.   45. jill] gill Q.   50.1. SD] *this edn; not in* Q.   55. invalued] *Shepherd;* in valued Q; unvalued *Dyce.*

---

40. *wagtail*] a wanton woman 'who, like the bird, keeps her tail in continual motion' (Williams, *Dictionary*, 3.1495).

41. *hairlaces*] 'braid or ribbon used before the invention of hairpins for tying about the head to bind up the hair' (Linthicum, 141).

44. *list*] please.

45. *wait upon*] serve, dance attendance upon (*OED* wait v. 10).

jill] familiar or contemptuous term applied to a woman; a wench or sexually promiscuous lass.

47. *will not*] will not have sex.

49. *will do*] will copulate, with the implication that all women are lusty in bed.

52. *abstract*] microcosm (*OED* n. B3a).

53. *a gem ... rare*] With Gerardine's image of Maria as a precious jewel compare Proverbs 31.10: 'Who shal finde a vertuous woman? for her price is farre above the pearles.' See also Chaucer, *Troilus and Criseyde*, 5.549: 'O ryng, fro which the ruby is out falle'.

55.] 'a price equal to her pricelessness' (Cleary). See Shakespeare, *A&C* 1.1.15: 'There's beggary in the love that can be reckoned.'

invalued] invaluable.

Lipsalve. Unvalued worth, ha, ha, ha! Why!
She's but a woman, and they are windy turning vanes;
Love light as chaff which, when our nourishing grains
Are winnowed from them, unconstantly they fly
At the least wind of passion! A woman's eye   60
Can turn itself with quick dexterity
And in each wanton glass can comprehend
Their sundry fancy suited to each friend.
Tut, their loves are all compact of levity,
Even like themselves, *nil muliere levius.*   65

56–7.] *lineation this edn;* Unvalued worth, ha, ha, ha! Why? shees but a woman, / And they are windy turning veins *Q;* Unvalued worth? ha, ha, ha! Why, she's but / A woman; and they are windy turning vanes *Dyce.* 57–8. A woman's eye / Can] *Dyce;* A womans eye, can *Q.* 63. friend] *Dyce;* fend *Q.*

56. *Unvalued ... ha!*] Lipsalve mishears Gerardine's 'invalued' and mocks the oxymoron he finds in 'unvalued worth', meaning 'not valuable value'. His ensuing speech (57–65) verges on prosiness, but the rhyming couplets indicate it is best rendered as verse. The rhyming and the Latin tag (65) are reminiscent of Freevill's mock oration in praise of prostitutes in Marston's *Dutch C.* 1.1.106–44.
57. *but*] only.
windy] probably winding or turning, rather than referring primarily to breezes.
vanes] weathervanes; constantly changing person or thing (*OED* 1b. fig.). Compare Nathan Field, *A Woman is a Weathercock* (1609).
58–60. *Love ... passion!*] Winnowing is a process of separating grain from chaff by exposing the grains to wind or a current of air (*OED* winnow v. 1a). Lipsalve depicts women as worthless *chaff* which blows from the winnowing basket, while the masculine *grains* remain.
60–1. *woman's ... turn*] demeaning reference to women's changeable erotic appetites, punning on *eye* = vagina (Williams, *Dictionary*, 1.453–4). Compare Shakespeare, *Oth.* 4.1.240–1: 'she can turn and turn, and yet go on / And turn again'.
62. *wanton glass*] seductive mirror.
comprehend] see, apprehend (*OED* v. 5).
63. *sundry*] various.
fancy] imaginary vision of themselves.
friend] lover.
64. *compact*] made.
levity] lightness, frivolity.
65. *nil ... levius*] 'nothing lighter (or more trivial) than a woman' (Lat.), reiterating women's inconstancy. The phrase is found, indirectly, in a fifteenth-century poem; see *A Selection of English Epigrams* (Boston: Joshua Belcher, 1812), no. 412; https://books.google.co.nz/books?id=SpEMAAAAYAAJ (accessed 18 April 2021).

Gudgeon. Tut, man, everyone knows their worth when they
    are at a rack-rent. In the term-time they bear as great a
    price as wheat when transportations are —
Gerardine. Peace! Let's draw near the window and listen if we
    may hear her.   70

    Enter MARIA [*with her lute*] *at the window* [*above,
            unaware of the men below*].

Maria. Debarred of liberty! Oh, that this flesh
    Could like swift-moving thoughts transfer itself
    From place to place, unseen and undissolved.
    Then should no iron ribs or churlish flint
    Divide my love and me. Dear Gerardine,   75
    Despite of chance or guardian's tyranny,

70.1–2. SD] *this edn; not in* Q.

66–7. *when ... rack-rent*] when competition makes the price of women exorbitantly high. A 'rack-rent' was an excessively high rent, making ownership of property, or even tenancy, impossible (*OED* n. citing this usage).
    67. *term-time*] when the law courts are active, increasing London's population as those bringing suits flood the town, creating more demand for housing. See 'To the Reader', 7.
    67–8.] The price of prostitutes during the legal terms is as high as the cost of wheat in London, inflated due to grain-hoarders. A royal proclamation of 1608 reports that 'all the straight provisions that are lately taken against transportation of grain' are still being infringed (Shepherd).
    68. *transportations*] actions of conveying or exporting goods from one place to another (*OED* n. 1a).
    70.1. SD *at the window*] 'Window' is a convenient term for a large opening in the upper stage wall. For the English and European tradition of the *Fensterlieder* or 'window songs', on which this scene draws, see Jill Colaco, 'The Window Scenes in *Romeo and Juliet* and Folk Songs of the Night Visit', *SP* 83 (1986), 140–5.
    71–3. *flesh ... undissolved*] Unlike Hamlet, Maria wishes that her flesh could be ethereal but remain intact; compare Shakespeare, *Ham.* 1.2.129–30: 'O that this too too solid flesh would melt, / Thaw, and resolve itself into a dew'. The soliloquy is studded with 'samples' from contemporary drama and poetry.
    74. *iron ribs*] curved bars of a window grate.
    churlish] unyielding.
    flint] hard stone, used in walls made of flint, a common building material in eastern England. Compare Shakespeare, *R2* 5.5.20–1: 'the flinty ribs / Of this hard world, my ragged prison walls'.
    76. *Despite*] in spite.

SC 2]   THE FAMILY OF LOVE   75

  I'd move within thy orb and thou in mine.
Lipsalve. [*Aside to Gerardine*] She'd move within thy orb,
  and thou in hers? — Blood, she talks
  bawdy to herself. — [*Whispers*] Gudgeon, stand close!
Maria. But in vain do I proclaim my grief,   80
  When air and walls can yield me no relief.
Gudgeon. [*Aside to Gerardine and Lipsalve*] The walls are the
  more stony-hearted then.
Lipsalve. [*Aside to him*] Peace, good Gudgeon, gape not so
  loud.
Maria. [*Taking her lute*] Come thou, my best companion,
  thou art sensible
  And canst my wrongs reiterate. Thou and I   85
  Will make some mirth, in spite of tyranny.

      [*She plays.*]

  The black-browed night, drawn in her pitchy wain
  In starry-spangled pride, rides now o'er heaven.

78–9. SD] *Dillon (subst); not in Q.*   78. talks] *Dyce;* talk *Q.*   79. SD] *this edn; not in Q.*   82. SD] *Dillon; not in Q.*   83. SD] *Dillon; not in Q.*   84. SD] *this edn; not in Q.*   86.1. SD] *this edn; not in Q.*   87. pitchy] *Dyce;* pithie *Q.*

 77.] Let us share our worlds, or conjoin sexually. The image hovers between the cosmographical and the sexual. Compare Donne, 'Air and Angels', 25: 'So thy love may be my love's sphere'.
 78. *Blood*] abbreviation of the common oath, 'By God's blood'.
 79. *stand close!*] stay hidden! (*OED* close adj. 4c). Gudgeon tries to sneak a peek at Maria.
 84–6. *Come thou ... tyranny*] No editor elucidates who or what Maria addresses as her 'best companion'. A musical instrument is 'sensible' (84), and capable of sounding Maria's 'wrongs' (85).
 84. *sensible*] capable of feeling.
 85. *reiterate*] articulate, echo.
 87. *black-browed night*] dark-faced; (also) frowning, scowling (*OED*), suggesting Maria's despair at ever reuniting with her lover, with whom a night should be joyful.
 pitchy wain] black chariot.
 88. *starry-spangled*] adorned with star-like diamonds, crystals or *spangle*[*s*] = thin pieces of silver or gold worn as bracelets, earrings or dangling pieces sewn to clothes (Miège 1677, *LEME*); probably referring to the underside of the upper stage at the Whitefriars, which, like the Globe and other theatres, was probably painted with stars like a heaven. Compare Marlowe, *1 Tamburlaine*, 5.1.185: 'the fiery spangled veil of heaven'.

76 THE FAMILY OF LOVE [ACT I

    Now is the time when stealing minutes tell
    The stole delight 'joyed by all faithful lovers; 90
    Now loving souls contrive both place and means
    For wishèd pastimes. Only I am pent
    Within the closure of this fatal wall,
    Deprived of all my joys.
Gerardine. [*Aloud*] My dear Maria, be comforted in this: 95
    The frame of heaven shall sooner leave to move,
    Bright Phoebus' steeds leave their diurnal race,
    And all that is forsake their natural being,
    Ere I forget thy love!
Maria. Who's that protests so fast? 100
Gerardine. [*Stepping forward*] Thy ever-vowèd servant,
    Gerardine.
Maria. Oh, by your vows it seems you'd fain get up.
Lipsalve. [*Aside*] Ay, and ride too.
Gerardine. I would, most loved Maria.

---

95. SD] *this edn; not in Q.* 101. SD] *this edn; not in Q.* 103. SD] *Dyce; not in Q.*

---

  89. *stealing minutes*] time passing stealthily. Locked up away from Gerardine, Maria is acutely conscious of the imperceptible passage of time, enjoyed by other lovers but bringing her no comfort.
  tell] (1) utter (*OED* v. 8a); (2) reveal (something secret or private) (*OED* v. 11a); (3) count (*OED* v. 17a).
  90. *stole*] stolen.
  'joyed] enjoyed.
  97. *Bright Phoebus*] The sun god Apollo, who drives his horse-drawn chariot daily across the sky. The image forms a gendered contrast with night's black chariot, invoked by Maria at 87.
  diurnal race] the sun's daily rotation.
  100.] Maria's three-beat question breaks the pentameter rhythm, suggesting that she is either surprised, scared, or seeking reassurance.
  fast] unshakably.
  102. *fain*] willingly
  103. *Ay ... too*] Bawdy quibble: 'up and ride' means mount for sexual intercourse (Partridge, ride, 226–7).

SC 2]   THE FAMILY OF LOVE   77

[*Lipsalve.*] [*Aside*] I knew it: he that to get up to a fair woman   105
  will stick to vow and swear may be accounted no man.
Maria.   But tell me
  Why hast thou chose this hour to visit me
  Which nor the day nor night can claim, but both,
  Or neither? Why in this twilight camest thou?   110
Gerardine. T'avoid suspicious eyes, I come, dear love,
  To take my last farewell, fitting this hour,
  Which nor bright day will claim nor pitchy night,
  An hour fit to part conjoinèd souls.
  Since that my native soil will not afford   115
  My wished and best content, I will forsake it
  And prove more strange to it than it to me.
  In time's swift course all things shall find event,
  Be it good or ill, and destinies do grant
  That most preposterous courses often gain   120
  What labour and direct proceedings miss.
Maria. Would thou forsake me then?
Gerardine. Let first blessed life forsake me! Be constant,

105. SH *Lipsalve*] *this edn; Ma. Q; Maria Dyce;* GUDGEON *Shepherd*. 105. SD] *this edn; not in Q; Aside to Lipsalve Cleary.* 107–8. But tell me / Why] *Shepherd;* but tell me why *Q (prose);* But tell me, / Why *Dyce.* 123–4. Be constant, / My absence] *Shepherd;* be constant / My absence *Q;* Be [thou] constant: / My absence *Dyce;* be constant. / My absence *Dillon.*

105–6.] Q assigns these lines to Maria; Bullen conjectured that they belong to Lipsalve. Maria is certainly capable of 'this shift in tone' (Dillon, 1.2.104–5n), but the interruption of the verse (resumed by Maria at 107) makes assignment to Lipsalve more plausible. Lipsalve's prose interruptions do not interfere with the lovers' poetic lines.
  106. *stick*] (1) hesitate (*OED* v. 15a); become embarrassed or nonplussed (*OED* 14a).
  107. *But ... me*] Completes Gerardine's line at 104, and might be spoken over Lipsalve's comment.
  108–10. *this hour ... this twilight*] 'the stress on the hour between night and day recalls [2.1 of] *R&J*' (Shepherd).
  117. *strange*] distant, unknown.
  118. *find event*] happen, transpire.
  120. *preposterous*] contrary to reason (*OED* 2).

78   THE FAMILY OF LOVE   [ACT I

   My absence may procure thy more enlarge,
   And then —   125
Maria. Desire's conceit is quick, I apprehend thee.
   Be thou as loyal as I constant prove,
   And time shall knit our mutual knot of love.
   Wear this, my love's true pledge. [*Throws it down.*] I
      need not wish,
   I know thou would return, nor will I say   130
   Thou mayst conceal thyself being returned
   Till I may make escape and visit thee.
   I prithee, love, attempt not to ascend
   My chamber window by a laddered rope;
   Th'entrance is too narrow, except this post,   135
   Which may with ease — yet that is dangerous.
   I prithee do it not. I hear some call. Farewell,
   My constant love let after-actions tell.   *Exit* MARIA.
Gerardine. Oh, perfection of women!
[*Lipsalve.*] A plague of such perfection!   140

---

129. SD] *Dyce; not in Q.* 130. nor will] *Dyce;* or will *Q.* 134. laddered] *Dyce;* lathered *Q.* 136. ease — yet] *Dyce;* ease, yet *Q.* 140–1. A ... shows] *lacking speech-headings and set as one line, separated by commas Q.* 140. SH] *Dyce; not in Q.*

---

124. *thy more enlarge*] greater freedom for you (*OED* enlarge n. citing this usage). Under cover of absence, Gerardine 'enlarges' Maria in the sense of making her pregnant; see above 1.1.32, and below, 126n (*quick*).

126. *Desire's ... thee*] My longing for you sharpens my mind; I understand you.
   conceit] process of understanding something (*OED* 2a obs.).
   quick] (1) Of the flesh or a part of the body: living; capable of sensation or movement (*OED* adj. 3); (2) of a fetus, quickening with life (*OED* adj. 5a).

129–37.] With Maria's tactics of negative persuasion compare Chapman, *May Day* (1604, pub. 1611), 2.2.143–5: 'But good cuz if you chance to see my chamber window open ... do not let him come in at it in any case'; see also the extended ploy used by Dulcimel to woo Tiberio in Marston, *Faun* (1605), 4.591–649.

129. *Wear this*] Maria throws Gerardine a ring or glove; compare *Dutch C.* 2.1.54: 'Wear this slight favour in my remembrance.'

133–6. *attempt not ... dangerous*] 'Probably ... refers to two locations: a fictitious barred window on a back or side wall; this "post," or location, the usual Swan-type opening'; Leslie Thomson, 'Window Scenes in Renaissance Plays: A Survey and Some Conclusions', *MaRDiE* 5 (1991), 232.

134. *laddered rope*] Compare Shakespeare, *TGV* 3.1.117: 'a ladder quaintly made of cords'.

SC 2] THE FAMILY OF LOVE 79

[*Gudgeon.*] How she woos, by negatives shows thee what to
do, under colour of dissuasion!
Gerardine. She's truly virtuous.
Lipsalve. Tut, man, outward appearance is no authentic
instance of the inward desires. Women have sharp falcons'   145
eyes, and can soar aloft, but keep them like falcons from
flesh and they soon stoop to a gaudy lure.
Gerardine. Why then, Huguenot women are admirable angels.
Gudgeon. But angels make them admirable devils.
Gerardine. My love's chaste smile to all the world doth speak   150
her spotless innocence.
Lipsalve. Women's smiles are more of custom than of courtesy. Women are creatures: their hearts and they are full
of holes, apt to receive but not retain affection. Thou wilt
tomorrow, thou sayst, be gone. If thou wilt know the   155
worst of a country's, marry before thou goest, for if thou

141. SH] *this edn; assigned to Gerardine, 139–41 up to* shows *Q.*   141–2. thee
... dissuasion!] *assigned to Gudgeon in Q.*   145. falcons'] *this edn;* faulcons
Q; falcon's *Dyce.*   150–1.] *prose in Q;* My love's ... doth speak / Her spotless
innocence. *Dyce.*   156. country's] *Bullen;* Cuntries *Q.*

146. *keep ... flesh*] make them hungry, i.e., deprive them sexually, drawing
on the commonplace association between food and sex.

147. *stoop*] swoop down, as the falcon descends swiftly on its prey (*OED*
v. 6a).

lure] mock-bird of the falconer, made of feathers and leather thongs, from
which the falcon is fed during training. Compare the proverb, 'In time all
haggard hawks will stoop to lure' (Tilley T298).

148. *Huguenot ... angels*] Huguenot women are seemingly expert at self-
denial. The Huguenots were particularly abstinent French Calvinists.

149. *But ... devils*] But if you pay them they will compromise their virtue.

angels] gold coins worth ten shillings, stamped with a device of the arch-
angel Michael killing the dragon.

admirable] egregious, ironically juxtaposing the sense of morally remarkable in 148.

152–3. *are more ... courtesy*] stem from force of habit as opposed to genuine
emotion. 'Common custom' was a term for 'whoring', as in Marston, *Dutch
C.* 2.1.171–4: 'When saw you ... Master Caqueteur, that prattling gallant of
a good draught, common custom, fortunate impudence, and sound fart?'

153–4. *their hearts ... holes*] women are like sieves, a misogynist commonplace.

154. *holes*] orifices, i.e., the vagina and anus.

apt ... affection] primed by nature to feel but not to retain desire. Drawing
on the same trope of women as leaky vessels, Shakespeare's Orsino opines
that women 'lack retention' (*TwN* 2.4.93).

155–6. *If ... country's*] if you will know the worst of a cunt's [habits].

80 THE FAMILY OF LOVE [ACT I

canst endure a cursed wife, never care what company
thou comest in.
Gerardine. Come, merry gallants, will you associate me to my
cousin Purge's the pothecary's, and take part of my 160
parting feast tonight?
Gudgeon. Oh, his wife is of the Family of Love. I'll thither:
perhaps I may prove of the fraternity in time; we'll thither,
that's flat. *Exeunt omnes.*

ACT I SCENE 3

Enter MISTRESS PURGE *[alone].*

[*Mistress Purge.*] What, Club, Club! Is Club within there?

Enter CLUB.

Club. Mistress.
Mistress Purge. I pray, what said Master Doctor Glister, will
'a come?
Club. 'A sent word 'a would, for 'a was but to carry a diet to 5
one of his patients — what call you her? She that paints
a daytimes, and looks fair and fresh on the outside, but
in the night-time is filthier than the inside of Bocardo,

---

161. feast] *Dyce;* feasts *Q.*

Act 1 Scene 3] *Q (Act.*I. *Sena.* 3*).* 1.3.0.1. SD *alone*] *this edn; Sola Q.*
1. SH] *Dyce; not in Q.*

---

157. *cursed*] shrewish.
159. *associate*] accompany.
160. *take ... of*] (1) share in (*OED* part n.1 P3a obs.); (2) participate in.
164. *that's flat*] that's decided (*OED* adj. 6b).

5. *diet*] prescribed course of food, esp. for medical reasons (*OED* 3).
6–9. *She ... her*] misogynist trope denigrating women for their application of cosmetics. The assumption about women who wear make-up is that 'All is not sweet, all is not sound', *Epicene*, 1.1.76. See Laurie Finke, 'Painting Women: Images of Femininity in Jacobean Tragedy', *TJ* 36 (1984), 356–70.
6. *paints*] applies cosmetics.
7. *a daytimes*] at daytime, during the day; an English regional usage (*OED* a prep. I 3a).
8. *Bocardo*] prison in the old north gate at Oxford, used of prisons generally. See Stubbes, lines 4707–9, 'to Bocardo goeth he as round [quickly] as a ball, where he shall be sure to lie, until he rot one piece from another'.

SC 3]   THE FAMILY OF LOVE   81

  and is indeed far more unsavoury to those that know her,
  forsooth.   10
Mistress Purge. Went 'a to her?
Club. 'A had a receipt for the grincomes in his hand, and 'a
  said 'a would take that in his way.
Mistress Purge. 'Tis well; and what guests besides him and his
  wife will be here at supper?   15
Club. The first in my account is Master Gerardine, your
  cousin; Master Doctor Glister and his wife; Master
  Dryfat, the merchant; Master Lipsalve, the courtier;
  Master Gudgeon, the gallant, and their pages. These, I
  take it, will be your full number.   20
Mistress Purge. Then belike my room shall be stuffed with
  courtiers and gallants tonight. Of all men I love not these
  gallants. They'll prate much but do little; they are people
  most uncertain. They use great words, but little sense;
  great beards, but little wit; great breeches, but no money.   25
Club. That was the last thing they swore away.
Mistress Purge. Belike they cannot fetch it again with swearing, for if they could, there's not a page of theirs but
  would be as rich as a monarch.
Club. There's nothing, mistress, that is sworn out of date that   30
  returns. Their first oath in times past was 'by the mass',
  and that they have sworn quite away. Then came they to

---

9. unsavoury to those that] *Dyce;* vnsauory that *Q.* 14. guests] *Dyce;*
guest *Q.* 20. take it] *this edn;* take will *Q.*

---

 9. *unsavoury*] i.e., grubby, insalubrious.
 10. *forsooth*] truly.
 12. *receipt*] prescription.
 grincomes] cant term for syphilis (*OED* grincome n. citing this usage).
 16. *account*] reckoning, tally.
 20. *full number*] all of the guests.
 21. *belike*] probably (*OED* adv.).
 room ... stuffed] obscene innuendo: *room* means 'vagina' (Williams, *Dictionary*, 3.1167–8), *stuffed*, 'penetrated sexually' (Williams, *Dictionary*, stuff, 3.1336). Compare Shakespeare, *MAdo* 3.4.57: 'A maid, and stuffed!'
 23–5. *prate ... money*] Mistress Purge aims to impress with her worldly insight, issuing a series of linked antitheses which elicit an easy laugh.
 24. *uncertain*] hard to judge.
 30. *out of date*] beyond its proper time, rendering an oath old-fashioned.
 31. *Their ... oath*] Compare Shakespeare, *AYL* 1.2.55–6: 'a certain knight that swore by his honour they were good pancakes'.

their faith, as 'by my faith, 'tis so'. That in a short time
was sworn away too, for no man believes now more than
'a sees. Then they swore by their honesties, and that, 35
mistress, you know is sworn quite away. After their honesties was gone, then came they to their gentility, and
swore as they were gentlemen, and their gentility they
swore away so fast that they had almost sworn away all
the ancient gentry out of the land, which indeed are 40
scarce missed, for that yeomen and farmers' sons, with
the help of a few Welshmen, have undertook to supply
their places — that at the last they came to silver, and
their oath was 'by the cross of this silver', and swore so
fast upon that, that now they have scarce left them a cross 45
for to swear by.

Mistress Purge. And what do they swear by now their money
is gone?

Club. Why, 'by the holy rood' and 'God refuse them'.

---

35. honesties] *Q* (honestyes); honesty *Dyce*. 49. 'by the holy rood'] *this edn;* by ( ) *Q*. 'God ... them'] *Dyce (subst); God ... them Q.*

---

35. *honesties*] truthfulness.

37. *gentility*] status or honour; gentlemen were entitled to a coat of arms, to bear a sword and to wear rich attire.

41. *yeoman ... sons*] Yeomen were freeholders under the rank of gentle-men who cultivated their own land. Club's counterpointing of 'ancient gentry' (40) with the small landholders who supplant them touches on the rising middleclass in England. Education at a university entitled such men to the status of a gentleman. Middleton also comments on 'farmers' sons' who 'wash their hands and come up gentlemen' (*RevT* 2.1.213–14).

42. *Welshmen*] Welshmen were reputed to be particularly proud of their gentility. See 'A Braggadocio Welshman', in Overbury, 215: 'Above all men he loves an herald and speaks pedigrees naturally'.

44. *'by ... silver'*] silver coin with the figure of a cross stamped on one side (*OED* cross n. 20).

49. *'by the holy rood'*] 'by the holy cross', or a similarly outrageous oath: 'by gad's lid' (God's eyelid); 'by the body of Christ'. Q's parentheses repre-sent 'either a censored oath or an invitation to the actor's imagination' (Shepherd). Jonson's *EMI* (F, 1616) registers a trend for 'dainty oaths' (1.4.62). Swearing 'by the holy rood' sustains Club's play on the silver 'cross' in 44–6. On extemporisation as represented in the early modern play text, citing this example, see Stern, 250–1.

SC 3] THE FAMILY OF LOVE 83

Mistress Purge. And can they not as well say 'Men refuse them', as 'God refuse them'?
Club. No, mistress, for men, especially citizens and rich men, have refused them their bonds and protestations already.
Mistress Purge. 'Tis well, see how supper goes forward, and that my shoes be very well blacked against I go to the Family.

Exit CLUB.

Enter MASTER PURGE.

— Now, sweet chick, where hast thou been? In troth, la, I am not well. I had thought to have spent the morning at the Family, but now I am resolved to take pills, and therefore, I pray thee, desire Doctor Glister that 'a would minister to me in the morning.
Purge. Thy will is known, and this for answer say,
'Tis fit that wise men should their wives obey.
And now, sweet duck, know I have been for my cousin Gerardine's will, and have it. 'A has given thee a legacy, but the total is Maria's.

Enter MASTER GLISTER, MASTER DRYFAT,
and MISTRESS GLISTER.

— Master doctor, your wife and Master Dryfat are most welcome. Now were my cousin Gerardine and Master Lipsalve here, our number were complete.

50–1. 'Men ... them'] *this edn;* men ... them *Q.* 51. 'God ... them'] *this edn;* God ... them *Q.* 53. refused them their] *Q;* refused their *Dyce.* 56.2. SD] *this edn; following 53 Q.* 57. In troth, la] *Dyce;* in troth law *Q.* 60. pray] *Dyce;* prey *Q.*

50–1. *And ... them'?*] Compare *Displaying*, Appendix 3, lines 45–6: 'They may not say, "God save" anything. For they affirm that all things are ruled by nature and not directed by God.'
   53. *bonds ... protestations*] oaths sworn by gallants in an effort to gain credit.
   54. *how ... forward*] that supper arrangements are advancing.
   55. *against*] before.
   57. *sweet chick*] term of endearment.
   la] exclamation used to accompany a conventional phrase (*OED* int. a).
   61. *minister to*] treat. The speech shows Mistress Purge's preference for Glister's sexual ministry over the religious fellowship provided by the Family.
   66. *total*] whole.

Glister. Is this frantic will done? Will Master Gerardine to sea? 70
Let me tell you, I am no whit sorry. Let such as will be headstrong bite on the bridle.
Purge. 'Tis here, master doctor. All his worth is Maria's and locked in a trunk, which by tomorrow sun shall be delivered to your custody. 75
Dryfat. Methinks 'twere a reasonable match to bestow your niece on Master Gerardine. 'A is a most hopeful gentleman, and his revenue such that, having your niece's portion to clear it of all encumbrances, 'twill maintain them both in a very worthy degree. 80
Glister. Tut, you are Master Dryfat, the merchant; your skill is greater in coney skins and wool-packs than in gentlemen. His lands be in statutes. You merchants were wont to be merchant staplers, but now gentlemen have gotten up the trade; for there is not one gentleman amongst 85 twenty but his land be engaged in twenty statutes staple.

---

70. *frantic*] lunatic.
71. *no whit*] not at all (arch.)
71–2. *Let ... bridle*] let impulsive young men champ at the bit like restless horses, eager to be off; let them take the bit in their teeth and run away (*OED* bite v. 16).
74. *tomorrow sun*] sunset tomorrow (*OED* sun n.1 4a obs.)
77. *hopeful*] promising, particularly with regard to financial assets.
78. *revenue*] income, esp. from lands (*OED* n. 1a).
79. *portion*] sum of money given by a woman's parents or guardian to contribute to her new household upon marriage.
encumbrances] (1) debts (Cleary); (2) liability attached to property, a specifically legal term (*OED* n. 4, but gives first usage as 1629).
79–80. *'twill ... degree*] they'll be able to live most comfortably, befitting their high social status.
82. *coney skins*] rabbit furs or pelts.
wool-packs] large bags of wool for transporting or sale, with an implication of woolsacks for judges to sit on, when invited to the House of Lords, a position of power to which a middleclass man such as Dryfat might aspire (*OED* n. 1b obs.).
84. *merchant staplers*] traders who buy wool from the grower to sell to the manufacturer = *OED* wool-stapler n., under wool-staple n.1.
86. *statutes staple*] legal term, meaning 'bond[s] of record, acknowledged before the mayor of the staple, by which a creditor has the power of seizing a debtor's lands in case of default' (*OED*, citing this usage). That is, gentlemen now only have value on paper, which they might forfeit at any moment. Gerardine's lack of hard cash is a major concern to Glister, who mentions the gallant's indebtedness at 1.1.3.

Enter LIPSALVE, GERARDINE, *and* GUDGEON.

Lipsalve. [*Singing*] Let every man his humour have —
　I do at none repine;
　I never regard whose wench I kiss,
　Nor who doth the like by mine.　　　　　　　　　　90
　Th'indifferent minds I hold still best,
　Whatever does befall;
　For she that will do with me and thee
　Will be a wench for all.
— And how goes the squares?　　　　　　　　　　　　95
Purge. Your stay, gentlemen, does wrong to a great many of
　good stomachs; your suppers expect you.
Gudgeon. And we our suppers.
Glister. And from what good exercise come you three?
Gerardine. From a play, where we saw most excellent Samson　100
　excel the whole world in gate-carrying.
Dryfat. Was it performed by the youths?
Lipsalve. By youths? Why, I tell thee we saw Samson, and I

---

87. SD *Singing*] *Dyce; not in Q.*　96. gentlemen] *Dyce;* gentleman *Q.*

---

　88. *repine*] fret.
　91. *Th'indifferent minds*] The men who are not picky; by implication, those who have inferior tastes.
　95. *how ... squares?*] how are things proceeding? The phrase refers to the squares of a board game (*OED* square n. 6a 6b, citing this usage).
　96. *stay*] delay (*OED* n.3).
　97. *expect you*] are ready and waiting for you.
　99. *exercise*] employment, customary practice (*OED* n. 2 obs.).
　100–1.] Two lost plays dramatised the Old Testament story of Samson: *The Story of Samson*, acted at the Red Lion in 1567 (*BD* 2.449); a play called *Samson* was acquired by the Admiral's Men in mid-1602, and its performance at the Fortune in September noted by a visitor to England (*BD* 4.395–6). Given *FoL*'s likely date of composition in 1605–06, this passage probably recalls the latter play.
　102. *the youths*] acting companies made up wholly of boys and young men such as the Children of the King's Revels who performed *FoL*. At the time of composition of *FoL*, the second wave of boy companies comprised the second Children of Paul's, the Chapel Children and the Children of the Queen's Revels.
　103–4.] (1) Lipsalve's deprecation of the youths' ability plausibly to enact the biblical strongman draws attention to the mimetic skill of the young actors on stage. For comparable passages of 'mock condescension', see Shapiro, 109–10; (2) Lipsalve 'makes a distinction aimed at mocking child

hope 'tis not for youths to play Samson. Believe it, we
saw Samson bear the town gates on his neck from the   105
lower to the upper stage, with that life and admirable
accord that it shall never be equalled, unless the whole
new livery of porters set their shoulders.
Mistress Purge. Fie, fie, 'tis pity young gentlemen can bestow
their time no better. This playing is not lawful, for I   110
cannot find that either plays or players were allowed in
the prime church of Ephesus by the elders.

---

performers by reference to the relative verisimilitude achieved by an adult
player in the role of Samson' (Taylor, Mulholland, and Jackson, 217).
    104–6. *we ... stage*] Lipsalve reports an enactment of the episode in which
Samson bears the gates of Gaza up to the mountain of Hebron (Judges 16.3).
This could have been enacted on the Fortune stage in various ways: (1) the
actor playing Samson ascends to the upper stage on 'a ladder ... specially
applied to the balcony' (Wilhelm Creizenach, *The English Drama in the Age
of Shakespeare*, trans. Cécile Hugon [1916] [New York: Russell and Russell,
repr. 1967], 375); (2) the actor ascends to the upper stage via an 'outer ...
visible staircase' (Lawrence, 20); (3) bearing the property gates, the actor
passes from one symbolic locus on the stage to another (Leslie Hotson,
Shakespeare's Wooden O [London: Hart Davis, 1959], 216); https://
www.lostplays.org/index.php?title=Samson (accessed 18 April 2021), and
Introduction, 'Staging'. Alfred Harbage saw Lipsalve's report of the Samson
action as a 'mocking allusion' to the physical prowess of actors in the public
theatres (*Shakespeare and the Rival Traditions* [New York: Macmillan, 1952],
106).
    104–8. *we ... porters*] Compare Shakespeare, *LLL* 1.2.65–7: 'Samson ...
he was a man of good carriage ... for he carried the town gates on his back
like a porter.'
    106. *life*] (1) vitality; (2) life-likeness.
    107. *accord*] agreement of parts.
    107–8. *unless ... shoulders*] To bear a load as heavy as Samson's, you'd
need a whole new breed of liverymen to form a new company. Thomas
Brewer's 'New Ballad ... in Commendation of the ... Company of the
Porters' was entered in the Stationers' Register in June 1605; see Introduction,
38–9. The woodcut accompanying the ballad shows three sturdy porters,
one setting his shoulders to a heavily loaded basket (figure 2).
    108. *livery*] city company (collective term as at *OED* livery 7c).
    109–12.] Mistress Purge's hostility to playing echoes Puritan writers
against the stage, for example Stubbes, ch. 36, 'Stage-Plays and Interludes,
with their wickedness'. With her reference to the early Church, compare Acts
19.31: when St Paul was in Ephesus, 'certain of the chief of Asia, which were
his friends, sent unto him, desiring him that he would not adventure into
the theatre'; the 1599 Geneva Bible also warns Paul to stay out of the forum.

SC 3]   THE FAMILY OF LOVE   87

Dryfat. Aha, I think she tickled you there.
Purge. Cousin Gerardine, shall the will be read before supper?
Gerardine. Before supper, I beseech you.   115
Lipsalve. Ay, ay, before supper, for when these women's bellies be full their bones will be soon at rest.
Dryfat. Well, master doctor, pity the state of a poor gentleman. It is in you to stay his journey, and make him and yourself happy in his choice.   120
Glister. Hold you content. — Shall this will be read?
Purge. It shall. — Read you, good Master Lipsalve.
Lipsalve. Command silence, then.
Gudgeon. Silence!
Lipsalve. In the name of God, Amen. *Know all men, by these*   125
presents, that I, Gerardine, being strong of body, and perfect in sense —
Dryfat. That's false: there's no lover in his perfect sense.
Gudgeon. Peace, Dryfat!
Lipsalve. Do give and grant to Maria Glister, daughter of John   130
Glister, and niece to Doctor Glister, physician, all my leases, lands, chattels, goods, and movables whatsoever. This is stark naught. You cannot give away your movables, for mistress doctor and Mistress Purge claim both shares in your movables by reason of their legacies.   135
Dryfat. That's true, for their legacies must go out of your movables.

---

126. presents] *Dyce;* presence *Q.*

---

113. *tickled*] (1) ironically, beat, chastised (*OED* v.1 6b); (2) vexed, provoked (*OED* v.1 7a obs.).

119. *stay*] halt, delay.

121. *Hold ... content*] Stay calm, take it easy; a reflexive usage (*OED* hold v. 7c).

125–6. *by ... presents*] by the contents of this document, i.e., Gerardine's will (*OED* present n.1 3b).

132. movables] items of personal property such as furniture, tableware, etc. as opposed to the inheritable real estate which Gerardine has left inclusively to Maria (*OED* 1a).

133. *stark naught*] total nonsense.

134. *claim both*] i.e., both of them claim.

136. *go out of*] be taken from.

Lipsalve. [*Writing*] I'll put it in: *all my movables, these following legacies being paid.*
Gerardine. Do so, good Master Lipsalve.
Lipsalve. 'Tis done.
Mistress Purge. I pray, read only the legacies, for supper stays.
Lipsalve. Well, the legacies. [*Reads.*] *First, I give to my cousin, Mistress Purge, a fair, large standing* — what's this? Oh, cup — *a fair, large standing cup, with a close-stool* —
Dryfat. 'Tis not so, 'tis not so.
Lipsalve. I cry you mercy, a close cover 'tis. *To Mistress Doctor I give a fair bodkin of gold, with two orient pearls attending the same: all which are in my trunk to be delivered to the keeping of Maria. In witness etc.* — Is this your will?
Gerardine. 'Tis.
Lipsalve. To it with your hand and seal.
Mistress Purge. How is it, chick? I must have the standing cup, and Mistress Glister the bodkin?
Purge. Right, sweet duck.
Gerardine. I pray, gentlemen, put to your hands.
Dryfat. Come, your fists, gentlemen, your fists.
Gerardine. [*While the witnesses sign the will*] Mistress Glister, I have found you always more flexible to understand the estate of a poor gentleman than your husband was willing; therefore, I have thought it a point of charity to reveal the wrongs you sustained by your husband's looseness. Let me tell you in private that the doctor cuckolds Purge

---

138. SD] *this edn; not in Q.*   143. SD] *Dillon; not in Q.*   144–5. Oh, cup] *Q (*O Cup*);* O, a Cup *Dillon.*   158. SD] *Dyce; not in Q.*

---

142. *supper stays*] dinner awaits (*OED* stay v. 19a).
144. *standing*] (1) of an erect penis (Williams, *Dictionary*, stand 3.1307–8); (2) of the stem and base of a goblet.
145. *close-stool*] privy; pan or chamberpot with a lid, set into a chair, for bodily wastes.
147. *close cover*] closed or closable cover (*OED* close adj. 1a).
148. *bodkin*] a short, pointed weapon like a dagger, with phallic innuendo.
pearls] punning on testicles, in relation to the bodkin (as penis).
156. *put ... hands*] sign it.
160. *estate*] situation.
162. *looseness*] lax behaviour.

SC 3]   THE FAMILY OF LOVE   89

  oftener than he visits one of his patients; what 'a spares
  from you, 'a spends lavishly on her. These pothecaries   165
  are a kind of panders — look to it! If 'a keep Maria long
  close, it is for some lascivious end of his own.
Mistress Glister. She is his niece!
Gerardine. Tut, these doctors have tricks. Your niceness is
  such that you can endure no polluted shows in your   170
  house. Take heed lest 'a make you a bawd before your
  time — look to it!
Lipsalve. Come, our hands are testimonies to thy follies.
  Shall's now to supper? We'll have a health go round to
  thy voyage.   175
Gudgeon. Ay, and to all that forswear marriage, and can be
  content with other men's wives.
Gerardine. Of which consort you two are grounds: one touches
  the bass, and the other tickles the minikin.
  But to our cheer; come gentles, let's away,   180
  The roast meat's in consumption by our stay.   *Exeunt.*

                    End of Act One

---

170. shows] *Q;* shoes *Dyce.*   181.1. End. . . One] *Q* (*Finis Act. Primi.*) *at right margin below Exeunt.*

  164–5. *'a ... you*] he keeps from you.
  166, 172. *look ... it!*] watch out!
  166–7. *keep ... close*] keeps Maria cooped up for a long time.
  169. *niceness*] fastidiousness.
  174. *We'll ... round*] We'll all drink a toast, perhaps implying the passing around of a cup from person to person at the table (*OED* to go round v. 1a).
  176. *forswear*] refuse.
  178–9. *consort ... bass ... minikin*] musical analogy; (1) the gallants are foundational players in a string consort: one of them plays the bass viol, or sounds a viol's bass string, the other plays the fiddle or lute, or touches the treble or highest string on that instrument (*OED* n.2 1); (2) 'grounds' as short recurrent themes, usually in the bass, upon which continuous variations arise. Compare Shakespeare, *R3* 3.7.43: 'on that ground I'll build a holy descant'; (3) bawdy innuendo, *tickles ... minikin* meaning 'caresses a young wife', as in Marston, *JDE* A3: 'when I was a young man and could tickle the minikin'. The juxtaposition of 'bass' and 'minikin' implies wives' lower and upper parts, i.e., genitals and breasts.
  181. *in consumption*] ruined by overcooking, dried out (*OED* consumption n. 1 3).

Act 2

ACT 2 SCENE 1

Enter MASTER PURGE.

[*Purge.*] The grey-eyed morning braves me to my face, and calls me sluggard. 'Tis time for tradesmen to be in their shops, for he that tends well his shop and hath an alluring wife, with a graceful 'what d'ye lack?', shall be sure to have good doings, and good doings is that that crowns 5
so many citizens with the horns of abundance. My wife, by ordinary course, should this morning have been at the Family, but now her soft pillow hath given her counsel to keep her bed. Master doctor should, indeed, minister to her, to whose pills she is so much accustomed that now 10

Act 2 Scene 1] *Q* (ACTVS SECVNDVS. / *Actus Secundus, scena prima*). 1. SH] *Dyce; not in Q.* 4. d'ye] *Dyce*; de *Q.*

---

1. *The ... morning*] It is daytime, but the sun is not yet shining. Purge has a confused smattering of Homer: the goddess Athena is traditionally 'glaucopis', often translated as 'grey-eyed', while dawn is 'rhododaktylos', 'rosy-fingered'.
braves] taunts (*OED* brave v. 1a).
2–5. *'Tis ... doings*] Tradesmen put their wives or daughters into the shop window as a lure to customers to enter the shop and be served by a pretty face. Compare Marston, *Dutch. C.* 3.3.13–17: 'a fine-faced wife in a wainscot carved seat is a worthy ornament to a tradesman's shop, and an attractive'.
4. *'what ... lack?'*] what do you need?
5. *good doings*] (1) prosperous trade (*OED* doing n. 2); (2) proficient coitus, a meaning the audience may hear but Purge may not intend (Williams, *Dictionary*, do 1.395).
6. *horns ... abundance*] horns of plenty (Lat., 'cornucopia'), with a satirical undertow created by the plural noun, suggesting the horns of a cuckold. This speech raises the question of whether Purge is a complacent cuckold. In the phrase 'wink at small faults' (22–3) he appears to shrug off any adultery as insignificant compared to the profit husband and wife make.
7. *ordinary course*] usual habit.
9–10. *minister to*] treat.
10. *pills*] euphemism for sexual attention.

her body looks for them as duly as the moon shakes off
the old and borrows new horns. I smile to myself to hear
our knights and gallants say how they gull us citizens,
when indeed we gull them, or rather, they gull themselves. Here they come in term time, hire chambers, and   15
perhaps kiss our wives — well, what lose I by that? God's
blessing on's heart, I say still, that makes much of my
wife; for they were very hard-favoured that none could
find in's heart to love but ourselves. Drugs would be dog
cheap, but for my private, well-practised doctor, and such   20
customers. Tut, jealousy is a hell, and they that will thrive
must utter their wares as they can, and wink at small
faults.   [*Exit.*]

---

23. SD] *Dyce; not in Q.*

11–12. *as duly ... horns*] as regularly, and appropriately, as the moon grows full and begins anew each month (*OED* duly adv. 3 1). The moon is at once feminised in its changeability, and made a figure of the cuckold ('old and ... new horns'), in that a crescent moon resembles the curved horns of an animal.
12–19. *I ... ourselves*] The plural pronouns 'our', 'us' and 'we' here provide evidence of direct audience address.
14. *gull*] trick, dupe.
15. *chambers*] rooms, lodgings.
17. *still*] always.
makes ... of] lavishes attention and money on, with a view to sex.
18. *they*] wives.
18–19. *they ... ourselves*] wives would have to be extremely ugly if loved only by their husbands.
19. *in's*] in his.
19–21. *Drugs ... customers*] Medicines would be little respected if it weren't for Glister's secret ('private') craftiness, which inflates the price of drugs (*OED* practise v. 1c 5c 9b 10a). 'Customers' suggests that Purge supplies and Glister applies medicines.
19–20. *dog cheap*] (1) figuratively, poorly esteemed (*OED* adj. 2 obs.); (2) dirt cheap.
22. *utter ... wares*] sell their goods (*OED* utter v.1 1a).
22–3. *wink ... faults*] ignore or close their eyes to small problems. See Tilley F123, citing Shakespeare, *H5* 2.2.53–4: 'If little faults ... / Shall not be winked at'.

Act 2 Scene 2

Enter DOCTOR GLISTER.

Glister. The tedious night is past and the jocund morn looks more lively and fresh than an old gentlewoman's glazed face in a new periwig. By this time my humorous lover is at Gravesend, and I go with more joy to fetch his trunk than ever the valiant Trojans did to draw in the Grecian   5
jade. His goods shall into the walls of my Troy, and be offered to a face more lively than ever was that thrice-ravished Helen, yet with such caution that no danger shall happen to me.   [*Exit.*]

Act 2 Scene 2] *Dyce (SCENE II); not in Q.*   2. lively] *Q;* lovely *Dyce.*   8. Helen] *Q;* Helen['s] *Dyce.*   9. SD] *Dyce; not in Q.*

---

1. *tedious*] excessively long.
jocund] cheerful, bright.
2. *glazed*] painted with cosmetics (Shepherd).
3. *periwig*] a full, stylised wig worn at this time mainly by women, but increasingly by men also from the mid-seventeenth century (*OED* n. 1).
humorous lover] i.e., impulsive Gerardine, melancholy over his rejection as Maria's husband. At 1.2.4–5, Lipsalve describes Gerardine exhibiting a posture associated with the fashionable lover's humour of melancholy: 'How thou goest crying up and down *with thy arms across* for a wife' (my emphasis).
4. *Gravesend*] port near the mouth of the river Thames.
4–6. *I ... jade*] Glister draws an analogy between Gerardine's trunk, which he supposes contains the young man's worldly 'goods' (6), and the gigantic Trojan horse by which the Greeks conveyed their best soldiers into Troy, enabling the city's sacking (*OED* Trojan adj. 1b). 'Grecian jade' also refers to Helen of Troy, whose abduction by Paris caused the Trojan war; the term places her contemptuously as inferior, a deceitful woman (*OED* jade n. 1a 2a).
7. *face ... lively*] i.e., Maria.
7–8. *thrice-ravished Helen*] Helen, queen of Sparta, daughter of Zeus and Leda, revered as the most beautiful woman of her time. She suffered three 'rapes': (1) abducted as a girl by Theseus, she was rescued by her brothers Castor and Pollux; (2) following her (possibly unwilling) marriage to the Greek Menelaus, she was seduced by Paris; (3) after whose death she married his brother Deiphobus, whom she then betrayed to Menelaus. After the Trojan war, Menelaus took Helen back to Sparta. The description challenges the audience to tot up the number of times Helen was exchanged between men.
8–9. *yet ... me*] Glister's exercise of 'caution' parallels the idea of Helen's destructive impact, as a raped woman, on the afterlives of ancient heroes such as Menelaus and Deiphobus.

ACT 2 SCENE 3

Enter LIPSALVE *and* GUDGEON *at several doors, with their pages,* SHRIMP *and* PERIWINKLE.

Gudgeon. Master Lipsalve, welcome within ken! We two are so nearly linked that if thou be'st absent but one two hours thy acquaintance grows almost mouldy in my memory.

Lipsalve. And thine fly-blown in mine. How dost thou do?

Shrimp. Fellow page, I think our acquaintance runs low too, but if it run not o'the lees, let's set it a-tilt, and give 'em some dregs to their mouldy fly-blown compliments. 5

Periwinkle. No, rather let's pierce the rundlets of our running heads and give 'em a neat cup of wagship to put down their courtship. 10

Act 2 Scene 3] *Dyce (SCENE III); not in Q.* 2.3.0.2. SH PERIWINKLE] *Dyce; Periwinde Q.* 4. thine] then *Q.* 5. too] *Q (to).*

0.1. SD *several*] different (*OED* adj. 2a).
1. *within ken!*] back home, within sight (*OED* ken n.1 2a).
2. *nearly*] intimately (*OED* adv. 3).
4. *fly-blown*] rotten, putrid (*OED* adj. 1).
6. *if ... lees*] if it isn't drunk to the last drop, *lees* being the dregs of wine left in bottle or glass (*OED* lee n. 2d). Compare Isaiah 25.6: 'a feast of wines on the lees'.
 set it a-tilt] (1) set the bottle of their acquaintance at an angle for pouring; (2) engage in a tournament of wit, from 'ride a-tilt', meaning to ride in an encounter on horseback with the thrust of a lance (*OED* a-tilt adv. 2).
6–7. *give 'em ... compliments*] offer our masters some competition for their tired, far-fetched phrases.
8–9. *pierce ... heads*] let us pour some wine, figuratively, let's have a bout of wit.
8. *rundlets*] roundlets, small casks or vessels often used for measuring wine or spirits (*OED* rundlet n.1 2, citing this usage).
8–9. *running heads*] (1) as opposed to running footmen who deliver messages; (2) lively wit of the pages' banter, continuing the metaphor of drinking begun in 6. A related usage in Beaumont and Fletcher's *Coxcomb* (1609), 4.3.69–70: 'These men have pestilence running heads', literalises *running heads* in the sense of 'flowing intelligence'; (3) term in printing for title line at the top of the page, punning on 'page' as 'boy' and as printer's product.
9. *wagship*] waggery, facetiousness, associated esp. with page roles following John Lyly's comedies (*OED* n. 1 obs., citing this line).

94 THE FAMILY OF LOVE [ACT 2

Shrimp. Courtship, cartship: for the tongues of complimenters run on wheels. But mark 'em, they ha' not done yet.
Gudgeon. And i'faith, how is't? Methinks thou hast been a
long vagrant.
Lipsalve. The rogation hath been long indeed; therefore we   15
may salute as ceremoniously as lawyers when they meet
after a long vacation, who, to renew the discontinued
state tale, they stretch it out with such length that whilst
they greet before, their clients kiss them behind.
Shrimp. If his nose were put i'the remainder of that state tale   20
he would say 'twere an unsavoury one.
Periwinkle. I wonder why many men gird so at the law.
Shrimp. I'll tell thee: because they themselves have neither
law nor conscience.

---

11. *cartship*] pun on 'courtship'. Criminals were taken to execution in open carts, while prostitutes were driven in public on the back of carts as a form of shameful display (see Boose, figure 5).

11–12. *complimenters*] flatterers.

12. *run ... wheels*] are fluent.

mark 'em] pay attention to what they are saying.

13–14. *thou ... vagrant*] you've been away a long time; a vagrant is a wanderer, or masterless man (*OED* n.1).

15. *rogation*] (1) beggar's activity of supplicating for alms, usually follow-ing a seasonal circuit; to rogue meant 'to play the vagrant' (Dyce); (2) pun on 'rogue' and 'rogation' days, named for the supplications chanted in processions on the three days before Ascension Day (*OED* 1a 1b).

16. *salute*] embrace, kiss as a greeting.

17. *long vacation*] three-month summer vacation taken by law courts, so called to distinguish it from Christmas and Easter vacations (*OED* long adj.1 and n.1).

17–18. *to ... tale*] to continue their interrupted political chat.

18. *state tale*] (1) talk about affairs of state; (2) discussion of legal judgements.

18–19. *they ... behind*] The lawyers talk for so long that their clients have to pay many times over for legal services, punning on '*kiss ... behind*' meaning 'to kiss (a person's) arse', 'to behave obsequiously towards (a person)' (*OED* kiss v. 6 l, but gives first usage as 1705). Compare *Club Law*, 3.9.1759: 'Kiss Mr Nifle behind'.

20. *tale*] pun on 'tail' as 'arse', continuing the scatological humour begun at 1.3.145.

21. *unsavoury*] (1) smelly; (2) unpleasant.

22. *gird*] gibe, sneer at (*OED* v. fig. 4a, citing this line, 4b).

23–4. *they ...conscience*] they obey neither the rule of law nor moral imperatives.

Gudgeon. But what news now? How stands the state of things   25
   at Brussels?
Lipsalve. Faith, weak and limber, weak and limber: nothing
   but pride and double-dealing. Virtue is vice's lackey;
   beggars suck like horse-leeches at the heart of bounty,
   and leaves him so tired and spur-galled that he can be no   30
   longer ridden with honesty.
Gudgeon. Well fare the City yet! There virtue rides a cock-
   horse, cherished and kept warm in good sables and fox

---

30. leaves him] *Dillon;* loues theame *Q;* leave him *Dyce.*

---

25. *what news*] standard set-up for clown routine in jigs and ballads, preparing the audience to laugh; see C.R. Baskervill, *The Elizabethan Jig and Related Song Drama* (1929) (New York: Dover, repr. 1965), 59–63, 67–8.

25–6. *the state … Brussels*] Probably refers to the ratification of the peace treaty between England and Spain that took place in Brussels on 1 May 1605, putting an end to the nineteen-year Anglo-Spanish War.

27. *limber*] sycophantic, willing to bow down to anyone (*OED* adj. 2 fig.); compare Marston, *Ant.&Mell.* 1.1.74: 'Confusion to these limber sycophants!'

28. *pride*] display of wealth and lavish ceremony.
   lackey] menial servant.

29. *horse-leeches*] large worms, popularly seen as great blood-suckers, hence 'rapacious, insatiable person[s]' (*OED* n. 2 3 fig.). Compare Shakespeare, *H5* 2.3.46–7: 'Let us to France, like horse-leeches … / To suck … the very blood to suck!'

30. *leaves him*] emended from Q's 'loues theame'. Bounty is personified as a 'heart' sucked of goodness, so that virtue is no longer of any use. Vice is riding, but the lackey virtue is running alongside.
   spur-galled] wounded by spurs attached to the rider's feet.

31. *honesty*] honour (*OED* n. 1a obs.).

32–3. *rides a cock-horse*] (1) is jubilant, like a child riding a hobby-horse (*OED* cock-horse n. 1); (2) rides a proud, fine horse; figuratively, occupies public office with arrogance (*OED* 2); see Cotgrave, 1611 (*LEME*): 'Il est à cheval, hee is set on cocke-horse; hee is all a hoight, hee now begins to flaunt it.' Gudgeon is sarcastic; city pride and ostentation are antithetical to virtue.

33. *good*] of superior quality (*OED* adj. 1h).
   sables] suit of black, trimmed with fur from the sable, a small furry mammal native to the Arctic and sub-Arctic regions of Europe and Asia (*OED* n.1 2a). Though often worn as mourning attire, Gudgeon envisages 'sables' as worn by professional figures such as lawyers and magistrates; compare *Ham.* 3.2.120–1: 'let the devil wear black, for I'll have a suit of sables'.

33–4. *fox fur*] associated with corruption, especially of usurers (Shepherd). Compare the cozening fox-protagonist of Jonson, *Volp.* (1606), 1.2.97: 'Give me my furs'.

fur, and with the breath of his nostrils drives pride and
covetousness before him, like's own shadow. Beggars   35
have whipping cheer; bounty obliges men to't, gives
money for scrips and scrolls, and liberality sealed with
strong arms and heraldry to outlive mortality. Love there
will see the last man born, never give over while there's
an arrow i'th' quiver.   40
Lipsalve. Now we talk of love, I do know not far hence so
good a subject for that humour that if she would wear
but the standing collar and her things in fashion our

---

36. to't] too't *Q*. 36–7. gives money ... liberality sealed] *Q;* and liberality gives money for scrips and scrolls, sealed *Dyce*.

34–5. *drives ... him*] subordinates pride and covetousness to his own purposes.

36. *whipping cheer*] flogging, flagellation; obsolete humorous usage (*OED* whipping n. C1b).

36–8. *bounty ... mortality*] open-handedness leads men to purchase coats of arms, with which they seal legal documents ('scrips and scrolls') that confirm liberal gifts to the next generations of gentlemen. Gudgeon expresses scorn for rich men who think they can purchase immortality via the appurtenances of heraldry rather than succouring 'beggars' to whom they give only 'whipping cheer' (36).

37. *liberality*] the quality of spending freely; generosity (*OED* n. 1a).

38. *strong*] (1) authoritative (*OED* adj. 5a); (2) firmly established (*OED* 15e); (3) financially well-endowed (*OED* 5e); (4) powerful in operative effect (*OED* 7). The arms are 'strong' because birth and high status may persist through generations, while individual lives are comparably short-lived.

38–40. *Love ... quiver*] Human charity will wait until nearly the end of the world before considering almsgiving (Dillon). The sexual import of 'love' is followed through in 'never ... arrow i'th' quiver', never cease while there's an ejaculating penis in a woman's vagina (*OED* arrow n. 2b).

40. *quiver*] (1) portable bag containing a huntsman's arrows (*OED* n. 1); (2) vagina (*OED* quiver n. 2 obs., citing Greene, *Disput. Cony-Catcher* (1592): 'the humour of an harlot, whose quiver is open to every arrow').

43. *standing collar*] upright collar made stiff with starching, a technique introduced to England in 1564 by a Dutch woman, Madame Dingham Vander Plasse, and worn by men and women until *c.* 1616: 'Let us have standing collars in the fashion, / All are become a stiff-neck generation', *Knave of Hearts* (1612), cited in Linthicum, 169, 2n. There is a bawdy quibble on 'standing', as at 1.3.144n.

in fashion] properly, or as in vogue at court.

SC 3]   THE FAMILY OF LOVE   97

    ladies in the court were but brown sugar-candy, as gross
    as grocery to her.   45
Gudgeon. She is not so sweet as a pothecary's shop, is she?
Lipsalve. A plague on you! Ha' you so good a scent? [*Aside*]
    For my life, he's my rival.
Gudgeon. Her name begins with Mistress Purge, does it not?
Lipsalve. True, the only comet of the city.   50
Gudgeon. Ay, if she would let her ruffs stream out a little
    wider. But I am sure she is ominous to me: she makes
    civil wars and insurrections in the state of my stomach.
    I had thought to have bound myself from love, but her
    purging comfits makes me loose-bodied still.   55

47. SD] *Dyce; not in Q.* 51. Ay, if] *Dyce;* I, if *Q.*

44. *sugar-candy*] sugar clarified and crystallised by slow evaporation. The first crystallisation produced brown or red sugar-candy, while the white version required reboiling and recrystallisation (*OED*).
  gross] (1) twelve dozen (*OED* n.3); (2) big, coarse (*OED* adj. 1a).
45. *grocery*] shop where the grocer (pun on 'grosser') buys and sells by the 'gross', a term of measure. The Grocers' Company was one of the top twelve City companies.
46. *sweet*] concocted from sugar. See below, 55, 57, for the 'purging comfits' and 'electuary' ministered to Gudgeon by Mistress Purge.
50. *comet ... city*] blazing star; compare 'some city star' (2.4.122).
51–2. *if ... wider*] 'if she would wear her clothes with more flamboyance'. Dryfat similarly uses sartorial style as a metaphor for temperament by describing female Familists as 'narrow-ruffed' (5.3.186).
51. *ruffs*] starched multi-pleated frills typically standing out around the neck (*OED* ruff n.3 2a). Ruffs varied enormously in size, ornamentation and style.
52. *ominous*] 'As a comet was formerly thought to be the harbinger of civil war or other insurrections in the state' (Dillon).
52–3. *she ... stomach*] With Mistress Purge's disruption of Gudgeon's physical equilibrium, compare Shakespeare, *JC* 2.1.67–9: 'the state of man, / Like to a little kingdom, suffers ... / The nature of an insurrection'.
54. *bound*] (1) made fast or sure; (2) made constipated (*OED* bind v. 3 4).
55. *purging comfits*] sweetmeats made of fruit and preserved with sugar, used medicinally as a laxative 'pill' (*OED* comfit n. a). Compare Fletcher, *Tamer*, 5.1.85–7: 'I gave him purging-comfits / At a great christening ... That spoiled his chamblet breeches'.
  loose-bodied] (1) physically unbound or liquid, brought about by laxative medicine, playing on 'bound' in 54; (2) wanton (*OED* loose-bodied adj.). A metaphor derived from the 'body' or bodice, an upper garment worn with a woman's skirt or gown made in two parts fastened at the sides, forming 'a pair of bodies'. A related usage occurs below at 5.3.186n.

98   THE FAMILY OF LOVE   [ACT 2

Lipsalve. What, has she ministered to thee then?
Gudgeon. Faith, some lectuary or so.
Lipsalve. Ay, I fear she takes too much of that lectuary to
   stoop to love: it keeps her body soluble from sin; she is
   not troubled with carnal crudities nor the binding of the   60
   flesh.
Gudgeon. Thou hast sounded her then, belike.
Lipsalve. Not I. I am too shallow to sound her; she's out of
   my element. If I show passion and discourse of love to
   her, she tells me I am wide from the right scope. She says   65
   she has another object and aims at a better love than
   mine.
Gudgeon. Oh, that's her husband.
Lipsalve. No, no, she speaks pure devotion. She's impenetrable. No gold, or oratory, no virtue in herbs, nor no physic   70
   will make her love.
Gudgeon. More is the pity I say, that fair women should prove
   saints before age had made them crooked. [*Aside*] 'Tis

---

58. Ay, I] *Dyce;* J, I *Q.*   73. SD] *Dyce; not in Q.*

---

   56. *ministered*] administered medicine (*OED* minister v. 8).
   57. *lectuary*] (1) electuary, a medicinal powder mixed with honey or syrup; (2) pun on electuary / lechery (Shepherd).
   59. *soluble ... sin*] free from sin. In medicine, soluble meant 'free from constipation' (*OED* adj. 1a).
   60. *carnal crudities*] (1) undigested pieces of meat in the stomach (*OED* crudity v. 2a); (2) 'imperfectly "concocted" humours' (*OED* crudity v. 2a pl.), here implying sexual longings.
   60–1. *binding ... flesh*] becoming constipated, see 54n.
   62. *sounded*] (1) measured the depth of, a nautical term (*OED* v. 2a), with figurative sense of 'penetrated'.
   belike] probably, perhaps.
   63–4. *I ... element*] Lipsalve admits he hasn't been able to have sex with Mistress Purge, as she is too wily for him to seduce.
   65. *I ... scope*] I deviate from the proper aim or subject (*OED* scope n. 2a 3a); compare the modern phrase 'wide of the mark'.
   66. *object*] goal, purpose.
   a ... love] love of God or the Spirit. Mistress Purge has rejected Lipsalve using Familist rhetoric.
   70. *virtue ... herbs*] power of plants that might work like a date-rape drug, or arouse her to a pitch of sexual desire.
   physic] medicine, or a course of medical treatment.
   73. *crooked*] bent with age (*OED* adj. 2a), therefore not worth assailing.

sc 3] THE FAMILY OF LOVE 99

my luck to be crossed still, but I must not give over the
chase. 75
Lipsalve. Come hither, boy, while I think on't.

Lipsalve and Shrimp confer.

Gudgeon. Faith, friend Lipsalve, I perceive you would fain
play with my love — a pure creature 'tis — for whom I
have sought every angle of my brain, but either she scorns
courtiers (as most of them do, because they are given to 80
boast of their doings) or else she's exceeding strait-laced.
Therefore, to prevent this smell-smock, I'll to my friend
doctor Glister, a man exquisite in the art magic, who hath
told me of many rare experiments available in this case.
— Farewell, friend Lipsalve. 85
Lipsalve. Adieu, honest Gregory, frequent my lodging. I have
a viola da gamba and good tobacco.

Exeunt GUDGEON *and* PERIWINKLE.

— Thou wilt do this feat, boy?
Shrimp. Else knock my head and my pate together.

87.1. SD] *Dyce; Exit Gud.and Periwind Q at 85.*

---

74. *crossed*] obstructed.
80. *for whom*] for whose seduction by me.
81. *doings*] sexual affairs. Compare 2.1.5n.
exceeding] exceedingly.
strait-laced] literally and metaphorically 'tightly corseted' or 'buttoned up'.
In this period women and some men wore bodices that were laced with
'points' (5.3.104) and eyelets.
82. *prevent*] anticipate, get a step ahead of.
smell-smock] a licentious man, i.e., Lipsalve (Shepherd); see Cotgrave,
1611 (*LEME*): 'Brigaille, a notable smellsmock or mutton-mungor, a cunning
solicitor of a wench'.
86–7. *I ... tobacco*] An unwitting invitation to watch Lipsalve's humiliation. In Jonson's *EMO* the dilettante courtier Fastidious Brisk tries to
impress the witty Saviolina by talking while puffing on tobacco and making
fumbling attempts to tune and play her viol da gamba (3.3). She spurns him.
87. *viola da gamba*] bass viol played between the knees (*gamba*, Ital., 'leg')
like a modern cello, implying sexual as well as musical practices.
89. *pate*] head, perhaps triggered by the homonym 'feat/feet' in 88.

Lipsalve. Away then, bid him bring his measure with him. 90
Exit SHRIMP.
Gerardine is travelled, and I must needs be cast into his mould. My flesh grows proud, and Maria's a sweet wench, etc. But yet I must not let fall my suit with Mistress Purge, lest — *sede vacanti* — my friend Gudgeon join issue. 95
I'll rather to my learnèd doctor for a spell,
For I have a fire in my liver burns like hell.
[*Exit* LIPSALVE.]

ACT 2 SCENE 4

Enter MISTRESS GLISTER, [*a* Servant], *and* MARIA.

Mistress Glister. [*To* Servant] I pray, let's have no polluted feet nor rheumatic chaps enter the house. I shall have my floor

---

90.1. SD] Dyce; Q follows line 89. 96–7.] Dyce; prose in Q.

Act 2 Scene 4] *this edn; not in* Q. 0.1. SD] *this edn; not in* Q.

---

90. *measure*] graduated rod or tape (*OED* n. 5b) used by the tailor ('him', 90). Lipsalve has requested Shrimp fetch a tailor to make him a suit of clothes resembling Gerardine's. Echoes Jonson's *EMO* 3.1 where Fungoso brings a tailor to see Brisk's outfit so that he can have a copy made.
91. *is travelled*] has gone overseas.
91–2. *be ... mould*] assume his shape or identity.
92. *proud*] sexually excited, erect (*OED* adj. obs. 7b). Compare Shakespeare, *Luc.* 712: 'The flesh being proud, desire doth fight with grace'.
92–3. *Maria's ... etc.*] Cue for the actor to improvise, possibly accompanied by 'hand gestures or comic measuring of Maria's body' (Dillon, ixx).
94–5. *lest ... issue*] lest Gudgeon court Mistress Purge for himself.
94. sede vacanti] Lat., 'the seat being vacant'; an ecclesiastical technicality describing the state of a bishopric while the see is vacant.
95. *join issue*] legal term: accept the concern tendered by the opposite party as a basis for argument (*OED* issue n. P2a).
97. *fire ... liver*] seat of love and violent passions such as Lipsalve's lust and possible venereal disease, with its symptom of burning.

2. *rheumatic*] overflowing with phlegm or catarrh (*OED* adj. 1b 2a 4a). See below 4.3.68n.
chaps] jaws, the mouth.
2–4. *I ... tables*] As well as hosting sumptuous banquets, the great halls of the Inns of Court were sometimes the scene of riotous behaviour by students. See A. Wigfall Green, *The Inns of Court and Early English Drama* (New York: Benjamin Blom, 1931), 35.

SC 4]   THE FAMILY OF LOVE   101

   look more greasy shortly than one of your inn of court
   dining tables. — And now to you, good niece, I bend my
   speech. Let me tell you plainly, you are a fool to be love-   5
   sick for any man longer than he is in your company. Are
   you so ignorant in the rules of courtship to think any one
   man to bear all the prick and praise? I tell thee, be he
   never so proper, there is another to second him.
Maria.   Let rules of courtship be authentic still   10
   To such as do pursue variety,
   But unto those whose modest thoughts do tend
   To honoured nuptials and a regular life,
   As far from show of niceness as from that
   Of impure thoughts, all other objects seem   15
   Respectless, of no proportion, balanced with esteem
   Of what their souls affect.
Mistress Glister.   No marvel sure you should regard these men
   with such reverend opinion; there's few good faces, and
   fewer graces, in any of them. If one among a multitude   20

   3–4. *inn of court*] set of buildings belonging to one of the four Inns of Court or legal societies of London: the Inner Temple, the Middle Temple, Lincoln's Inn and Gray's Inn. Established around the end of the thirteenth century, the inns functioned as a cheaper alternative to Oxford and Cambridge by providing education for gentlemen's sons, many of whom did not enter the legal profession but became statesmen, civil servants, secretaries or servants in the royal household. John Marston, John Ford, Thomas Middleton and (through fraternisation) Ben Jonson were among the writers whose literary and theatrical talents were fostered by the Inns of Court and their revels tradition. On the inns' social and literary milieu, see Ostovich, 28–38. Bly, 53, notes that 'The liberty of the Whitefriars shared a gate with the Inner Temple, and law students undoubtedly dominated the audience.'
   4. *bend*] direct.
   8. *prick and praise*] selection and commendation for excellence, with bawdy innuendo. Compare 1.1.25n.
   9. *proper*] (1) handsome, attractive; (2) sexually well equipped.
   10. *authentic*] authoritative, appropriate (*OED* 3a).
   still] always, on every occasion (*OED* adv. 3a).
   11. *variety*] variety of sexual partners.
   14. *niceness*] coyness (Cleary).
   16. *Respectless*] Unworthy of respect, contemptible (*OED* 2b). Omitted by Dyce to make a pentameter line.
   proportion] importance.
   17. *affect*] love (*OED* v. 4a).
   19–20. *faces ... graces*] The rhyme adds a kick to Mistress Glister's judgement of men.

have a good pair of legs, he never leaves riding the ring
till he has quite marred the proportion. Nay, some, as I
have heard, wanting lineaments to their liking and calf to
support themselves, are fain to use art, and supply themselves with quilted calves, which oftentimes in revelling   25
fall about their ankles. And for their behaviour, wit, and
discourse (except some few that are travelled), it is as
imperfectious and silly as your scholars new come from
the university. By this light, I think we lose part of our
happiness when we make these weathercocks our equals.   30
Maria. Disgrace not that for which our sex was made,
  Society in nuptial beds. Above these joys
  Which lovers taste, when their conjoinèd lips
  Suck forth each other's souls, the earth, the air,

---

31. sex] *this edn;* sect Q.   32. Society ... beds. Above] *Dillon (subst);*
Society ... beds aboue Q.   nuptial beds] Q; nuptials: 'bove *Dyce.*

---

21. *riding the ring*] (1) a form of jousting in which two men-at-arms
mounted on horseback encountered each other, aiming to carry away a ring
on their lances; compare Webster, *DM*, 1.1.87: 'Who took the ring oftenest?';
(2) bawdy innuendo, *riding* referring to a man mounted for coitus (Partridge,
ride, 226); *ring* meaning pudenda (Partridge, 227).

22. *marred*] impaired.
proportion] shapeliness of his legs.
wanting] lacking.
lineaments] body parts (*OED* lineament n. 2a).

25. *quilted calves*] padded stockings.
revelling] dancing.

28. *imperfectious*] imperfect; a malapropism. Like Marston's Mistress
Mulligrub, Mistress Glister's pretentious discourse betrays her social
aspirations.

30. *weathercocks*] changeable, inconstant men (*OED* n. 2b fig.).

31. *sex*] Q's 'sect' was a current synonym for 'sex' (*OED* sect n.1 1d) or
gender (*OED* sect n.1 1a). Q's use of 'sect' and 'society' (32) in successive
lines suggests a subliminal religious sense for 'sect' (*OED* 1b 4a, 4b).

32. *Society*] (1) lovemaking; (2) companionship (*OED* n. 5a), perhaps
remembering the marriage service from the Book of Common Prayer: '[mat-
rimony] was ordained ... for the [partners'] mutual society'; (3) worship
(*OED* 11a).

nuptial beds] emended by Dyce to 'nuptials', weakening the frankness of
Maria's reference to physical love.

33. *conjoinèd*] joined.

34. *Suck ... souls*] kiss passionately. Compare Marlowe, *Dr Faust.* 5.1.93:
'Her lips sucks forth my soul'.

SC 4] THE FAMILY OF LOVE 103

  Yea, gods themselves know none. Elysium's sweet, 35
Ay, all that bliss which poets' pens describe,
Are only known when soft and amorous folds
Entwine the corps of two united lovers,
Where what they wish they have, yet still desire,
And sweets are known without satiety. 40

     Enter VIAL

[*Vial.*] Here's Club, forsooth, and his fellow prentice have
 brought Master Gerardine's trunk.
Mistress Glister. Let them come in if their feet be clean.
              [*Exit* VIAL.]
So then, your best beloved is gone — fair weather after
 him! All thy passions go with him! Recomfort thyself, 45
 wench, in a better choice: his love to thee would have
 been of no longer continuance than the untrussing of his
 hose. Then why shouldst thou pine for such a one?
Maria. [*Aside*] She's foolish, sure. With what imperfect
  phrase
And shallow wit she answers me. 50

---

36. Ay] *Dyce;* J *Q.*   40. satiety] *Dyce;* society *Q.*   40.1. SD] *Dyce; Enter Wall Q.*   41. SH] *Dyce; Nun. Q.*   43. SD] *Ex. Q.*   49. SD] *Dyce; not in Q.*   50. SD1–2] *Dyce (subst); Enter Club and another with the Trunke Q.*

---

 35. *Elysium's*] belonging to Elysium, the home of blessed spirits in the classical world.
 sweet] pleasure(s), sweetness. Adjectives were commonly used for nouns in early modern English (Abbott, 5). The singular form avoids obtrusive sibilance.
 37. *folds*] (1) folds of flesh; (2) ambience in a spiritual sense (*OED* n. 2b).
 38. *corps*] bodies (*OED* n.1).
 41. SH] Q's '*Nun.*' is short for 'Nuntius' (Lat.) or messenger, commonly used in early modern prompt books for a servant delivering information.
 44–5. *fair ... him!*] alludes to the proverb 'After a storm comes a calm (fair weather)' (Tilley S908). See also 4.3.133.
 45. *passions*] Maria's myriad feelings. Mistress Glister hopes that now Gerardine is gone, Maria will stop being in love with him and move on to other prospects.
 Recomfort] Console, hearten.
 47–8. *no ... hose*] no longer duration than the undoing of his flies. Men wore close-fitting leg coverings which were tied or 'trussed' with 'points' or thongs fastening the hose to the doublet. 'Hose' could refer either to the legging-like article of clothing, or to breeches (Linthicum, 204–6, 282).

104   THE FAMILY OF LOVE   [ACT 2

        Enter CLUB *and another* [Prentice] *with the trunk.*

Mistress Glister. Honest Club, welcome. Is this Master Gerardine's trunk? He is gone, then?
Club. Ay, indeed, Mistress Glister, he is departed this transitory City, but his whole substance is here enclosed, which, by command, we here deliver to your custody, to   55
the use of Mistress Maria according to the tenure of the premises.
Mistress Glister. Place it here, my honest Club, well done. And how does thy mistress? Was she at the Family today? [CLUB *spits.*] Spit not, good Club, I cannot abide it.   60
Club. Not today, forsooth, she hath overcharged herself and her memory. She means to use a moderation, and take no more than she can make use of.
Mistress Glister. And I prithee, Club, what kind of creatures are these Familists? Thou art conversant with them.   65
Club. What are they? With reverence be it spoken, they are the most accomplished creatures under heaven; in them is all perfection.
Mistress Glister. As how, good Club?
Club. Omitting their outward graces, I'll show you only one   70
instance, which includes all other: they love their neighbours better than themselves.

---

56. tenure] *Q;* tenour *Dyce;* tenor *Shepherd.*   60. SD] *Dyce; not in Q.*

53–4. *departed ... City*] (1) euphemism for 'dead', in that life is transitory; (2) perhaps a recondite echo of St Augustine, *The City of God* (413–27 CE), with its two cities: the earthly Babylon and the heavenly Jerusalem. Club may see London as the modern Babylon of worldly transitoriness.

54. *his ... enclosed*] equates the City and Gerardine's trunk with the opposition of body and soul. The material 'substance' inside the trunk represents Gerardine's spiritual essence.

56. *tenure*] holding good to Gerardine's will, read aloud in 1.3 (*OED* n. 1b).

57. *premises*] legal term: 'the matters stated previously' (*OED* n. 2a).

61. *over-charged*] over-taxed, by listening to too much religious discourse.

62. *memory*] consciousness, mind (*OED* n. 6a 7a).

68. *perfection*] (1) completion, in the sense of consummation; (2) spiritual flawlessness (*OED* n. 1a 2). Human perfectibility was a tenet of Niclaes' writings.

71–2. *they ... themselves*] See Leviticus 19.18: 'Thou ... shalt love thy neighbour as thy self'. Club suggests that female Familists sleep with one another's husbands. The Bible speaks of husband and wife as 'one flesh' (Ephesians 5.31).

Mistress Glister. Not than themselves, Club.
Club. Yes, better than themselves, for they love them better than their husbands, and husband and wife are all one; therefore, better than themselves.
Mistress Glister. This is logic. But tell me, doth she not endeavour to bring my doctor of her side and fraternity?
Club. Let him resolve that himself, for here he comes.

Enter DOCTOR GLISTER.

Glister. Oh, hast thou brought the trunk, honest Club? I commend thy honest care — [*Tipping him*] here's for thy pains.
Club. I thank you, master doctor, you are free and liberal still. You'll command me nothing back?
Glister. Nothing but commendations, farewell.
                    [*Exeunt* CLUB *and* Prentice.]
[*To Maria*] Your sweetheart Gerardine is by this time cold of his hope to enjoy thee; he's gone, and a more equal and able husband shall my care ere long provide thee. [*To Mistress Glister*] What clients have been here in my absence, wife?
Mistress Glister. Faith, mouse, none that I know, more than an old woman that had lost her cat and came to you for a spell in the recovery.
Glister. I think egregious ignorance will go near to save this age; their blindness takes me for a conjurer. Yesterday a

---

81. SD] *this edn; not in Q.* 85.1. SD] *Dyce; Exit Q opp. 84.* 86. SD] *this edn; not in Q.* 89. SD] *this edn; not in Q.*

77–8. doth ... fraternity] isn't Mistress Purge trying to persuade my husband around to her religious viewpoint; isn't she trying to seduce Glister? With its connotation of 'brotherhood', *fraternity* refers to the Family of Love.
83. liberal] generous.
86–7. Your ... thee] By now your boyfriend's lost interest in you. Mistress Glister uses 'cold of' in a physiological and psychological sense, suggesting that, with distance, Gerardine's sexual ardour for Maria has evaporated (*OED* cold adj. 6a, 7a).
87. equal] financially equal, wealthy.
88. able] physically and sexually able.
91. mouse] term of sexual endearment (Partridge, 194). Compare Shakespeare, *Ham.* 3.4.184: 'call you his mouse'.
95. conjurer] magician or wizard.

justice of peace salutes me with proffer of a brace of
angels to help him to his footcloth, some three days
before stolen, and was fain to use his man's cloak instead
on't.

Enter VIAL.

Vial. Here's a gentleman craves speech with you, sir. 100
Glister. Go in, sweet wife, and give my niece good counsel.
　　　　　　　Exeunt MISTRESS GLISTER *and* MARIA.
His name?
[*Vial.*] He will not tell it me.
Glister. His countenance?
[*Vial.*] I can see nothing but his eyes. The rest of him is so 105
wrapped in cloak that it suffers no view.
Glister. Admit him.　　　　　　　　　　　[*Exit* VIAL.]
　What should he be for a man?

Enter LIPSALVE.

What, Master Lipsalve, is it you? Why thus obscured?
What discontent overshadows you?
Lipsalve. A discontent indeed, master doctor, which to shake 110
off, I must have you extend your art to the utmost bounds.
You physicians are as good as false doors behind hangings
to ladies' necessary uses. You know the very hour in

99.1. SD] *Dyce; Enter Viall Q, towards right margin.* 101.1. SD] *Dyce; new line at right margin after 100 Q.* 103. SH] *Dyce; Nun. Q.* 105. SH] *Dyce; Nun. Q.* 107. SD] *Dyce; not in Q.* 107.1. SD] *Dyce; at end of 106, Q.*

---

96. *brace*] pair (*OED* n.2 15c)
97. *help ... to*] find or retrieve. Magicians or witches assisted clients to find lost or stolen things.
　footcloth] large, richly ornamented cloth, considered a mark of dignity and high status, laid over the back of a horse so as to hang down to the ground on each side (*OED* n. 1); hence, a desirable item for thieves.
98. *fain*] forced, obliged (*OED* adj. 2b).
107. *What ... man?*] Who is it? Compare Middleton, *Mad World* 5.2.287–8: 'what is she for a fool would marry thee?'
108. *obscured*] muffled, hidden.
112. *false doors*] secret doors facilitating the entry and exit of illicit lovers (*OED* false adj., adv. and n.).
　hangings] tapestries.

which they have neither will to deny nor wit to mistrust.
Faith now, by the way, when are women most apt?   115
Glister. Shall I unbutton myself unto you? After the receipt of
  a purgation, for then are their pores most open. But what
  creature of a courtier is it hath drawn your head into the
  woodcock's noose?
Lipsalve. A courtier? Nay, by this flesh, I am clean fallen out   120
  with them; they have nothing proportionable.
Glister. Oh, I perceive then 'tis some city star that attracts
  your aspect.
Lipsalve. [*Aside*] He knows by his art. — [*Aloud*] In plain
  terms, a certain pothecary's wife.   125
Glister. Upon my life, Master Purge! I smell you, sir.
Lipsalve. You may smell a man after a purgation, indeed. Sir,
  'tis she. Now, for that fame hath bruited you to be a man
  expert in necromancy, I would endeavour myself to you
  forever would you vouchsafe to let one of your spirits   130
  bring Mistress Purge into some convenient place where
  I might enjoy her. I have heard of the like — can you
  perform this?

---

124. SD] *Dyce; not in Q.*   SD] *this edn; not in Q.*   126. Master] *Q;* mistress *Dyce.*   Purge!] *this edn;* Purge's *Bullen.*   129. endeavour] *Q;* endear *Dyce.*

---

   115. *apt*] ready for sex.
   116. *Shall ... you?*] Shall I tell you what I mean?
   119. *woodcock's noose*] bird caught with a snare: (1) a woodcock is a large migratory bird, common in Europe and Britain, with a long bill and variegated plumage, much esteemed as food; (2) allusively, from the ease with the woodcock is captured, a fool, simpleton. See Shakespeare, *Ham.* 1.3.114: 'springes to catch woodcocks' (Dillon).
   120. *clean*] completely (*OED* adv. 4 obs.).
   121. *proportionable*] attractive, well-proportioned (*OED* adj. 2).
   123. *aspect*] (1) gaze (*OED* n. 1); (2) planetary position, in relation to Mistress Purge as a 'star' (*OED* n. 4).
   126. *smell*] understand, but with secondary literal meaning associated with a purgation of the bowels (as at 127).
   Master Purge!] that is, Master Purge's [wife].
   128. *bruited*] proclaimed widely, a conversion from Fr. *bruit* = noise (*OED* v. 1 obs.).
   129. *endeavour*] (1) malapropism for 'endear'; (2) use effort or pains for (*OED* v. 4a obs.).
   132. *enjoy*] have sex with.

Glister. With much facility, I assure you. But you must understand that the apparition of a spirit is dreadful, and withal covetous, and with no small sum of gold hired to such feats.

Re-enter VIAL

Vial. Sir, here's another gentleman, muffled too, that desires present conference with you.
Glister. [*To Lipsalve*] Walk you into that room; I will bethink myself for your good, and instantly resolve you.
                                                    [*Exit* LIPSALVE.]
  Let the gentleman come in.   [*Exit* VIAL.]
Lipsalve — in love with my vessel of ease? Come to me to help him to a morsel most affected by my own palate? No more but so — I have shaped it. The conceit tickles me!

Enter GUDGEON.

Sir, as a stranger, I welcome you. [*Recognizing him*] What, Master Gudgeon, have I caught you? I thought it was a gallant that walked muffled. Come, let me behold you at full — here are no sergeants, man.
Gudgeon. Master doctor, this my obscure coming requires an action more obscure — and in brief, this 'tis. Sir, you are held a man far seen in nature's secrets. I know you can effect many things almost impossible. Know then I love Mistress Purge, and opportunity favours me not, nor indeed is she so tractable as I expected. If either by medi-

---

137.1. SD] *Dyce; not in Q.* 138. SH] *Dyce; Nun. Q.* 140. SD] *this edn; not in Q.* 141.1. SD] *Dyce; not in Q.* 142. SD] *Dyce; not in Q.* 146. SD] *this edn; not in Q.*

---

135. *withal*] moreover (arch.).
139. *present*] immediate.
143. *vessel of ease*] toilet, then called a 'close-stool'; here figuratively, Mistress Purge, in whom Glister eases himself of lust in the form of semen.
144. *affected*] desired.
145. *tickles*] excites.
149. *sergeants*] men who arrested offenders or summoned them to appear before the court (*OED* sergeant n. 4a).
152. *far seen*] expertly informed about, shrewd (*OED* far-sighted adj., but gives earliest usage as 1641).
155. *tractable*] compliant.

cine or your art magical you can work her to my will, I
have a poor gallant's reward, sir.

Glister. [*Aside*] That's just nothing. — But how, sir, would
you have me to procure you access to Mistress Purge?
You never knew a physician a bawd.   160

Gudgeon. Why, by conjuration, I tell you, wherein you are
said to be as well practised as in physic. [*Offering him
money*] Here's the best part of my present store to effect
it.

Glister. Not a penny for myself, but my spirits, indeed, they   165
must be fee'd. Walk you by here, while I think upon a
spell. [*Aside*] What mystery should this be, Lipsalve and
Gudgeon both in love with Mistress Purge, and come to
me to help 'em by art magic? 'Tis some gullery, sure; yet,
if my invention hold, I'll fit them. — Who's within there?   170

Enter [*Servant*].

Fetch me in all haste two good whips — I think you may
have them not far hence.

[*Exit* Servant.]

It shall be so. — Now tell me, Master Gudgeon, does no
man know of your love to Mistress Purge?

Gudgeon. Not a man, by my gentry.   175

Glister. Then, sir, know I'll effect it. But understand withal,
the apparition will be most horrid, if it appear in his
proper form, and will so amaze and dull your senses that
your appetite will be lost and weak, though Mistress

---

158. SD] *Dyce; not in Q.* 162–3. SD] *this edn; Giving money Dyce.* 166. fee'd] *Dyce (feed);* fed *Q.* 167. SD] *this edn; not in Q.* 170.1.] *Dyce; following* 170 *I'll ... them Q.* SD Servant] *Dyce; one Q.* 172.1. SD] *Dyce; not in Q.*

---

156. *work ... will*] make her submit to my desire (*OED* will n.1 2).

160. *You ... bawd*] disingenuous. Physicians were often considered lascivious, as, like bawds, they 'set bones together'; see Middleton, *RevT* 1.3.44.

161. *by conjuration*] by invoking spirits or devils to make his wishes come true.

169. *art magic*] the art of magic, magical art.

gullery] deception, trick (*OED* n.1 obs.).

170. *if ... them*] if my trick works, I will be avenged. *Fit* means 'punish' (*OED* v.1 12). Compare Kyd, *SpT* 4.1.70: 'Why then I'll fit you'.

178. *proper*] own.

Purge should attend it naked. Now, sir, could you name   180
a friend with whom you are most conversant, in his likeness should the spirit appear.
Gudgeon. Of all men living, my conversation is most frequent
with Lipsalve, the courtier.
Glister. 'Tis enough, I'll to my spirit. — Are these whips come   185
there?

Enter [Servant] *with whips.*

[*Servant*] Ready here, sir.   [*He puts down whips and exit.*]
Glister. So, lie thou there. [*Aside*] My noble gallants, I'll so
firk you! [*To Gudgeon*] Sir, my spirit agrees in Lipsalve's
shape. Tomorrow, 'twixt the hours of four and five shall   190
Mistress Purge be rapt with a whirlwind into Lipsalve's
chamber — that's the fittest place, for by the break of day
Lipsalve shall be mounted, and forsake the City for three
days, so my spirit resolves me. Now, sir, by my art, at
that very hour shall his chamber door fly open, into which   195
boldly enter in this sort accoutred: put me on a pure clean
shirt, leave off your doublet (for spirits endure nothing
polluted), take me this whip in your hand, and being
entered you shall see the spirit in Lipsalve's shape, in the
self-same form that you appear. Speak these words here   200
ready written [*Giving a paper*], take three bold steps

186.1. SD] *this edn; Enter one with whips* Q.   187. SH] *Dyce;* Man Q.
187. SD] *this edn; not in* Q.   188. SD] *Dyce; not in* Q.   189. SD] *this edn;
not in* Q.   201. SD] *Dyce; not in* Q.

---

181. *a friend ... conversant*] the friend you talk to most frequently.
188. *thou*] addressing the whips.
189. *firk*] (1) rouse (*OED* v. 2b); (2) whip, trounce (*OED* v. 4a). Compare
Barry, *Ram Alley* 1.3.111n, 'An action, boy, called firking the posteriors'.
189–90. *my ... shape*] my spirit agrees to appear as Lipsalve.
191. *rapt*] carried away by force (*OED* v. 1 obs.).
193. *mounted*] on his horse.
196. *sort*] manner.
   accoutred] dressed, equipped (*OED* accoutre v.), a borrowing from
French.
196–8. *put me ... take me*] for me, archaic dative usages, enlivening the
situation by making it more immediate between speaker and listener.
Compare Shakespeare, *John* 4.1.1: 'Heat me these irons hot'.

SC 5]   THE FAMILY OF LOVE   111

    forward, then whip him soundly, who straight vanisheth
    and leaves Mistress Purge to your will.
Gudgeon. Ay, but shall your spirit come armed with a whip
    too?   205
Glister. He shall, but have no power to strike.
Gudgeon. Is this infallible? Have you seen the proof?
Glister. Probatum, upon my word, I have seen the experience.
    If it fail, say I am a fool and no magician.
Gudgeon. Master doctor, I would you had some suit at court;   210
    by the faith of a courtier, I would beg it for you. Fare you
    well, sir. I shall report of you as I find your charm.
Glister. And no otherwise, sir. Let me understand how you
    thrive.   *Exit* [GUDGEON.]
    Ha, ha, ha! Now to my friend Lipsalve. I must possess   215
    him with the same circumstance, wherein I am assured
    to get perpetual laughter in their follies, and my revenge.
                                         Exit.

ACT 2 SCENE 5

Enter MARIA *over the trunk.*

Maria. Oh, which way shall I turn or shift or go
    To lose one thought of care? No soothing hope
    Gives intermission or beguiles one hour
    Of tedious time, which never will have end
    Whilst love pursues in vain my absent friend.   5

        [*She addresses the trunk.*]

---

214. SD] *Dyce; following 212 Q.*

Act 2 Scene 5] *this edn; not in Q.*   5.1. SD] *this edn; not in Q.*

---

    208. Probatum ... experience] proved; from Lat., *probare*, to test. Here, 'experience' has the obsolete sense of 'experiment', 'practical demonstration' (*OED* n. 1a 2).
    215–16. possess ... circumstance] give him the same instructions.

    0.1. SD] The trunk containing Gerardine was carried on stage at 2.4.50.1. Q's stage direction indicates the prop's prominence.
    1. shift] continue living (*OED* v. 5b).
    5. friend] lover (Williams, *Dictionary*, 1.553).

Thou continent of wealth, whose want of store,
For that it could not peise th'unequal scale
Of avarice, giv'st matter to my moan.
O dross, the level of insatiate eyes,
The devil's engine and the soul's corrupter, 10
Thou playest th'attorney 'gainst the lawful force
Of true affection, dost interpose a bar
'Twixt hearts conjoined. Cursed be thy seed of strife,
Whose progress chokes the natural course of life!

> GERARDINE *rising out of the trunk, she seems fearful and flies.*

Oh, help, help, help! 15
Gerardine. Stay, sweet Maria, I bring thee ample joy
To check that sudden fear. Let thy sweet heart,
That constant seat of thy affection,
Repay that blood exhausted from thy veins.
Fear not, sweet wench! I am no apparition, 20

---

6. *continent*] container, receptacle (Schmidt, 1.242).
want] lack.
store] accumulated goods or money (*OED* n. 5a); compare 2.4.163: 'Here's the best part of my present store'.
7. *peise*] counterbalance (*OED* v. 4a [lit. and fig.], citing this usage, obs.).
9. *dross*] money, wealth.
level] that which is aimed at; a mark (*OED* n. 9b obs.).
9–14.] This scene's 'overly ornate rhetorical style' parodies the language of romantic love plots (Cleary).
13–14. *strife ... life*] whose interference cuts off the cycle of love, marriage and reproduction.
14.2. SD *flies*] retreats in alarm (Bullen). '*She seems fearful and flies*' struck Dillon as 'the only stage direction which might indicate a remnant of an authorial admonition' (xvii). Beaumont parodied Gerardine's rising out of the trunk and alarming Maria in *KBP*, where Jasper '*ris[es] out of [a] coffin*' and alarms his lover, Luce (4.283 SD). See Maxwell, 'Twenty Good-Nights', 234–7.
15–21. *Oh ... friend*] In *KBP*, Luce exclaims 'Save me, heaven!' and makes as if to flee on seeing Jasper emerge from the coffin; when Jasper appeals to Luce to recognise him, she addresses him as 'dear shadow of my friend', that is, his ghost; to which he answers 'Dear substance; / I swear I am no shadow' (4.283–7). Beaumont's debt to Barry is clear in the stage action and in the words 'substance' (21) and 'friend' (21).
18. *constant seat*] loyal residence.
19.] return the colour drained from your veins, instead of looking pale with fear.

SC 5]   THE FAMILY OF LOVE   113

    But the firm substance of thy truest friend.
    Knowst thou me now?
Maria.   Gerardine, my love!
    What unheard of accident presents
    Thy unexpected self, and gives my heart
    Matter of joy, mixed with astonishment?   25
    I thought thou hadst been cabined in thy ship,
    Not trunked within my cruel guardian's house.
Gerardine. That cruelty gives fuel to desire,
    For love suppressed fares like a raging fire
    Which burns all obstacles that stop his course,   30
    And mounts aloft. The ocean in his source
    May easier hide himself and be confined
    Than love can be obscured, for in the mind
    She holds her seat, and through that heavenly essence
    Is near when far remote; her virtual presence   35
    Fills, like the air, all places, gives delight,
    Hope in despair, and heart 'gainst fell despite.
    That worst of men, thy cruel guardian, may

---

    21. *firm substance*] material reality.
    26. *cabined*] confined (*OED* cabin v. 3a).
    30.] Because suppressed love (kept down by authority) eventually behaves like a fire out of control. Arguably Gerardine refers here to Cupid, the Roman boy-god of erotic desire (28), whereas at 34, love anchored in the mind is feminine ('She holds her seat').
    31–2. *The ocean ... himself*] The ocean may conceal itself more easily in its own source (place of origin).
    33–5. *for ... remote*] Gerardine conceives love in loosely neoplatonic terms as a powerful force whose throne or location ('seat', 33) is the mind. Compare Castiglione, *The Courtier*, trans. Thomas Hoby, 1561 (1603), 4.X7v, in *EEBO*: 'to avoid therefore the torment of [the beloved's] absence, and to enjoy beauty without passion, the courtier, by the help of reason, must full and wholly call back ... the coveting of the body and beauty alone, and ... behold [beauty] in itself simple and pure ... and frame it within in his imagination sundered from all matter'.
    34. *holds*] occupies.
    heavenly essence] spiritual substance. Compare Marlowe, *Hero and Leander*, 269–71: 'This idol which you term Virginity / Is neither essence subject to the eye ... nor to any one exterior sense'.
    35–6. *her ... places*] compare 'Life-stirring Venus' in Lucretius, *The Nature of Things*, trans. A.E. Stallings (London: Penguin, 2007), line 1.
    37. *fell*] fierce, cruel.

   Keep down a while, but cannot dissipate
   What heav'n hath joined, for fate and providence   40
   Gave me this stratagem, to let him know
   That love will creep where 'tis restrained to go.
Maria. I apprehend the rest. Oh, rare conceit!
   I see thy travel happily was feigned
   To win access, which with small ease thou hast gained.   45
   This trunk, which he so greedily supposes
   Contains thy substance (as it doth indeed),
   Upon thy fair pretence, in lieu of love
   Bequeathed to me, if death should stop the course —
   This trunk, I say, he hugs. Sink thou or swim,   50
   So he may feed his wolf, that root of sin,
   His avarice. But heaven, that mocks man's might,
   Gives this close means t'insist upon our right.
Gerardine. Ingenious spirit, true oracle of love,
   Thou hast prevented me. This was my plot,   55
   Whose end and scope I long to imitate

---

50. hugs. Sink] *this edn;* hugs; sink *Q.*

---

 39. *keep down*] suppress, obstruct.
 40. *what ... joined*] echo of the marriage ceremony in the Book of Common Prayer: 'Those whom God hath joined together, let no man put asunder'.
 42. *love ... go*] proverbial; 'Kindness (Love, Kind) will creep where it cannot go' (Tilley K49); compare Shakespeare, *TGV* 4.2.19–20: 'love / Will creep in service where it cannot go'.
 restrained to go] prohibited from walking (*OED* go v. 1a obs.).
 45. *small ease*] little comfort. Anticipates Maria's naming of the trunk 'little-ease'; see below, 3.1.9n, 178.
 46. *he*] Here, and at 50–1, Glister.
 48. *fair pretence*] ostensibly admirable ploy.
 in lieu] instead, in the place.
 49. *course*] i.e., of Gerardine's life.
 50. *Sink ... swim*] proverbial; Glister doesn't care whether you drown or swim to safety (Dent S485). Compare Marlowe, *JM* 1.2.268–9: 'since you leave me in the ocean thus / To sink or swim'.
 51–2. *wolf ... avarice*] a common emblem of greed. Gerardine depicts avarice as the source ('root') of sin in general. Compare Shakespeare, *Lear* (F) 3.4.86–7: 'wolf in greediness'.
 53. *close*] (1) closed (*OED* adj. 1a); (2) narrow (*OED* adj. 2a); (3) hidden, secret (*OED* adj. 4a). Senses (1) and (2) are physical properties of the trunk.
 55. *prevented*] anticipated (Bullen).
 56. *scope*] object, goal (*OED* n.2 2a).

SC 5]   THE FAMILY OF LOVE   115

   With accents free and uncontrolled with fear.
   Does opportunity stand fair?
Maria.   Not now.
   Danger stands sentinel.
Gerardine.   Then I'll retire.
   We must be cautelous.   60

        [GERARDINE *re-enters the trunk.*]

Maria.   So, so [*Closing and securing the trunk*], and time
   Shall not oft turn his hourglass ere I'll find
   Peace and occasion fitting to thy mind.   *Exeunt.*

                  End of Act Two

---

60. cautelous] Q *(cautilous)*. 60.1. SD] *this edn; He goes again into the trunk* Dyce; *not in* Q. SD] *this edn; not in* Q. 62. Peace] Q; Place *Dyce*. 62.1. End of Act Two] Q *(Finis Actus Secundi)*.

---

57. *accents*] speech.
58. *opportunity*] (1) circumstances (*OED* n. 1a); (2) in Renaissance iconography, the winged figure of Opportunity or Occasion was bald behind with a single forelock that had to be seized as she approached; otherwise, she vanished. With this clustering of opportunity, occasion (62) and time (60), compare Middleton, *RevT* 1.1.55, 99; 1.3.23–5.
60. *cautelous*] (1) crafty, artful (*OED* adj. arch. 1); see Shakespeare, *Cor.* 4.1.34: 'With cautelous baits and practice'; (2) cautious.
60–2. *time ... mind*] (1) evokes the emblem of (Old) Father Time, a winged, aged man carrying an hourglass and sometimes a scythe; (2) time as *kairos*, or the decisive moment; see Middleton, *RevT* 1.3.23–4n.
62. *Peace*] freedom from anxiety (*OED* n. 3a); a desirable resolution to Maria's fright earlier in the scene. 'Dyce's and Bullen's emendation to "Place" is tempting ... in light of the next lines of Act 3, as well as the possible argument that this exchange between Gerardine and Maria ... has just happened in the room where the trunk was left and that for 3.1. it has been moved to Maria's room ... ultimately this ... issue ... involves a modern bias toward realism that the staging of the time did not have' (Cleary).

Act 3

ACT 3 SCENE 1

Enter GERARDINE *and* MARIA.

Gerardine. The coast is clear, and Argus' wakeful eyes
   Securely sleep; time turns to us his front.
   Come, sweet Maria, of th'auspicious hours
   Let's take advantage.
Maria.   With all my heart,
   I do embrace the motion with thyself.   5
   Welcome, sweet friend, to liberty of air
   Which now, methinks, doth prompt our breaths to move
   Sweet accents of delight, the joys of love.
   How dost thou brook thy little-ease, thy trunk?

Act 3 Scene 1] *Q (ACTVS TERTIUS./Actus Tertius scena prima)*. 4–5. With ... heart, / I] *lineation follows Dyce; set as one line Q.*

   0.] Dyce and Dillon envisage 1–63 taking place on the upper stage. However, there is no SD requiring this location, and the extended romantic dialogue between Maria and Gerardine would be more engaging, because closer to the audience, on the main stage. The action is fluid: Maria and Gerardine remove to the upper stage or 'window' (62) at 63, whereupon the main stage becomes the street.
   1. *coast .... clear*] proverbial (Dent C469).
   Argus' wakeful eyes] Argos 'Panoptes' ('all-seeing'); monster of classical myth sometimes depicted as covered in eyes and unsleeping.
   2. *front*] (1) forehead. Like the emblems Occasion and Opportunity, Time was sometimes depicted as bald except for a single lock of hair (*OED* time n. 34b); (2) face (*OED* n. 2).
   7. *move*] utter, put forth (*OED* v. 29a).
   9. *brook*] cope with, endure (*OED* v. 3a).
   little-ease] (1) a place or bodily position that is very uncomfortable to be held in; narrow place of confinement (*OED* 1); (2) instrument of torture, whether a cell in which the prisoner cannot stand or lie at full length (such as a dungeon in the Tower) or a simpler device such as stocks.

SC I]   THE FAMILY OF LOVE   117

Gerardine. That trunk confines this chest, this chest contains   10
   Th'unbounded speculation of our love
   Incomprehensible. Grief, joy, hope, and fears
   — Th'affections of my mind — are like the spheres,
   Which in their jarring motions do agree
   Through th'influence of love's sweet harmony.   15
Maria. Are not inferior bodies here on earth
   Produced and governed by those heavenly ones?
Gerardine. They are.
Maria. They jar, you say, yet in that strife maintain
   Perpetual league. Why should their influence   20
   In rational souls be checked by erring sense?
   Or why should mutual love, confirmed by heav'n,
   B'infringed by men? Methinks 'tis most uneven.
Gerardine. Thou argu'st well, Maria, and this withal,

10–11. *That ... love*] gesturing to his heart, Gerardine represents their love as limitless (*unbounded*) and beyond mortal powers of discernment (*speculation*). Compare Davies, *Nosce Teipsum*: 'casket of thy breast' (1890); 'What heavenly treasure in so weak a chest' (1892) (Shepherd).

12. *Incomprehensible*] (1) immense, unable to be contained (*OED* 1); (2) beyond the reach of intellect (*OED* 2a); (3) religious term; see the Athanasian Creed in the Book of Common Prayer: 'the father incomprehensible, the son incomprehensible, and the holy ghost incomprehensible'.

13–15. *spheres ... harmony*] In the Ptolemaic universe, nine concentric *spheres* carried the planets and stars in harmonic revolution around the sublunary world. Gerardine compares the salvific influence of love on 'Th'affections of [his] mind' to the influence of Boethius' 'music of the spheres', composed of the sounds emitted by each celestial body, 'that harmony standing as the foundation of all the world about us, not only that on earth, but that of the stars and planets, as well as heaven itself' (Albert Seay, *Music in the Medieval World* [Englewood Cliffs, NJ: Prentice-Hall, 1965], 21).

14. *jarring*] (1) discordant, clashing; (2) audibly vibrating (*OED* jar v.1 5).

16–17.] Maria expresses the Renaissance understanding that astronomical bodies govern the material world.

19. *They jar*] (1) Maria plays teasingly on Gerardine's pronunciation of 'They are' in 18. Her response may incorporate a joke about contemporary pronunciation; (2) Maria mishears Gerardine's 'They are'.

20. *league*] union (*OED* n.2 2).

21. *erring sense*] meaning that wanders away from that intended; 'Davies attacks the errors of sense in *Nosce Teipsum*, 397ff' (Shepherd).

23. *uneven*] unjust (Bullen).

24. *this withal*] this point as well.

> That brutes nor animals do prove a thrall 25
> To such servility; souls that are wards
> To gold opinion, or th'undue regards
> Of broking men, wolves that in sheepskin bands
> Prey on the hearts to join th'unwilling hands,
> Ruin fair stocks, when generous houses die, 30
> Or propagate their name with bastardy.
> Maria. Sterility and barrenness ensue
> Such forcèd love; nor shall erroneous men
> Pervert my settled thoughts, or turn mine eye
> From thy fair object, which I will pursue, 35
> Rich in thy love, proud of this interview.

---

25. brutes] *Q* (Bruites). 27. gold opinion] *Q;* gold, opinion *Dyce*. 29. Prey] *Q* (Pray).

25–6. *brutes ... servility*] neither beasts nor animals lacking in reason experience such bondage, i.e., are restrained from mating with whom they wish.
   26. *wards*] (1) guards, wardens (*OED* n.1 obs.); (2) people under the sway of a higher authority; (3) 'wards of court' were minors under the care of a legally appointed guardian (*OED* n.2 6a).
   27. *gold*] golden, with allusion to the monetary value of gold or its use as currency (*OED* golden adj. fig.1b). The word choice was probably dictated by metrical considerations. For uninflected adjectival forms such as 'gold' for 'golden', see Hope, 1.2.4, and compare Shakespeare, sonnet 18, 6: 'gold complexion'.
   gold opinion] judgements based upon money. Compare Shakespeare, *Mac.* 1.7.32–3: 'I have bought / Golden opinions from all sorts of people'. The parallel phrasing is striking, but the senses are different. Macbeth's 'golden opinions' means 'glowing estimations', while Gerardine's 'gold opinion' is strongly negative. Dyce's pointing is possible, but predictable.
   28. *broking*] (1) bargaining (*OED* broke v. 1); (2) base-dealing, 'peddling', contemptible (*OED* adj.).
   wolves] men such as Glister.
   sheepskin bands] parchment bonds (Bullen), i.e., legal documents detailing property or money exchanged between families upon the marriage of their children.
   29. *hearts*] punning on 'harts', deer, preyed on by 'wolves' (28).
   30. *stocks*] (1) trunk or stem of a (living) tree (*OED* stock n.1 2a); (2) descendants of a common ancestor (*OED* n. 2c).
   generous houses] noble families (*OED* generous adj. 1a obs.).
   31. *propagate*] reproduce, multiply, continuing the 'stock' metaphor in 30.
   32. *ensue*] are born of, issue from (*OED* v. 6c).

SC I]   THE FAMILY OF LOVE   119

Gerardine. I'll suck these accents; let our breaths engender
   A generation of such pleasing sounds,
   To interchange delights. [*They kiss.*] Oh, my blood's on
      fire!
   Sweet, let me give more scope to true desire.   40
Maria. What, wouldst thou more than our minds' firm
      contract?
Gerardine. Tut, words are wind. Thought unreduced to act
   Is but an embryon in the truest sense.
Maria. I am beleaguered; I had need of sense,
   You make me blush. Play fair yet, above board.   45
Gerardine. Hear me exemplify love's Latin word
   Together with thy self,
   As thus: hearts joined, *Amore.* Take *a* from thence,
   Then *more* is the perfect moral sense,
   Plural in manners, which in thee do shine   50
   Saintlike, immortal, spotless, and divine.
   Take *m* away, *ore* in beauty's name
   Craves an eternal trophy to thy fame.

---

39. SD] *this edn; not in Q.*   42. unreduced] *Shepherd;* vnreduct *Q.*   act] *Dyce;* Art *Q.*   44. beleaguered] *Dyce (*beleague[r]'d*);* beleagued *Q.*

37–9. let ... delights] Compare Shakespeare, *R2* 5.5.6–8: 'My brain I'll prove the female to my soul, / My soul the father, and these two beget / A generation of still-breeding thoughts' (Cathcart, *Marston*, 118).

39. *my ... fire!*] I am aroused!

40. *let ... desire*] let me make love to you. Compare Barry, *Ram Alley* 1.2.169: 'give thy love free scope, embrace and kiss'.

42. *words ... wind*] proverbial: 'Words are but wind' (Tilley W833).

unreduced ... act] not realised in action.

43. *embryon*] embryo (*OED* n. 1a).

44. *beleaguered*] embarrassed, confused; a word that is military in origin, literally meaning 'besieged' (*OED* beleaguer v. 1). Maria feels Gerardine is coming on too strongly.

45. *above board*] openly, without subterfuge (*OED* adv. 2 fig.); term derived from gambling at cards (cf. 'Play fair'), meaning to play with one's cards visible above the playing table, so as to avoid suspicion of cheating (*OED* adv. 1 obs.).

46–7. *exemplify ... self*] explain with examples the meaning of *amore* in relation to Maria (*OED* exemplify v. 1).

48. Amore] love, from *amor, amoris* (Lat.).

49. more] manners, from *mos, moris*, habit, custom (Lat.).

52. ore] face, mouth, from *os, oris* (Lat.).

120   THE FAMILY OF LOVE   [ACT 3

   Lastly, take *o*, in *re* stands all my rest,
   Which I in Chaucer style do term a jest.   55
Maria. You break all modest bounds, away, away!
Gerardine. So when men come behind, do women say.
Maria. Come, come, I say —
Gerardine.   Ay, that's the word, indeed,
   Men that come bold before are like to speed.

           Enter LIPSALVE [*disguised as Gerardine*]
                and SHRIMP, *his page.*

55. style] Q *(stile)*.   58. I say —] *Dyce;* I say Q.   59.1–2. SD] *Dyce; Enter Lipsalue and Shrimp his Page* Q.

   54. *take* o]   (1) take away the *o* from *ore*; (2) grab the vulva; female genitals were often linked to the shape of a zero.
   in re]   (1) literally, in the thing, from Lat. *res, rei*, thing, object; (2) in your vagina; 'thing' as euphemism for female genitals (Partridge, 259–60). Compare Chaucer, 'Wife of Bath's Prol.', 447: 'my *bele chose*'; (3) in reality (legal phrase) (*OED* in prep. 2 23a).
   stands]   (1) remains; (2) referring to an erect penis (Williams, *Dictionary*, stand 3.1305).
   55. *Chaucer style*]   Chaucerian style, i.e., the bawdy puns on *o, re* and 'stands' in 54. On nouns as premodifiers in early modern English, as in 'music vows', Shakespeare, *Hamlet*, ed. G. R. Hibbard (Oxford: Oxford University Press, 1987), 3.1.157, see Abbott, 22. Middleton links Chaucer with lewdness in *More Diss.* 1.4.36–7: ''Tis not good to jest, as old Chaucer was wont to say, that broad famous English poet'.
   jest]   (1) joke, witticism (*OED* n. 5a); (2) piece of raillery or banter (*OED* n. 4); (3) allusive of copulation (Williams, *Dictionary*, 2.734). Chaucer uses *gest* to mean a story told expressly for entertainment, which may be how the word acquired the sense of mockery that Gerardine intends here. See *Melibeus*, Prol. 15: 'Lat se wher thou kanst tellen aught in geeste'. Compare 5.3.3: 'grand jury of jests'.
   57. *come behind*]   (1) approach or embrace women from behind, with hints of rear entry or anal intercourse; compare Mason, *Turk* (1607) 5.1., I3, in *EEBO*: 'S'foot my office is italianated, I am fain to come behind'; (2) reach orgasm after their sexual partners (Partridge, come 102–3).
   58. *Come, come*]   spoken reprovingly, but Gerardine interprets the phrase to mean 'come hither'.
   59. *come ... before*]   (1) accost or embrace women from the front; (2) reach sexual climax early (*OED* before adv. 5a).
   like]   likely.
   speed]   (1) succeed sexually; (2) prosper, attain their purpose (*OED* v. arch. 1a).

But who comes here? *Monstrum horrendum!* My nostrils 60
have the rank scent of knavery. Maria, let's remove ourselves to the window, and observe this piece of man's
flesh.   *Exeunt.*
Lipsalve. Now, Mistress Maria, ward yourself. If my strong
   hope fail not, I shall be with you to bring —   65
Shrimp. To bring what, sir? Some more o'your kind?
Lipsalve. Faith, boy, that's mine aim.
Shrimp. I'll be sworn, sir, you have a good loose, you let fly
   at 'em apace.
Lipsalve. I have shot fair and far off, but now I hope to hit   70
   the mark indeed.

---

65. bring —] *Dyce*; bring *Qc;* bring. *Qu.* 69. at 'em] *Dyce;* at 'hem *Qc;* at chem *Qu.*

---

60. *Monstrum horrendum!*] Dreadful monster! (Lat.); echoes Aeneas' description of the cyclops Polyphemus, a one-eyed giant, *Aeneid*, 3.658: *monstrum horrendum, informe, ingens, cui lumen ademptum* ('a monster awful, hideous, huge and eyeless').

61. *rank ... knavery*] Altieri, 56, proposes that Gerardine and Maria are 'overcome by the stench of Lipsalve's bout with Ms. Purge's laxative candies', and that Maria's wandering senses (98) are caused not by 'her passion', as Lipsalve assumes (101), but by his noxious 'odour'. Her reading assumes that Gerardine smells Lipsalve here without actually seeing him. However, it is Gudgeon, not Lipsalve, who speaks of Mistress Purge's 'comfits mak[ing] him loose-bodied' (2.3.55), which casts some doubt on Altieri's interpretation.

64. *ward*] guard.
strong] resolute, steadfast (*OED* adj. 3).

65. *be ... to bring* —] come to get you. In support of this sense, see Brome, *Late Lancashire Witches*, ed. Helen Ostovich, 2.2.269: 'I'll have one smooch at thy lips, and be with thee to bring'. Whereas the example from Brome suggests 'some mutually satisfying consequence' (Ostovich), Lipsalve's warning to Maria to 'ward [her]self' gives the phrase an overtone of sexual coercion. https://www.dhi.ac.uk/brome/viewTranscripts.jsp?type=BOTH&play=LW&act=2 (accessed 20 April 2021).

66. *more ... kind*] more Lipsalves (*OED* kind n. 7a). Shrimp draws out the sexual reference of Lipsalve's pledge to deflower Maria, and to make her give birth to Lipsalve's baby (or babies).

68. *loose*] the discharging of an arrow (Dyce), introducing a spate of archery terms.

69. *at 'em*] The 'c' in 'chem' in Qu looks more like a damaged or over-inked 't' than it does a 'c' (compare the 't' in 'thee', D2r, line 3).

70–1. *shot ... mark*] I've had good results from the bow ('shot fair'), and missed the bull's eye ('far off'), but now I hope to score ('hit the mark') successfully.

Shrimp. God save it!
Lipsalve. But where's the sign?
Shrimp. [*Pointing*] Why, there.
Lipsalve. That's a special thing to be observed. 75
Shrimp. I have heard talk of the Gemini; methinks that should be a star favourable to your proceeding.
Lipsalve. The Gemini? Oh, I apprehend thee; that's because I am so like Gerardine. Ha, is't not so, boy?
Shrimp. As if you were spit out on's mouth, sir. You must 80 needs be like him, for you are both cut out of a piece. But lord, sir, how you hunt this chase of love! Are you not weary?
Lipsalve. Indefatigable, boy, indefatigable.
Shrimp. 'Fatigable', quoth you. You may call it 'leanable' well 85 enough, for I am sure it is able to make a man lean.
Lipsalve. 'Tis my vocation, boy, we must never be weary of well-doing. Love's as proper to a courtier as preciseness to a puritan.

Enter MARIA *above* [*and* GERARDINE *unseen by* LIPSALVE *and* SHRIMP].

---

74. SD] *this edn; not in Q* 76. talk] *Qc;* alke *Qu.* 80. on's] *Qc;* ons *Qu.*
85. 'Fatigable'] *this edn;* Fattigable *Q.* 'leanable'] *this edn;* leaneable *Q.*

---

73. *sign*] (1) Maria, as the 'target' of Lipsalve's love, an extension of the archery metaphor in lines 68–72 (Cleary); (2) astrological sign.

81. *cut ... piece*] cut from the same cloth. Lipsalve is wearing a suit of clothes identical to Gerardine's.

88. *well-doing*] (1) doing good to others; (2) with libertine inflection, 'copulating with panache'; compare 2.1.5n. and 4.3.26. Tilley cites this line as a variant on the proverb 'Everyone must walk ... in his own calling' (C23); see Glister's version of the same proverb at 5.1.99.

88–9. *preciseness ... puritan*] moral propriety, strictness in religious observance (*OED* preciseness n.), as practised by self-termed 'precisians' (*OED* n.); *puritan* is a colloquial term. Compare Shakespeare, *MM* 1.3.50–3: 'Lord Angelo is precise [i.e., a precisian] ... scarce confesses / ... that his appetite / Is more to bread than stone.'

89.1–2. SD] Gerardine comments audibly on the ensuing action, but remains out of sight of Lipsalve, 'standing back or ... behind [Maria]' (Dillon, 3.1.60.1n). Dyce conjectured that Gerardine conceals himself behind curtains suspended before the upper stage. Lopez, *Convention*, 68–72, argues convincingly that Gerardine remains visible to the audience throughout the sequence.

Shrimp. [*Aside*] Love: *subaudi* lust. A punk in this place,   90
    subintelligitur.
Lipsalve. Boy, I have spied my saint.
Shrimp. Then down on your knees.
Lipsalve. Fly off, lest she take thee for my familiar.
                                    [*Shrimp moves aside.*]
    — Save thee, sweet Maria.   95
    Nay, wonder not, for thou thyself art wonder,
    To see this unexpected gratulation.
Maria. Whom do I see? Oh, how my senses wander!
    Am not I Hero? Art not thou Leander?
Gerardine. Th'art in the right, sweet wench, more of that vein.   100
Lipsalve. Her passion overcomes her, 'tis the kindest soul.
    [*Aside to Shrimp*] Oh, excellent device, it works, it works,
    boy!
Shrimp. It does indeed, sir, like the suds of an ale vat or a
    washing bowl.   105

---

90. SD] *Dyce; not in Q.* 90. *subaudi*] *Qc (subbaudy);* subbandy *Qu.* 94.1. SD] *this edn; not in Q.* 100. Th'art] *Shepherd;* Thar't *Q;* Thou'rt *Dyce.* vein] *Qc* (vayne;); vayne? *Qu.* 102. SD] *this edn; not in Q.*

---

90. *subaudi*] that implies, from Lat. *subaudio*, 'to understand (a word implied but not expressed' (*OED* subaud v.).
  punk] prostitute.
  91. *subintelligitur*] is understood (but not stated) as subtext (Lat.). Shrimp assumes from Maria's position at the window that she is sexually available. Compare Barry, *Ram Alley* 1.2.0.1 SD.
  92. *saint*] Compare Marlowe, *Hero and Leander*, 177–9: 'He kneeled, but unto her devoutly prayed; / Chaste Hero to herself thus softly said: / "Were I the saint he worships, I would hear him."'
  94. *familiar*] demon, attendant spirit (Schmidt, 1.398).
  97. *gratulation*] happy greeting (*OED* n. 4).
  99. *Am ... Leander?*] Maria mocks Lipsalve, likening her position above him to the mythical Hero's ensconcement in her tower at Abydos. On burlesque treatments of the Hero and Leander story, including this scene, see Scott.
  101. *'tis*] 'it is', for 'she is'. Use of the third person pronoun to refer affectionately or familiarly to a precocious child or to/about a lover.
  103. *excellent device*] i.e., Lipsalve's trick of disguising himself as Gerardine.
  104. *suds*] the froth produced by the fermenting process involved in making beer.
    ale vat] a large cask or other vessel in which beer is brewed (*OED* ale n. 2; vat n.1).
  105. *washing bowl*] vessel for washing laundry.

Lipsalve. [*To Maria*] Joy not too much, extremes are perilous.
Maria. Oh, weather-beaten love! [*Calling offstage*] Cicely, go make a fire. Go fetch my ladder of ropes. Leander's come! 110
Lipsalve. [*To Shrimp.*] Mark how prettily in her ropture she harps upon Gerardine's travel. [*Aloud to Maria*] Let the ecstasy have end, for I am Gerardine.
Gerardine. [*Aside*] The devil you are!
Maria. Ha! Let me see; my love so soon returned? 115
Lipsalve. I never travelled farther than thine eyes,
   My bruited journey was a happy project
   To cast a mist before thy jealous guardian,
   Who, now suspectless, gives some hope t'attain
   My wished delight, before pursued in vain. 120
Gerardine. [*Aside to Maria*] Ask if he strained not hard for that same project.
Maria. Has not that project over-racked thy brain,
   And spent more wit than thou hast left behind?
Shrimp. [*Aside*] By this light, she flouts him.

---

106. SD] *this edn; not in Q.* 108. SD] *this edn; not in Q.* 111. SD] *this edn; not in Q.* 111. ropture] *Qc;* rapture *Qu.* 112. SD] *this edn; not in Q.* 114. SD] *Dyce; not in Q.* 117. bruited] *Q* (bruted). 121. SD] *Dillon; not in Q.* 124. SD] *Dyce; not in Q.*

106–7. *extremes are perilous*] Compare Marston, *Dutch C.* 2.1.49–50: 'be not so passionate; / Nothing extreme lives long'.

108. *Cicely*] servant presumed to be offstage.

111. *ropture*] neologism for 'rapture', punning on 'ropes' in 103. Noted by Dillon as 'a careful revision' by the typesetter to the printed proofs of Q (xxvi).

113. *ecstasy*] rapturous delight, i.e., Maria's vision of (Lipsalve as) Gerardine as Leander.

117. *bruited*] rumoured (*OED* bruit v. 2b).

happy] lucky, successful (*OED* adj. 2 1a).

119. *suspectless*] not suspecting (i.e. Glister).

122. *over-racked*] over-strained (*OED*), from 'rack' meaning 'to stretch' (*OED* v.1), anticipating the image of Lipsalve's wit being stretched like cloth 'on tenterhooks' at 126f.

123. *spent ... wit*] expended more intelligence.

124. *flouts*] mocks.

SC I]   THE FAMILY OF LOVE   125

Lipsalve. No, wit is infinite. I spent some brain;   125
    Thy love did stretch my wit upon the tenters.
Gerardine. [*Aside to Maria*] Then is't like to shrink in the
    wetting.
Maria. [*Aside to Gerardine*] It cottons well, it cannot choose
    but bear
    A pretty nap. [*To Lipsalve*] I tender thy capacity;
    A comfortable caudle cherish it.   130
    But where's my favour that I bid thee wear
    As pledge of love?
Gerardine.   Now dost thou put him to't.
    More tenters for his wit, he's nonplus quite.
Lipsalve. I wear it, sweet Maria, but on high days,
    Preserve it from the tainting of the air.   135
    [*Aside*] What should I say — [*Aloud*] 'tis in my tother
    hose.

127. SD] *Dyce; not in* Q.   128. SD] *this edn; not in* Q.   129. SD] *this edn;
not in* Q.   132. to't] *Dyce;* toot *Q.*   136. SD] *Dyce; not in* Q.   SD] *this
edn; not in* Q.

125. *spent ... brain*] thought hard.
126.] My love for you inspired me to surpass my natural intelligence.
upon ... tenters] extremely. *Tenters* were wooden frames on which cloth
was stretched after being milled, so that it could set and dry evenly and
without shrinking (*OED* n.1 1).
128. *cottons*] (1) forms a down or nap on (*OED* v.1 1); (2) succeeds, goes
on – a metaphor derived from the finishing of cloth (*OED* v.1 2 4, citing this
line). Maria refers to the performance she is orchestrating, in which she is a
knowing actress and Lipsalve an unwitting actor.
129. *pretty*] (1) cleverly done, artful (*OED* adj.1b); (2) with ironic or
condescending sense, in reference to Lipsalve as both a potential suitor and
wit (*OED* adj. 2a).
nap] a special pile given to cloth, by artificially raising, cutting and
smoothing the short fibres (*OED* n.2 1b).
tender ... capacity] cherish your mental ability (*OED* capacity n. 5),
punning on 'tenters' (126); ironic.
130.] may you be rewarded with a comforting bedtime drink (of wine and
honey) for your wit.
133. *nonplus*] in a state of perplexity (*OED* n. Lat.).
134. *high days*] holidays, days of festivity.
136. *'tis ... hose*] a mocking or evasive answer (Tilley H723). Compare
Ford, Dekker, Middleton and Rowley, *Spanish Gipsy*, 3.2.67: 'Your answer
will be, "in your t'other hose".'
tother] the other (of two).

Maria. How! In your tother hose? He that I love
　　Shall wear my favour in those hose he has on.
Lipsalve. [*Aside*] Fiends and furies! Block that I am!
Shrimp. In your tother hose? [*Aside*] She talked of a ladder of　140
　　ropes; if she would let it down, for my life he would hang
　　himself in't. — In your tother hose? Why, those hose are
　　in lavender; besides, they have never a codpiece. But
　　indeed, there needs no ivy where the wine is good. In
　　your tother hose?　145
Maria. I said you were too prodigal of wit.
Lipsalve. Expostulate no more, grant me access,
　　Or else I'll travel to the wilderness.
Maria. Your only way. Go travel till you tire,
　　Be rid, and let a gull discharge the hire.　150
Shrimp. Master, the doctor, the doctor!
Lipsalve. Where? Which way?
Shrimp. This way. That way, some way — I heard him
　　coming.
Lipsalve. Oh, boy, I am abused, gulled, disgraced, my credit's　155
　　cracked.

---

139. SD] *Dyce; not in Q.*　140. SD] *Dyce; not in Q.*　153. some way — I heard] *this edn;* some way I heard *Q.*

---

　143. *in lavender*] pawned (Tilley L96).
　codpiece] bag-like appendage attached to the front of men's hose or breeches, often conspicuously ornamented. As codpieces were no longer worn at this date, the word might suggest Lipsalve's attachment to fancy clothing.
　144. *there ... good*] proverbial, meaning 'good wine needs no advertising' (Tilley W462); by extension, able penises need no flaunting. Signs bearing an ivy bush were found above the doors of vintners; ivy was sacred to Bacchus, the Greco-Roman god of wine.
　150. *Be rid*] (1) be carried about or paraded (on or in a cart, hurdle, rail) as a punishment (*OED* ride v. 4b); (2) be ridden upon, as legend has it Socrates was by his wife, Xanthippe. The contemptuous expression drives home Maria's dominance.
　let ... hire] let some fool pay for your expenses, whether of hiring a horse or coach to get out of town, or generally covering Lipsalve's debt accrued as a gallant. The 'gull' is not necessarily Lipsalve himself.
　155–6. *my ... cracked*] 'My reputation is ruined'; proverbial. See Tilley C814: 'Credit lost is like a Venice glass broke'. Compare *Club Law*, 3.8.1486–7: 'my credit was never cracked yet'.

SC I]   THE FAMILY OF LOVE   127

Shrimp. You know that's nothing new for a courtier.
Lipsalve. Oh, I shall run beside myself.
Shrimp. No, sir, that's my office. I'll run by your side.
Lipsalve. My brain is out of temper. What shall I do?   160
[*Shrimp.*] Take her counsel, sir: get a cullis to your capacity,
   a restorative to your reason, and a warming-pan to your
   wit. He comes, he comes!
Lipsalve. Follow close, boy, let him not see us.
                        [*Exit* LIPSALVE *and* SHRIMP.]
        [*Maria and Gerardine remain above.*]
               Enter DOCTOR GLISTER.

Glister. What? More flatterers about my carrion? More battery   165
   to my walls? Shall I never be rid of these Petronel Flashes?
   As for my friend Gerardine, the wind of my rage has
   blown him to discover countries, and let the sea purge
   his love away, and him together, I care not. Young
   wenches now are all o'the hoigh. We that are guardians   170

---

157. new for a] *Dyce;* for a new *Q.*   161. SH] *Qc;* omitted *Qu.*   161.
Take] *Qc;* ke *Qu.*   164.1. SD] *Q* (*Exeunt*).   164.2. SD] *this edn; not in Q.*
165. What? More] *Qc;* What more *Qu;* What, more *Dyce.*   166. Petronel
Flashes] *Q;* petronel-flashes *Dyce.*

---

   158. *beside myself*] out of my wits (*OED* beside prep. 5. fig. a).
   159. *No ... side*] Shrimp gives his job description as a running footman, delivering messages, attending on his employer's person or his coach (*OED* running adj. 3a hist.).
   160. *out of temper*] disturbed, disordered (*OED* temper n. 3 4a obs.). In a 'tempered' self, the humours were in balance.
   161. *cullis*] a nourishing food for sick persons (*OED* n.1).
   capacity] ability to receive or recuperate physical strength.
   162. *restorative*] a food, cordial or medicine which has the effect of restoring health or strength (*OED* n. 1a).
   warming-pan] a long-handled covered pan of metal to contain live coals, etc., used at this time for warming beds.
   165. *flatterers*] referring to Lipsalve, whom Glister has just seen leave.
   carrion] Maria's body as flesh for predatory men.
   166. *Petronel Flashes*] rifle shots, a term describing blowhards or 'huffing gallants' (Bullen). See the blustering knight Sir Petronel Flash in Chapman, Jonson, and Marston's *EHo!* (1605).
   170. *o'the hoigh*] eager, volatile (*OED* hoigh n. obs.), punning visually on the nautical 'hoy', used to call aloft on a ship; Maria is similarly aloft in the theatre (*OED* hoy int.).

must respect more besides titles, gold lace, person, or
parts; we must have lordships and manors elsewhere as
well as in the man. Wealth commands all, and wealth I'll
have, or else my minion shall lead apes in hell. I must
after this gallant too; I'll know his rendezvous and what 175
company he keeps.   *Exit.*
Maria. Now must we be abrupt. Retire, sweet friend,
To thy small-ease. What more remains to do
We'll consummate at our next inteview.
Gerardine. So shall I bear my prisonment with pleasure. 180
Look thou but big, our cruel foe will yield,
And give to Hymen the honour of the field.
                                   Exeunt [above].

ACT 3 SCENE 2

Enter MISTRESS PURGE, *and* CLUB *before her with
a link [and carrying a book].*

Mistress Purge. Fie, fie, Club, go a'tother side the way! Thou
collowest me and my ruff. Thou wilt make me an unclean
member i'the congregation.

181. big, our] *Dyce;* big or *Qu;* big, nor *Qc.*   182.1. SD] *Dyce; Exeunt. Q.*

Act 3 Scene 2] *Shepherd (*III ii*); not in Q.*   0.1–2. SD] *this edn; not in Q.*

---

171. *gold lace*] 'The term "lace" was used of two products; a braid or cord,
and an ornamental, openwork fabric'; both kinds of lace could be made of
gold or silver threads. Like clothing in general, gold laces were a status
symbol, 'in demand by gallants both for their own garments and those of
their servants' (Linthicum, 128, 134–5).
   person] physical attributes.
   172. *parts*] talents.
   174. *lead ... hell*] proverbially the old maid's fate. See Shakespeare, *TS*
2.1.33–4: 'I must dance barefoot on her wedding day / And, for your love to
her, lead apes in hell' (Tilley M37).
   175. *rendezvous*] habitual meeting places (*OED* 3a); a newish word in the
seventeenth century, first introduced in a military sense (*OED* 2a 2b).
   177. *abrupt*] hasty.
   181. *big*] (1) threatening; (2) pregnant (*OED* adj. 6a); making Maria 'big
with child' is a key part of Gerardine's intrigue. See 5.3.364n.
   182. *Hymen*] Greco-Roman god of marriage.
   0.2. SD *link*] torch made of flax fibre and pitch, used for lighting people
along the streets (*OED* link n.1, citing 88–9 of this scene).
   2. *collowest*] blacken, dirty (*OED* collow v.), alluding to the smoke of the
link.

Club. If you be unclean, mistress, you may pure yourself. You have my master's ware at your commandment; but what am I, then, that does all the drudgery in your house?
Mistress Purge. Th'art born to't. Why, boy, I can show thy indentures; thou giv'st no other milk. We know how to use all i'their kind.
Club. You're my better in bark and rind, but in pith and substance I may compare with you. You're above me in flesh, mistress, and there's your boast, but in my tother part, we are all one before God.

Enter DRYFAT.

Mistress Purge. All one with me? Dost thou swear, too? Why then, up and ride!
Dryfat. Whither away, Mistress Purge?
Mistress Purge. To the Family, Master Dryfat, to our exercise.

---

7. Th'art] *Dillon;* Thart *Q;* Thou'rt *Dyce.* 8. indentures; thou] *Dyce;* Indentures thou *Q.* 10. rind] *this edn;* Rhyne *Q;* rine *Dyce.* 11–12. above ... in flesh] *Qc;* above flesh *Qu.*

---

4. *pure*] to make morally and spiritually pure; to purify oneself from sin (*OED* v. 2, citing this usage). The word hints at Club's interest in unorthodox religious and political ideas. See *Displaying*, C4v: 'The true freedom is ... that the man ... be wholly released, purged, and purified from all wicked nature and sin.'

8. *indentures*] contract by which an apprentice is bound to the master who undertakes to teach him a trade (*OED* n.).

thou ... milk] that's the natural work of an apprentice, i.e., manual labour; perhaps a twist on the proverb 'as natural to him as milk to a calf' (M 930).

9. *use*] treat.

10. *bark ... rind*] (1) things of the flesh, in the Pauline sense; as opposed to the spirit. See Romans 8.5; (2) external appearance (Shepherd).

12–13. *tother part*] the soul.

13. *we ... God*] Compare *A Supplication of the Family of Love* (1606), 19: Familists 'are all equal among themselves' (cited in Shepherd). The idea originates in Galatians 3.28: 'there is nether bonde nor fre ... for ye are all one in Christ Jesus'. Club subversively channels the questioning of social hierarchy that was part of Familist beliefs.

14–15. *Dost ... ride!*] Mistress Purge hears Club's words 'before God' (11–12) as an oath. As distinct from 1.2.103, 'up and ride!' here refers to riding on a rail as punishment for misdemeanours such as swearing (compare 3.1.150).

17. *exercise*] (1) religious observance (*OED* n. 10a); (2) weekday sermon (Bullen).

Dryfat. What, by night?
Mistress Purge. Oh, lord, ay, sir, with the candles out, too; we fructify best i'th' dark. The glance of the eye is a great matter; it leads us to other objects besides the right.
Dryfat. Indeed, I think we perform those functions best when we are not thrall to the fetters of the body.
Mistress Purge. The fetters of the body? What call you them?
Dryfat. The organs of the body, as some term them.
Mistress Purge. Organs? Fie, fie, they have a most abominable squeaking sound in mine ears; they edify not a whit, I detest 'em. I hope my body has no organs.
Dryfat. To speak more familiarly, Mistress Purge, they are the senses: the sight, hearing, smelling, taste, and feeling.
Mistress Purge. Ay, marry. — 'Mary', said I? Lord, what a word's that in my mouth! — You speak now, Master Dryfat, but yet let me tell you where you err, too. This feeling I will prove to be neither organ nor fetter; it is a thing — a sense, did you call it?
Dryfat. Ay, a sense.
Mistress Purge. Why, then, a sense let it be — I say it is that we cannot be without, for, as I take it, it is a part belonging to understanding. Understanding, you know, lifteth up the mind from earth; if the mind be lift up, you know the body goes with it. Also it descends into the conscience, and there tickles us with our works and doings, so that we make singular use of feeling.

---

18. *by night?*] Compare *Displaying*, Appendix 3, line 15: 'They are called together ever in the night time'.

20. *fructify*] (1) bear spiritual fruit; (2) copulate.

25–8. *organs ... organs*] 'Organs' is a dangerous pun for a Familist, invoking the musical instruments with which most English churches were equipped before the Reformation. Compare the 'organs' jokes at the end of Middleton, *Mad World* 2.1.163–7.

29. *familiarly*] in everyday language (*OED* adv. 1b).

31. *marry*] a mild oath, invoking the Virgin Mary, used to give emphasis to one's words (*OED* int. 1 arch.).

31–2. *'Mary' ... mouth!*] pun; an alarmed Mistress Purge fears: (1) she may have betrayed her marriage by saying 'marry'; (2) she may have betrayed her faith by pronouncing a Catholic oath.

35. *thing*] punning on 'genitalia', see 3.1.54n.

39. *understanding*] intellect.

43. *singular*] special (*OED* adj. 8c).

Dryfat. And not of the rest?
Mistress Purge. Not at that time; therefore we hold it not amiss   45
to put out the candles, for the soul sees best i'th' dark.
Dryfat. You come to me now, Mistress Purge.
Mistress Purge. Nay, I will come to you else, Master Dryfat.
These senses, as you term them, are of much efficacy in
carnal mixtures, that is, when we crowd and thrust a man   50
and a woman together.

Enter PURGE *and overhears them.*

Purge. [*Aside*] What, so close at it? I thought this was one end
of your exercise. Byrlady, I think there is small profit in
this. I'll wink no more, for I am now tickled with a conceit
that it is a scurvy thing to be a cuckold.   55
Dryfat. I commend this zeal in you, Mistress Purge. I desire
much to be of your society.
Mistress Purge. Do you indeed, blessing on your heart! Are
you upright in your dealings?
Dryfat. Yes, I do love to stand to anything I do, though I lose   60
by it. In truth, I deal but too truly for this world. You

---

52. SD] *Dyce; not in Q.*

47. *You ... now*] Now you're talking in a way I understand (*OED* to come to v. 2).
48. *else*] more, further (*OED* adv. 1a).
52. *close*] privately (*OED* adj. 4b obs.).
53. *exercise*] (1) religious practice as at 17; (2) copulation (Williams, *Dictionary*, 1.452–3).
Byrlady] contraction of 'by Our Lady', used as an oath or strong exclamation of surprise, still in regional use (*OED* byrlady n. int.).
55. *scurvy*] contemptible (*OED* adj. 2a). Compare Shakespeare, *Oth*. 4.2.139: 'some scurvy fellow'.
56. *zeal*] a word often associated with fervent Puritans, e.g., Zeal-of-the-Land Busy in Jonson's *Bart.Fair* (Shepherd).
57. *society*] (1) acquaintance; (2) religious group or fellowship (*OED* 11a).
59. *upright*] (1) honest; (2) sexually erect, triggering pun on 'stand' (55).
60–73.] Dryfat's self-portrait resembles satirical representations of the stage Puritan. See Patrick Collinson, 'The Theatre Constructs Puritanism', in D.L. Smith et al. (eds), *The Theatrical City: Culture, Theatre, and Politics in London, 1576–1649* (Cambridge: Cambridge University Press, 1995), 151–69.
60. *stand to*] (1) obey, be bound by (*OED* stand to v. PV2, 1 obs.); (2) fight stoutly (PV2, 3 obs.); adhere to, insist upon (PV2, 9, 10b obs.); (3) maintain an erection; compare Shakespeare, *Mac*. 2.3.28–9: '[drink] ... makes him stand to and not stand to'.

shall hear how far I am entered in the right way already.
First, I live in charity and give small alms to such as be
not of the right sect; I take under twenty i'th' hundred,
nor no forfeiture of bonds unless the law tell my con-   65
science I may do't; I set no pot on a Sundays, but feed
on cold meat dressed a Saturdays; I keep no holy days
nor fasts, but eat most flesh o'Fridays of all days i'the
week; I do use to say inspired graces able to starve a
wicked man with length; I have Aminadabs and Abrahams   70
to my godsons, and I chide them when they ask me blessing; and I do hate the red letter more than I follow the
written verity.

Purge. [*Aside*] Here's clergy.

Mistress Purge. These are the rudiments indeed, Master Dryfat.   75

Dryfat. Nay, I can tell you, I am or will be of the right stamp.

---

70. Abrahams] *Dyce;* Abrams *Q.*   74. SD] *Dyce; not in Q.*

---

62. *entered ... way*] embarked on the spiritually correct lifestyle, but with sexual quibble to follow up pun on 'stand to'.

63–4. *give ... sect*] Family of Love rule. Compare *Displaying*, Appendix 3, lines 85–6: 'They hold that they are bound to give alms to none other persons but to those of their sect.'

64. *twenty ... hundred*] 20 per cent interest on loans.

66. *set ... on*] don't cook.

a] on.

67. *dressed*] prepared.

68. *flesh o'Fridays*] Dryfat exaggerates his Puritan leanings by rejecting the Anglican and Roman Catholic bar on eating meat on Fridays. Compare Marston, *Dutch C.* 1.2.23–4: 'I trust I am none of the wicked that eat fish o'Fridays'.

69–70. *graces ... length*] Puritans were known to offer long prayers before meals; compare Marston, *Certain Satires*, Satire 2, lines 61–2: 'a solemn grace / Of half an hour'.

70. *Aminadabs ... Abrahams*] pious names; ancestors of Christ (Matthew 1–2, 4), intended to suggest a Puritan. Compare *Dutch C.* 3.3.72–3: 'Oh, Sir Aminadab Ruth bade me kiss him methodically'.

72. *red letter*] red print indicating saints' days in the ecclesiastical calendar, hence a sign of Catholicism (*OED* red letter n. 1a 2, citing this usage).

73. *verity*] truth.

74. *clergy*] learning.

76. *right stamp*] (1) correct character or kind, appropriate to the person's stated belief or behaviour (*OED* stamp n.3 13e); (2) certifying mark, authorising the bearer (*OED* stamp n.3 13a).

SC 2]   THE FAMILY OF LOVE   133

Purge. [*Aside*] A pox o'your stamp.
Mistress Purge. Then learn the word for your admittance, and
     you will be much made on by the congregation.
Dryfat. Ay, the word, good Mistress Purge.   80
Mistress Purge. 'A brother in the Family'.
Dryfat. Enough, I have my lesson.
Purge. [*Aside*] So have I mine: 'A brother in the Family'. I
     must be a Familist today. I'll follow this gear while 'tis
     on foot, i'faith.   85
Mistress Purge. Then shore up your eyes, and lead the way to
     the goodliest people that ever turned up the white o'th'
     eye. — Give me my book, Club, put out thy link, and
     come behind us.

                         They knock.

Answer within. Who's there?   90
Dryfat. Two brothers and a sister in the Family.
                                            [*They are*] *let in.*

---

77. SD] *Dyce; not in Q.* 83. SD] *this edn; not in Q.* 91.1. SD] *Dillon (subst);* Let in. *Q in right margin;* MISTRESS PURGE, DRYFAT, *and* CLUB *enter the House: then* PURGE *knocks at the door. Dyce.* 91.2. SD] *this edn; Purge knocks at left margin Q.*

---

  78. *word*] password.
  79. *you ... congregation*] Compare *Displaying*, Appendix 3, lines 11, 14–16: a 'new elected brother ... is admitted with a kiss, viz., all the company, both men and women, kiss him, one after another'.
     much made on] made a big fuss of.
  81. *'A brother ... Family'*] punning on the term used for a fellow member of a Christian sect, here the Familists, and a male sibling in a 'family' (*OED* 3a). With the password used for entry to the meeting, compare *Displaying*, Appendix 3, lines 19–21: 'when they come to the house of meeting, they knock at the door, saying, "here is a brother in Christ", or "a sister in Christ"'.
  84. *gear*] business, matter.
  85. *on foot*] alive, active.
  86. *shore*] lift up, raise (*OED* v.1, citing this line). Turning the eyes heavenwards was an affectation associated with Puritans.

134   THE FAMILY OF LOVE   [ACT 3

PURGE *knocks.*

Answer within. Who's there?
Purge. A Familiar brother.
Answer within. Here's no room for you nor your familiarity.
Purge. How? No room for me nor my familiarity? Why, what's   95
the difference between a familiar brother, and a brother
in the Family? Oh, I know: I made eclipses of 'in' in this
place where it should have been expressed, so that the
want of 'in' put me clean out. Or let me see: may it not
be some mystery drawn from arithmetic? For my life,   100
these Familists love no substraction, take nothing away,
but put in and add as much as you will, and after addition
follows multiplication of a most Pharasithypocritical
crew. Well, for my part I like not this Family, nor indeed
some kind of private lecturing that women use. Look to't,   105
you that have such gadders to your wives; self- willed they

92. SH] *Q* (— *Within*).   94. SH] *Q (Within).*

93–4. *Familiar ... familiarity*] Purge bungles the password. As well as 'of the family' (*OED* 2a) and 'friendly' (*OED* 1b), 'familiar' carries connotations of closeness and intimacy, especially inappropriate sexual intimacy (*OED* 3a, 3b). Compare *Club Law*, 2.5.921–3: 'and you would but look on us ... and love us ... that there might be some familiarity between us'. The voice '*within*' (94 SH) rejects the association of Familism with sexual intimacy.

97. *eclipses*] (1) obliterations, obscurings; (2) malapropism for 'ellipses'.

100–3. *arithmetic ... multiplication*] Purge riffs on 'arithmetic' as the science of numerical calculation, encompassing the malapropism 'substraction' (101).

103. *multiplication*] (1) mathematical process of multiplying quantities; (2) production of offspring, as in God's injunction to 'Be fruitful, and multiply' (Genesis 1.22)

Pharasithypocritical] hypocritically taking credit to themselves for piety (*OED* pharisee v.), as did the Pharisees of the New Testament. Purge reiterates a common criticism of Familists.

105. *private lecturing*] giving of weekday lectures by independent Protestant preachers. Lectures tackled doctrinal matters in greater depth than sermons (Gerald R. Cragg, *Puritanism in the Period of the Great Persecution 1660–1688* [Cambridge: Cambridge University Press, 1957], 163, 210). 'Private' indicates nonconformist venues other than churches, but also implies extramarital affairs.

105–6. *Look ... you*] Purge may address men in the audience directly at this point.

106. *gadders*] those who go to many social events or travel to many places for pleasure; gadabouts (*OED*, n. 1). Compare Marston, *Dutch C.* 3.3.173: 'Whither are you a-gadding?'

are as children, and i'faith capable of not much more
than they, peevish by custom, naturally fools. I remember
a pretty wooden sentence in a preamble to an exercise
where the reader prayed that men of his coat might grow   110
up like cedars to make good wainscot in the house of
sincerity. Would not this wainscot phrase be writ in brass,
to publish him that spake it for an animal? Why, such
wooden pellets out of earthen trunks do strike these
females into admiration, hits 'em home, sometimes,   115
perhaps, in at one ear and out at tother, and then they
depart, in opinion wiser than their neighbours, fraught
with matter, able to take down and mortify their husbands. Well, I'll home now, and bring the true word next
time. I shall expect my wife anon, red-hot with zeal and   120
big with melting tears, and this night do I expect, as her
manner is, she will weep me a whole chamberpot full.
Loquor lapides? Do I cast pills abroad? 'Tis no matter what

---

129. a] *Q;* a[n] *Dyce.*   horner-able] *this edn;* hornorable *Q;* honourable *Dyce.*

---

107. *custom*] habit.
109. *wooden*] (1) dull (*OED* 1b); (2) anticipating 'wainscot' (101).
sentence] pithy saying (*OED* 4a).
110. *reader*] person leading religious worship. Purge has accompanied his wife to religious lectures.
110–12. *grow up ... sincerity*] Compare Psalm 92.12–13: 'The righteous shal florish like a palme tre, and shal growe like a cedre in Lebanon. / Suche as be planted in the House of the Lord, shal florish in the courts of our God' (Cleary).
112. *wainscot*] panelling used to line a room, usually of oak rather than 'cedar' (*OED* n. 3 fig.).
wainscot phrase] clumsy or wooden expression. The reader's mixed metaphor, 'like cedars ... good wainscot', attracts Purge's derision.
114. *earthen trunks*] (1) human bodies or speakers; (2) pun on tree trunks, continuing the tree metaphor at 110–11; (3) tubes, pea-shooters, firing 'pellets' of wisdom (114) (Bullen).
118. *take down*] (1) get the better of in religious argument; (2) sexual innuendo; reduce a man's tumescence.
121. *big ...tears*] swollen with bodily fluids and religious fervour.
121–2. *this ... full*] 'identification of the [zealous] female body with incontinence and physical uncontrol', Paster, 'Humor', 57–8.
123. *Loquor lapides?*] Am I speaking harshly? (Lat.), metaphor of words as missiles adapted from Plautus, *Aulularia*, 152: *lapides loqueris*, 'Your words are stones'.

I say, I talk like a pothecary, as I am. I have only purged
myself of a little choler and passion, and am now armed   125
with a patient resolution. But how? To put my horns in
my pocket? No.
What wise men bear is not for me to scorn;
'Tis a horner-able thing to wear the horn.   *Exit.*

ACT 3 SCENE 3

Enter LIPSALVE *with his whip.*

Lipsalve. Fortune, devil's turd i'thy teeth! I'll turn no more
o'thy wheel; art is above thy might. What though my
project with Mistress Maria failed? More ways to the
wood than one: there's variety in love. It is believed I am
out of town; my door is open, the hour is at hand; all   5
things squared by the doctor's rule; and now I look for
the spirit to bring me warm comfort, to clothe my naked-
ness, and that is Mistress Purge, the cordial of a Familist.

Act 3 Scene 3] *Shepherd* (III iii); *not in* Q.   0.1. SD] *Q; Enter* LIPSALVE
without his doublet, a whip in his hand Dyce.

---

129. *a horner-able thing*] an act worthy of a cuckold. The pronunciation
puns on 'honourable'; Q's use of the indefinite article 'a' instead of 'an'
perhaps facilitates this pun by telling the actor how to say the word to get
the most impact.

0.] The encounter between Lipsalve and Gudgeon devised by Glister as
a punishment for their lust takes place shortly before dawn in Lipsalve's
chamber (2.4.190–2).

1–2. *Fortune ... wheel*] In Renaissance iconography Fortune is pictured as
a blindfolded woman, turning a wheel which raises humans to prosperity
and lowers them to misery.

2. *o'thy*] on your.

3–4. *more ... one*] proverbial, 'There be more ways to the wood than one'
(Tilley W179).

6. *squared ... rule*] directed by Glister's course of proceeding. The phrase
puns on 'square' and 'rule' both as actions of, and implements for, measuring
in carpentry (*OED* square v. 1a b, 4 fig.; rule n. 13a); compare Shakespeare,
T&C 5.2.131–3: 'stubborn critics, apt ... to square the general sex / By
Cressid's rule'.

8. *cordial*] person who provides succour, comfort or stimulation, here, of
a specifically sexual kind (*OED* n. 2b fig). More commonly used of a restorative food, drink or medicine (*OED* n. 1).

SC 3]   THE FAMILY OF LOVE   137

   And come quickly, good spirit, or else my teeth will
chatter for thee.   10

            [LIPSALVE *stands aside*.]
            Enter GUDGEON *with his whips*.

Gudgeon. Oh, the naked pastimes of love, the scourge of dull-
ness, the purifier of uncleanness, and the hot-house of
humanity! I have taken physic of Master Purge any time
this twelve months to purge my humour upon's wife, and
I have ever found her so fugitive, from exercise to exer-   15
cise, and from family to Family, that I could never yet
open the close-stool of my mind to her, so that I may well
say with Ovid, *Hei mihi, quod nullus amor est medicabilis
herbis*! Now am I driven to prove the violent virtue of
conjuration; if it hit, and that I yerk my Familist out of   20
the spirit, I'll hang up my scourge-stick for a trophy and
imparadise my thoughts. Though the doctor go to the
devil, 'tis no matter. Ha, let me see, Lipsalve's door open,
and himself out of town? Excellent doctor, soothsaying
doctor, oraculous doctor!   25

            Enter DOCTOR GLISTER *above*.

10.1. SD] *this edn; Scene shuts.* Dyce; *not in* Q. 10.2. SD] Q; *Enter*
GUDGEON *without his doublet, a whip in his hand.* Dyce. 16. family to
Family] Q (*subst*); Family to Family Dyce. 25.1. SD] Q;LIPSALVE *discovered as before*: GLISTER *watching above* Dyce.

   10.2. SD] Q's stage direction affords some Pythonesque humour as
Gudgeon enters carrying not one, but two whips.
   12. *hot-house*] brothel (*OED* n. 1b). Compare Shakespeare, *MM* 2.1.61–2:
'Now she professes a hothouse, which I think is a very ill house, too.'
   16. *from ... Family*] from her household with its servants (*OED* family n.
1a) to religious meetings of the Family of Love.
   18–19. Hei ... herbis!] Woe to me, because no love is treatable with herbs.
Gudgeon (or Barry, or the compositor) have fused two lines from separate
works of Ovid, *Met.* 1. 523 and *Her.* 5.149.
   20. *yerk*] whip (*OED* v. 2a).
   21. *scourge-stick*] whip.
   22. *imparadise*] (1) to place in paradise; (2) to bring into a state of rapture
or supreme happiness. See Florio, 1598 (*LEME*): '*imparadisare*, to
emparadize, to bring to paradise'.

Glister. I have taken up this standing to see my gallants play
at barriers with scourge-sticks for the honour of my punk;
and in good time I see my brave spirits shining in bright
armour, nakedly burning in the hellfire of lechery, and
ready for the hot encounter. Sound trumpets! The com- 30
batants are mounted.
Gudgeon. [*Seeing Lipsalve*] The apparition — Mistress Purge
peers through him, I see her.
Lipsalve. [*Seeing Gudgeon*] The spirit appears — but he might
have come sooner. I am numbed with cold; a shivering 35
ague hath taken away my courage.
Glister. [*To the audience*] They are afraid one of another. Look
how they tremble — the flesh and the devil strengthen
'em! Ha, ha, ha!
Gudgeon. Has 'a no cloven feet? What a laxative fever shakes 40
me.
Lipsalve. Will 'a not carry me with him to hell? Well, I must
venture: *Clogmathos.*
Gudgeon. My cue: *Clogmathathos.*
Lipsalve. My cue: *Garrazin.* 45
Gudgeon. Garragas.

---

32. SD] *this edn; not in Q.*   34. SD] *this edn; not in Q.*   37. SD] *this edn; not in Q.*   46, 48.] *to right side of 45 & 47 Q.*

---

26. *standing*] position, vantage point (*OED* n. 2c).

27. *barriers*] martial combat and entertainment at which men fought with 'bated' or blunted weapons across a central barrier either outdoors in a tilting yard or in the middle of a hall. Glister's speech readies the audience for a mock-duel in the manner of that staged in Shakespeare's *TwN* 3.4, and recounted by Brisk in Jonson's *EMO* 4.3.

punk] whore, side-hoe, i.e., Mistress Purge.

30. *hot*] lustful.

31. *mounted*] i.e., figuratively, on horseback (as in a jousting competition); with a pun on a sexual sense.

40. *laxative fever*] trembling and high fever such as that brought about by medically induced diarrhoea. The gallants' symptoms here are caused by fear and their state of semi-undress.

43–50.] With this dialogue compare Cocledemoy's 'bogus Greek', Marston, *Dutch C.* 4.3.12–20n.

43. *Clogmathos*] a greeting?

45–7. *Garrazin ... Garrazinos*] 'guard yourself' (from 'garrison')?

46. *Garragas*] 'you guard *your*self'?

Lipsalve. Garrazinos.
Gudgeon. Ton tetuphon.
Lipsalve. Tes tetuphes.
Both. With a *whirley twinos*.   50

They lash one another.

Both. Hold! hold! hold! Gog's nowns! Gog's blood! A pox! A
  plague! The devil take you! Truce! Truce! I smart, I
  smart!
Glister. Ha, ha, ha! Oh, for one of the hoops of my Cornelius'
  tub. I must needs be gone, I shall burst myself with laugh-   55
  ing else.
  Magic hath no such rule. Men cannot find
  Lust ever better handled in his kind.   *Exit* DOCTOR.
Gudgeon. What art thou? With the name of Jove I conjure
  thee!   60
Lipsalve. With any name, saving the whip. I'll no more of that
  conjuration, a plague on't.
Gudgeon. Speak! Art not a spirit, in the likeness of my friend
  Lipsalve, that should transform thyself to Mistress Purge?
Lipsalve. How? A spirit? I hope spirits have no flesh and   65
  blood, and I am sure thou hast drawn blood out of my
  flesh with the spirit of thy whip.

---

50. SH] *Dyce; Ambo. Q.*   50.1. SD] *Dyce; in roman following long dash after 50 Q.*   51. SH] *Dyce; Ambo. Q.*   51–3. *Both.* Hold! ... I smart!] *Q;* LIPS. Hold ... hold! / GUD. Gogs ... blood! / LIP. A pox ... you! / GUD. Truce ... I smart. *Dyce.*

---

  47. Garrazinos] 'we both guard ourselves'?
  48. Ton tetupon] 'I set upon you'?
  49. Tes tetuphes] 'We set upon each other'?
  50. whirley twinos] 'whirling twines', i.e., whips.
  51. *Gog's nowns!*] God's wounds!
  54. *hoops*] metal bands encircling, and supporting, wooden barrels or tubs.
  54–5. *Cornelius' tub*] sweating-tub formerly used to treat venereal disease, also called '(Mother) Cornelius' tub' (*OED* tub n.1 †b, obs.). The barrel-making joke has extended meaning for Lipsalve and Gudgeon, who have been acting like lechers, and deserve the lecher's torment of syphilis and its 'cure' of mercury baths.
  56. *else*] otherwise.
  58. *in ... kind*] according to its type, or breed (*OED* kind n. 1c 7a 7c).
  65. *hope*] in Chaucer, 'hope' = 'think' is a northern dialecticism.

140   THE FAMILY OF LOVE   [ACT 3

[*Gudgeon.*] Then shall we prove to be honest gulls, and the
  doctor an errant knave.
Lipsalve. A plague upon him for a glister, he has given our 70
  loves a suppositor with a *recombentibus*. I'll tell thee,
  sirrah —
Gudgeon. Tell not me, let me prevent thee. The wind shall
  not take the breath of our gross abuse. We feel the gullery.
  Therefore let us swear by our naked truths, and by the 75
  hilts of these our blades, our flesh-tamers, to be revenged
  upon that paraperopandemical doctor, that pocky doctor.
Lipsalve. Agreed, we'll cuckold him, that he shall not be able
  to put his head in at's doors, and make his precise, puri-
  tanical, and peculiar punk, his pothecary's drug there, a 80
  known cockatrice to the world.
Gudgeon. If report catch this knavery, we have lost our reputation forever, wherefore let's be secret.
  Ill tax we women of credulity,
  When men are gulled with such gross foppery. 85

---

68. SH] *Dyce; not in Q.* 77. paraperopandemical] *this edn;* Paraperopandenticall *Q.* 83. wherefore ... secret] *prose in Dyce; verse in Q.*

---

70. *glister*] i.e., clyster, materialising the pun in Glister's name. See Names of the Characters, 1n.

71. *suppositor*] suppository. Compare Sharpham, *Cupid's Whirligig*, 1607 (1616 edn), C4r, in *EEBO*: 'do you never make no suppositors sir?' Glister has purged the gallants' lust by orchestrating their whipping of each other.
  recumbentibus] Lat., powerful knockdown blow (*OED*).

73. *prevent*] anticipate, forestall (*OED* 1a obs.).

73–4. *The ... abuse*] We will not utter one word more about our humiliating treatment.

74. *gross*] flagrant (*OED* adj. 4a).

76. *blades*] swords.

77. *paraperopandemical*] causing widespread 'pandemic', or sweeping disease, an appropriate epithet for a doctor (*OED* gives the earliest recorded usage of *pandemic* as 1666). Q could represent a compositorial misconstruction of *paraperopedantical*, 'thoroughly pedantic', in prescribing the punishment the gallants have just experienced. Dillon explains Q as an 'invented word' implying 'that slippery and far-reaching doctor, who has maimed us and our hopes' (3.3.74n).

pocky] (1) infected with the pox, usually syphilis (*OED* 1a); (2) worthless, contemptible (*OED* 1b colloq.).

80. *peculiar*] belonging only to Glister (*OED* adj. 2a).

81. *cockatrice*] cant term for prostitute.

85. *foppery*] trickery.

SC 4]   THE FAMILY OF LOVE   141

Lipsalve. Come, let us in and cover both our shames!
   This conjuration to the world's a novelty:
   Gallants turned spirits and whipped for lechery.
                                                    Exeunt.

                       ACT 3 SCENE 4

                       Enter MARIA.

Maria. Gerardine, come forth, Maria calls!
   Those ribs shall not enfold thy buxom limbs
   One minute longer. The cincture of mine arms
   Shall more securely keep thy soul from harms.

   [*Enter* GERARDINE *out of the trunk.*]

Gerardine. What heavenly breath of Phitonissa's power,   5
   That raised the dead corpse of her friend to life,

Act 3 Scene 4] *Q (Act. 3. Scen.4.).* 0.1. SD] *Dyce; Enter Maria and Gerardine out of the Trunke.* Q. 4.1. SD] *this edn; before 1* Q. 5. Phitonissa's] *this edn;* Phitonessaes *Q.*

---

   86. *our shames*] both men are dressed only in their shirts, without their doublets, the equivalent of being naked in the early modern period.

   2. *ribs*] of the trunk.
   buxom] (1) lively, attractive (*OED* adj. 3). Compare Shakespeare *H5* 3.7.22–3: 'a soldier ... / Of buxom valour'; (2) in vigorous good health, plump, sexy (*OED* 4: the definition says the word is used in this sense '[c]hiefly of women', but see the citation from Cotgrave, 1711 (*LEME*): 'at matineux, an early man is buxom'; (3) flexible, pliant (*OED* 2). *OED* allows 'wanton' in a 'contextual' sense under sense 1 above (*OED* 3); see also B.E., 1699 (*LEME*): 'Bucksom, wanton, merry'. Since we last saw them in 3.1 Maria and Gerardine have consummated their love; Maria's appreciation of Gerardine's physical attractiveness is part of her character. The consciously literary language in this scene dignifies the couple's love.
   3. *cincture ... arms*] enclosure of my embrace (*OED* 1a, from Lat. cincture, 'girdle', but gives first usage as 1615). Compare Marston, *JDE* C4v: 'the cincture of a faithful arm' (Freebury-Jones, Tarlinskaja, and Dahl, 61).
   5–10.] I feel no less magical force work on me than that with which Phitonissa raised Samuel, for this coffin-like trunk releases my whole self to Maria's presence, liberating me in my imprisonment.
   5. *Phitonissa's*] woman with powers of divination who lived at Endor and raised the spirit of Samuel to speak to Saul (1 Samuel 28.7–19); also known as the witch of Endor. Compare Chaucer, *Friar's Tale*, 1510.

    Prevails no less on me, for even this urn,
    The figure of my sadder requiem,
    Gives up my bones, my love, my life, and all
    To her that gives me freedom in my thrall.   10
Maria. Be brief, sweet friend, salute and part in one,
    For niggard time now threats with imminent danger
    Our late 'joyed scope. Thy earnest, then, of love,
    Ere Sol hath compassed half the signs, I fear,
    Will show a blushing fault, but 'twas thy plot, thine aim,   15
    T'enforce consent in him that bars thy claim.
Gerardine. Love salves that fault. Let time our guilt reveal;
    I'll ne'er deny my deed, my hand and seal.
    The elements shall lose their ancient force,
    Water and earth suppress the fire and air,   20
    Nature in all use a preposterous course,

---

15. 'twas thy plot, thine aim] *Q;* 'twas thine aim *Dyce.*

---

  7. *this urn*] i.e., the trunk.
  8. *figure ... requiem*] symbol of my death.
  12. *niggard*] stingy.
  13. *late ... scope*] recently enjoyed desires (*OED* scope n.2 2a).
  earnest] (1) pledge (the couple's lovemaking); (2) specifically, Gerardine's sperm, an 'earnest' realised in Maria's pregnancy.
  14. *Ere ... signs*] before the sun has passed through six of the twelve signs of the zodiac, i.e., before six months have elapsed. Compare *Gesta Grayorum*, 15: 'the glorious planet Sol, coursing through the twelve signs of the zodiac' (Shepherd).
  15. *blushing fault*] (1) a fault (her pregnancy) prompting blushes from Maria and Gerardine; (2) a fault that blushes, perhaps prompted by 'Sol' (14). See below, 5.1.25, 'the blushing sun'.
  aim] plan.
  16. *him*] Glister, who opposes Gerardine's suit to Maria.
  17. *salves*] heals.
  18. *deed ... seal*] (1) the couple's lovemaking; (2) 'deed' as a legal document, 'hand and seal' as the conventional, legal form of witnessing and oath-taking, as in swearing 'by this hand' (*OED* hand n. P4), or acting on personal 'faith' (23) as a gentleman.
  19–20.] Gerardine envisages an apocalyptic upheaval in which the usual order of the elements is reversed; Renaissance thinkers understood God as having placed the elements in the order of earth, water, air, and fire. See E. M.W. Tillyard, *The Elizabethan World Picture* (London: Chatto and Windus, 1943), 55–7.
  21. *preposterous*] back to front (*OED* 1a).

  Each kind forget his likeness to repair,
  Before I'll falsify my faith to thee.
Maria. The humorous bodies' elemental kind
  Shall sooner lose th'innated heat of love,   25
  The soul in nature's bounds shall be confined,
  Heaven's course shall retrograde, and leave to move,
  Ere I surcease to cherish mutual fire
  With thoughts refined in flames of true desire.
Gerardine. These words are odours in the sacred shrine   30
  Of love's best deity; the marriage god
  Longs to perform these ceremonious rites
  Which terminate our hopes; till mine grow full
  I'll use that intercourse amongst my friends

 22.] Each animal fail to return to his mate (Dillon).
 23. *falsify*] break, violate; compare Greene, *Never Too Late* (1590), Part 2, I3v, in *EEBO*: 'Aeneas ... falsified his faith to Dido' (*OED* v. 5 obs.).
 faith] honourable promise (here, of marriage).
 24. *humorous bodies'*] bodies subject to motions of the four 'humours' or bodily moistures: blood, phlegm, choler or yellow bile, and melancholy or black bile (*OED* humour n. 1a). The humours were held to derive from combinations of the four 'elements' (19) that made up all matter; the proportion of humours in any one body determined the degree of heat, cold, moisture, or dryness in an individual's temperament or 'complexion'. See C.S. Lewis, *The Discarded Image* (1964) (Cambridge: Cambridge University Press, 1994), 169–74.
 elemental kind] essential composition (the four elements).
 25. *innated*] imbued with by nature (*OED* innate v.1 b, obs.).
 heat of love] God's love as the force that gives both living beings and the universe order and motion (Dillon).
 27. *Heaven's course*] the direction of the sun and the planets.
 retrograde] (1) go backwards; (2) of the sun: show apparent motion southwards after reaching the most northerly position of the year. Compare Guillaume de Salluste Du Bartas, *Divine Weeks and Works* (1605), trans. J. Sylvester, 482, 'southward Sol doth retrograde' (*OED* v. 3b).
 leave ... move] stop moving.
 28. *surcease to*] stop.
 cherish] (1) nurse, give sustenance to; perhaps anticipating the birth of their child (*OED* 2a); (2) entertain kindly (of a guest) (*OED* 3).
 mutual fire] reciprocated passion.
 31. *love's ... deity*] Cupid.
 marriage god] Hymen; compare 3.1.171.
 33. *grow full*] are realised, achieved. Gerardine personifies his hopes as living things that will mature as Maria's and his child grows in her womb.

        That erst I did; then in the height of joy   35
        I'll come to challenge interest in my boy.
        Till then, farewell.
Maria.   You'll come upon your cue?
Gerardine. Doubt not of that.
Maria.   Then twenty times adieu.
                                  Exeunt.

              End of Act Three

38.2. *End of Act Three*] Q (*Finis Actus Tertis*).

  35. *erst*] formerly.
  36. *challenge interest*] claim legal ownership of his son (*OED* interest n. 1a).
    interest] legal concern in a thing; esp. right or title to property.
  37. *cue*] signal by word or action that an actor is to respond on time by playing his role.
  38. *twenty times*] parodied by Beaumont in *KBP* (1607), 2.64–5: 'Good night, twenty good nights, and twenty more, / And twenty more good nights; that makes threescore.'

Act 4

ACT 4 SCENE I

Enter LIPSALVE *and* GUDGEON, SHRIMP *and* PERIWINKLE.

Gudgeon. Come, boys, our clothes, boys. And what is the most current news, Periwinkle?
Periwinkle. Faith, sir, Fortune hath favoured us with no news, but what the pedlar brought from Norfolk.
Lipsalve. Is there nothing stirring at court, Shrimp? 5
Shrimp. Faith, there is, sir, but nothing new.
Lipsalve. Good wag, faith; thou smellest somewhat of a courtier, though thy mother was a citizen's wife. [*To Gudgeon*] Off with that filthy great band, nay, quick, on with your robe of sanctity — nay, suddenly, man! 10
Gudgeon. And why must we shift ourselves into this demure habit? Is't impossible to be of the Family, and keep our own fashion?

Act 4 Scene 1] *Q* (ACTVS QVARTVS./ *Actus Quartus, scena prima*).
8. SD] *this edn; not in Q.* 12. habit?] *this edn;* habite, *Q.* Is't impossible] *this edn;* if impossible *Q.*

---

1. *our clothes*] The 'robe[s] of sanctity' (10) with which the gallants are to pass as Familists.
1–2. *what ... news*] see above, 2.3.25n.
3–4. *no news ... Norfolk*] (1) Compare the proverb, 'Norfolk wiles, many men beguiles' (Tilley S857), the first part of which is cited in Barry, *Ram Alley* 4.4.80; (2) relevant news in 1605 might have been 'the appointment to the hitherto vacant post of Lord Lieutenant of the Catholic and pro-Spanish Henry Howard' (Shepherd).
5. *nothing stirring*] no news circulating (*OED* stir v. 13b).
7–8. *smellest ... courtier*] you show a touch of the courtier (*OED* smell v. 9b).
9. *filthy great*] obscenely large (*OED* filthy adv. 2 colloq.); possibly an instance of the later adverbial use of 'filthy' in phrases such as 'filthy rich'.
band] neck-band, collar or ruff (Shepherd).
10. *suddenly*] quickly.
11. *shift*] change.
11–12. *demure habit*] pious costume.

145

Lipsalve. Tut, man, the name of a gallant is more hateful to them than the sight of a corner-cap. Hadst thou heard the protestations the wife of a bellows-mender made but yesternight against gallants, thou hadst for ever abjured crimson breeches. She swore that all gallants were persons inferior to bellows-menders, for the trade of bellows-making was very aerial and high, and what were men and women but bellows, for they take wind in at one place, and do evaporate at another. 'Evaporate' was her very phrase.

Gudgeon. Methinks her phrase flew with somewhat too strong a vapour.

Lipsalve. Nay, she proves farther that all men receive their being chiefly from bellows, without which the fire burns not; without fire, the pot seethes not; the pot not seething, powdered beef is not to be eaten, of which she then averred our nation was a great devourer, and without which they could neither fight for their country abroad,

---

22. 'Evaporate'] *this edn;* euaporate *Q.*

---

15. *corner-cap*] cap with corners, worn by divines and members of the universities (*OED*); the cap here is used to represent the whole man, who had authority over the (resentful) uneducated. See *Club Law*, 3.3.1158–9: 'these corner-cap slaves in the town'.

15–23. *Hadst ... phrase*] Lipsalve's anecdote 'parodies the Familists' stress on inspiration' (Chakravorty, 28).

16. *bellows-mender*] one of the peripatetic trades, scorned by those of fixed address. An Elizabethan attack on Familists by the schoolmaster William Wilkinson 'describes the chief elders of the Family as weavers, basketmakers, musicians, and others who wander about in their occupations' (Moss, 'English Critics', 41).

20. *aerial*] (1) composed of air or gas (*OED* adj. 6); (2) lofty, elevated (*OED* 3a, citing this line).

high] (1) physically elevated; (2) dignified.

22. *evaporate*] expel air, fart.

25. *vapour*] (1) moisture created by exhalation (*OED* n. 2a); (2) smelly emission of air, i.e., fart; (3) pretentious or senseless wording (*OED* 4, but gives earliest usage as 1631); compare the games of vapours in Jonson, *Bart. Fair*, 2.5 and 4.4.

28. *seethes*] boils (*OED* v. 1a).

29. *powdered*] salted (to preserve the meat for longer use).

SC I]   THE FAMILY OF LOVE   147

 nor get children at home. For, said she, powdered beef
is a great joiner of nerves together.
Gudgeon. What answer madest thou?
Lipsalve. Marry, that I thought a bawd was a greater joiner of   35
nerves together than powdered beef. With that she pro-
tested that a bawd was an instrument of the devil, and as
she had proved that bellows-makers were of God's trade,
so bawds were of the devil's trade, for (and thereupon
she blew her nose) the devil and bawds did both live by   40
the sins of the people.

    Enter CLUB *and* MISTRESS PURGE.

Gudgeon. No more. Mistress Purge is at hand.
Lipsalve. Vanish, boys, away, make haste.
    [*Exeunt* SHRIMP *and* PERIWINKLE.]
Before Jove, she'll be with us ere we can be provided for
her.   45

    [*They move aside.*]

Mistress Purge. Advance your link, Club. At what time wert
thou bound, Club? At gut-tide, Hollantide, or Candletide?

43.1. SD] *this edn; following* away *Dyce; not in* Q. 45.1. SD] *Dillon;* They
retire *Dyce; not in* Q. 47. gut-tide] *this edn;* Guttyde *Q;* Guttide *Dyce.*

 32. *get*] beget, father – the implicit subjects of the verbs 'fight' and 'get'
are patriotic Englishmen.
 33. *nerves*] sinews, tendons (*OED* n. 2).
 35–6. *a bawd ... beef*] Compare Cocledemoy's defence of bawds in
Marston, *Dutch. C.* 1.2.31–59.
 40. *blew her nose*] sneezing was a sign of the devil; blowing the nose was
voluntary. The bellows-mender's wife takes care to differentiate herself from
bawds.
 44. *provided*] dressed in their costumes (*OED* v. 9b).
 47. *bound*] indentured as an apprentice (*OED* bind v. 20).
 47–50. *gut-tide ... Michaeltide*] Mistress Purge refers to Church holidays
as markers of *time*, the literal meaning of 'tide' (as in *OED* n. 1 6), rather
than '-mas', which designates the Roman Catholic celebration of the Mass:
gut-tide, Shrove Tuesday, a time of feasting (*OED* n. obs. and dialect.);
Hollantide, All-Hallows (1 November); *Candletide,* Candlemas (2 February);
Michaeltide, Michaelmas (29 September).

148   THE FAMILY OF LOVE   [ACT 4

Club. I was bound, indeed, about Midsummer.
Mistress Purge. And when hath thy prenticeship end? At
    Michaeltide next?   50
Club. So I take it.
Mistress Purge. They say, Club, you fall very heavy on such
    you love not; you never learned that of me.
Club. Indeed, mistress, I must confess, my falling is rustic,
    gross, and butcherlike; marry, yours is a pretty, foolish,   55
    light, courtlike falling. Yet, believe me, my master smells
    somewhat too gross of the purgation; he wants tutoring.
Mistress Purge. And why, I pray?
Club. My master being set last night in his shop, comes
    Master Doctor Glister, as his manner is, squirting in sud-   60
    denly, and after some conference tells my master that by
    his own knowledge you were young with child, to which

---

56. courtlike] *Dyce;* Courttake *Q.*

---

48. *Midsummer*] the day of the summer solstice, usually 21 June; a period of feasting and merrymaking in early modern Britain.
51. *take*] understand.
52. *fall*] attack, beat (Dillon).
54. *rustic*] physically robust (*OED* adj. 2c).
55. *gross*] (1) rough (*OED* adj. 13b obs.); (2) brutally unrefined (*OED* 15a).
butcherlike] strongly physical, as a butcher pounds meat.
56. *light*] (1) tripping, as in 'light of step' (*OED* adv.1); (2) unchaste (*OED* adj.1 14b).
falling] with the suggestion of falling backwards for sexual intercourse. Compare Middleton, *RevT* 1.2.183–4: 'when they risse / Were merrily disposed to fall again'.
56–7. *smells ... purgation* (1) is too absorbed in his business (implicitly, to notice his wife's adultery with Glister); (2) scatalogical subtext: stinks of taking his own laxatives or of cleansing the bowels of others (figuratively, releasing them from crime or sin).
57. *tutoring*] schooling in the ways of the world, telling off (*OED* tutor v. 2); in 'wink[ing]' at his wife's adultery (2.1.22–3), Purge is not fulfilling his role as husband and head of the household.
59. *set*] seated (*OED* v.1 4a, 5a).
60. *squirting*] (1) darting (*OED* squirt v. 2a); (2) spurting, like the thin excrement of someone with diarrhoea (*OED* 1a b).
61. *conference*] chat.
62. *knowledge*] (1) information learned through observation; (2) carnal knowledge of Mistress Purge.
young ... child] in the early stages of pregnancy.

SC 1]   THE FAMILY OF LOVE   149

my master replied, 'Why, master doctor, will you put me
to more charges yet?'
Mistress Purge. Thou art a fool, in that my husband spake as   65
wisely as if the master of his company had spoke. He
knows doctors have receipts for women, which makes
them most apt to conceive, and, he promising 'a had
ministered the same lately to me, thereupon spake it.
Lead on with your link!   70
Lipsalve. [*To Gudgeon*] Art ready?
Gudgeon. [*To Lipsalve*] Ready.
Lipsalve. [*To Gudgeon*] Then speak pitifully, look scurvily, and
dissemble cunningly, and we shall quickly prove two of
the fraternity. [*Stepping forward to Mistress Purge*]   75
Benediction and sanctity, love and charity, fall on Mistress
Purge, sister of the Family.
Mistress Purge. And what, I pray, be you two?
[*Lipsalve.*] Two newly converted from the rags of Christianity
to become good members in the house of the Family.   80

---

63. 'Why] *this edn;* why Q.   64. yet?'] *this edn;* yet Q.   71. SD] *this edn; Aside Dillon; not in* Q.   72. SD] *this edn; Aside Dillon; not in* Q.   73. SD] *this edn; Aside Dillon; not in* Q.   75. SD] *this edn; Advancing with* GUDGEON *Dyce; The Gallants walk up to Mistress Purge Dillon; not in* Q.   79. SH] *Dyce;* Sa. Q.

63–4. *put ... charges*] (1) burden me with more expenses in the cost of your diagnosis; (2) increase my household costs by getting my wife pregnant; (3) force me to raise more children, punning on 'charges' as expenses and bastard children entrusted to Purge's care. Legally a married woman's children belonged to her husband, whether the children were his or not.
  65–9.] Mistress Purge skilfully deflects Club's charge of her husband's ignorance of her adultery with Glister.
  66. *master*] head officer of a livery company or guild (*OED* n.1 24).
  company] corporation. London apothecaries became an incorporated company in 1606.
  67. *receipts*] medicines made according to a prescription; remedies (*OED* n. 12 hist. or arch.).
  68. *apt ... conceive*] ready to get pregnant, fertile. See 2.4.115n.
  68–9. *he ... me*] i.e., Glister swearing that he, Glister, had given the identical fertility drug recently to Mistress Purge.
  69. *thereupon ... it*] that's why Master Purge said it.
  73. *scurvily*] contemptibly. See 3.3.60n.
  80. *members*] possible pun on 'sexual organs' (Williams, *Dictionary*, member 2.873–4).

Mistress Purge. Who, I pray, converted you?
[*Gudgeon.*] Master Dryfat, the merchant.
Mistress Purge. And from what sins hath he converted you?
[*Lipsalve.*] From two very notorious crimes. The first was
  from eating fish on Fridays, and the second from speak-   85
  ing reverently of the clergy. But 'a resolved us your talent
  in edifying young men went far beyond his.

Enter MASTER PURGE [*unobserved*].

[*Mistress*] *Purge.* A talent I have therein, I must confess, nor
  am I very nice at fit times to show it. For your better
  instructions, therefore, you must never hereafter frequent   90
  taverns nor tap-houses, no masques nor mummeries, no
  pastimes nor playhouses.
Gudgeon. Must we have no recreation?
Mistress Purge. Yes, on the days which profane lips call holidays, you may take your spaniel and spend some hours   95
  at the ducking-pond.

---

82. SH] *Dyce; not in Q.*   84. SH] *Dyce; Sa. Q as catchword only.*   87. SD *unobserved*] *this edn; Enter* PURGE *behind. Dyce; Enter Mayster Purge. / [He stands back] Dillon; not in Q.*   88. SH *Mistress*] *Dyce; Ma. Pur Q.*

---

87. *edifying*] (1) morally or spiritually improving; (2) with innuendo of seducing.
  89. *nice*] shy (*OED* adj. 6a).
  91. *tap-houses*] alehouses.
  masques] Presented mainly at court but also in some aristocratic households, masques involved spectacular scenery, costumes, music, dancing and a histrionic element, usually played by professional actors. The masque became a defined genre in the early Stuart period, under the aegis of Jonson and his collaborator Inigo Jones. See Martin Butler, *The Stuart Court Masque and Political Culture* (Cambridge: Cambridge University Press, 2008).
  mummeries] festive performances by masked or disguised actors taking place in private houses, at court or in the city of London from the thirteenth century onwards. 'The term "mumming" is not clearly distinct from mask or disguising.' Such entertainments had 'a processional element, bringing in representative or allegorical figures in sequence' (Janette Dillon, *Cambridge Introduction to Early English Theatre* [Cambridge: Cambridge University Press, 2006], 39). The early form of mumming should be distinguished from the British 'mummers' play' or St George play, a form of pantomime that was revived in the eighteenth and nineteenth centuries (*OED* mummers play n.).
  96. *ducking-pond*] (1) pond on which ducks were hunted or shot (*OED*, n. a); (2) pond for ducking offenders in the parish (*OED* b).

SC I]   THE FAMILY OF LOVE   151

Lipsalve. What are we bound unto, during the time we remain
   in the Family?
Mistress Purge. During the light of the candle you are to be
   very attentive, which being extinguished, how to behave   100
   yourselves I will deliver in private whisper.

                    [*They whisper.*]

Purge. 'Tis now come to a whisper. What young Familists be
   these? I'faith, I'll make one. I'll trip you, wife, I scent
   your footing, wife.
   For Galen writes, Paracelsus can tell,   105
   Pothecaries have brains, and noses eke, to smell.
Lipsalve. We shall with much diligence observe it.
Purge. [*Aside*] I fear I shall have small cause to thank that
   diligence, but do your worst.
   He that hath read five herbals in one year   110
   Can find a trick which shall prevent this gear.
   They are going. Follow, Purge, close, close and softly, like
   a horsekeeper in a lady's matted chamber at midnight.

              [*Mistress* PURGE *knocks.*]

101.1. SD] *this edn; not in* Q.   105. Galen] *Dyce; Gallus* Q.   108. SD] *Dyce; not in* Q.   110–11.] *verse as in Dyce; prose in* Q.   113.1. SD] *Shepherd; Exeunt Gudgin, Lipsalue, and Mistrisse Purge.* Q; *Mistress* PURGE *knocks at the door of the Meeting-house.* Dyce.

---

   97. *bound unto*] obliged to do.
   103. *make one*] join the group (*OED* make v.1 25b obs.).
   103–4. *scent ... footing*] I see what you're up to. Hunting metaphor: to 'scent' is 'to perceive as if by smell' (*OED* scent v. 2a, fig.); 'footing' means a footprint (*OED* n. 7a).
   105. *Galen*] second-century Roman physician (129–c. 200 CE). The London College of Physicians, which rivalled the apothecaries, was devoted to Galen, whose medical theories depended on the four humours.
   Paracelsus] Swiss-German physician and natural philosopher (1493–1541). He opposed Galen's humoral theory of diseases, advocating a more experimental approach.
   106. *eke*] also.
   110. *herbals*] treatises describing herbs and plants, and their uses in healing. John Gerard's *Herbal* (1597) was the best known of the period.
   112–13. *like ... midnight*] Purge fantasises equine workers as expert at sexually servicing aristocratic women. Compare Webster, *DM* 2.5.42: 'some strong thigh'd bargeman'.

152   THE FAMILY OF LOVE   [ACT 4

Answer within. Who knocks?
Mistress Purge. Brethren and a sister in the Family.   115
Answer within. Enter in peace.

Exeunt GUDGEON, LIPSALVE,
and MISTRESS PURGE [*with* CLUB].

Purge. Brethren and a sister, that's the word. How beastly was I mistaken last day. I should have said, 'A brother in the Family', and I said, 'A familiar brother', for which I and my family were thrust out of doors. But, as Titus   120
Silus of Holborn Bridge most learnedly was wont to say, *quasi dicat* —

He knocks.

Answer within. Who's there?
Purge. A brother in the Family.
Answer within. Enter, and welcome.   [*Exit* PURGE.]   125

ACT 4 SCENE 2

Enter GERARDINE [*disguised as a porter*].

[*Gerardine.*] Thou sacred deity, Love!
Thou power predominate, more to be admired

---

114. SH] *Q (Within).* 116. SH] *Q (Within).* 116.1–2. SD] *moved from 113.1 in Q;* MISTRESS PURGE, LIPSALVE, GUDGEON, *and* CLUB *enter the house.* Dyce. 122. *quasi dicat*] *this edn; qd—— Q.* 123. SH] *Q (Within).* 125. SH] *Q (Within).* 125. SD] *Dillon;* PURGE *enters the house* Dyce; *not in Q.*

Act 4 Scene 2] *Q (Act.4 Scena.2).* 0.1. SD *disguised as a porter*] *Dyce; not in Q.* 1. SH] *Dyce; not in Q.*

120–1. *Titus Silus*] satirical invocation of London tradesman via a bombastic name. Embellished by Rudyerd, *Le Prince d'Amour, or the Prince of Love* (1660), 38, in *EEBO*: 'What said Silus Titus, the soap maker of Holborn Bridge?' Compare an apothecary named 'Rhadamanthus' in Jonson, *Poet.* 3.1.121. A Silus Titus was born in St Katherines in 1571, and died in 1637; https://www.geni.com/people/Silus-Titus-II/6000000000112117885 (accessed 20 April 2021).
121. *Holborn Bridge*] ancient stone bridge crossing the Fleet river (a tributary of the Thames), lost when the river was culverted in 1732.
122. quasi dicat] as if one should say (Lat.), what I really meant, of course …

2. *predominate*] having prevailing influence over others (*OED* adj.).
admired] wondered at.

SC 2]   THE FAMILY OF LOVE   153

    Than able to be expressed, whose orb includes
    All terrene joys which are; all states which be,
    Pay to thy sacred throne, as tribute fee,   5
    Their thoughts and lives. Like Jove's, so must thy acts
    Endure no question — why, thy hidden facts
    The gods themselves obey; heaven synod holds
    No gods but what thy awful power controls.
    The Delphian archer, proud with Python's spoil,   10
    At Cupid's hand was forced to take the foil;
    Not Mars his warlike adamantine targe
    Could free his warlike breast at Cupid's charge;
    And Jove, whose frown all mortal lives bereaves,
    His marble throne and ivory sceptre leaves,   15
    And in the likeness of a bull was seen,
    As forced by him to bear the Tyrian queen

---

6. lives. Like] *Dyce;* liues like *Q*.   8. heaven synod] *Q (Heauen Synod);* heaven-synod *Dyce*.   12. warlike] *Q;* star-like *Dyce*.   15. His] *Dyce;* This *Q*.

---

    3. *orb*] sphere, region of action or activity (*OED* 5a).
    4. *terrene*] earthly (Dillon).
    states] ranks (*OED* state n. obs).
    7. *hidden*] secret (*OED* adj.), because immortal.
    facts] (1) deeds, exploits (*OED* n. 1a, 1b); (2) laws under Venus's jurisdiction, this sense supported by 'synod' (8).
    8. *heaven synod*] the assembly of gods in heaven (*OED* n. 2). Compare Shakespeare, *AYL* 3.2.138: 'heavenly synod'.
    10. *Delphian archer*] the god Apollo, whose oracular shrine was situated at Delphi; his weapon was the bow. See 1.2.93n.
    Python's spoil] Apollo's destruction of Python, a mythical serpent who once lived in the caves of Parnassus.
    11. *take ... foil*] accept defeat (*OED* foil n.2 2a) in the combat of love, referring to Apollo's futile pursuit of Daphne. Apollo's scorning of Cupid's prowess with arrows led Cupid to pierce him with a love-kindling dart (Ovid, *Met*. 1.452-74).
    12. *Mars his*] An example of the use of 'his' after a noun to show possession, often after a proper name, especially one ending in –s. Mars, the god of war, fell in love with Venus.
    adamantine targe] impenetrable shield.
    13. *charge*] onset, assault.
    14–18. *Jove ... kingdom*] Jove (Zeus) changed himself into a bull in order to seduce Europa.
    17. *him*] Cupid.
    Tyrian queen] Europa, daughter of Agenor, king of Tyre. See 4.4.15n.

Through Neptune's watery kingdom. If these submit,
My metamorphose is not held unfit.

Enter DRYFAT.

And see, in most wished occasion, Dryfat the merchant 20
presents himself. — Sir, in the best of hours met; my
thoughts had marked you out for a man most apt to do
them the fairest of offices.
Dryfat. What, art thou a Welsh carrier, or a northern landlord,
th'art so saucy? 25
Gerardine. Is't possible, sir, my disguise should so much fool
your knowledge? How, a northern landlord? Can you
think I get my living by a bell and a clack-dish?
Dryfat. By a bell and a clack-dish? How's that?
Gerardine. Why, by begging, sir. Know you me now? 30
Dryfat. Master Gerardine, disguised and ashore! Nay, then,
I smell a rat.
Gerardine. Master Dryfat, shall I repose some trust in you?
Will you lay by awhile your City's precise humour? Will
you not deceive me? 35
Dryfat. If I deceive your trust, the general plague seize me!
That is, may I die a cuckold.
Gerardine. And I say thou shall die a true citizen, if thou
conceal it. And thus in brief: it stands with thy knowledge

---

25. th'art] *Dillon;* thart *Q;* thou'rt *Dyce.*

---

18. *If ... submit*] (1) If these deities subjected themselves to the force of love; (2) If these gods changed themselves to pursue their love objects.

19. *metamorphose*] metamorphosis, change; i.e., Gerardine's porter's disguise. *held unfit*] viewed as indecorous.

23. *offices*] services (*OED* n. 3a).

24. *Welsh*] part of a popular tradition of anti-Welsh humour that coincided with the 'steady flow of Welsh immigrants [into England] from the second quarter of the sixteenth century' (Spufford, 183).

carrier] bearer of a message or letter.

northern landlord] (1) 'stupid bumpkin (being in the north, he is very far from court)' (Shepherd); (2) compare Barry, *Ram Alley* 5.3.165: 'That oath doth show you are a northern knight'. '"Northern" could mean "Scottish"' (Fraser, '*Ram Alley*').

27–8. *Can ... clackdish*] Do you really think I'm a beggar, clanging a bell and clacking my wooden dish to ask for alms?

34. *precise*] see 3.1.88–9n.

SC 2]   THE FAMILY OF LOVE   155

    how seriously I have and do still affect Maria. Now, sir, 40
    I have so wrought it that if thou couldst procure me a
    fellow that could serve in stead of a crier, I myself would
    play Placket the paritor, and summon Doctor Glister and
    Maria to appear at thy house, and as I play the paritor,
    so wouldst thou but assume the shape of a proctor, I 45
    should have the wench, thou the credit, and the whole
    City occasion of discourse this nine days.
Dryfat. How's this, how's this? I should procure a fellow to
    play the paritor and I myself should play the proctor —
    but upon what occasion should they be summoned? 50
Gerardine. Upon an accusation that Doctor Glister should get
    Maria his niece with child, and have bastards in the
    country — which I have a trick to make probable.
Dryfat. And now I recall it to memory, I heard somewhat to
    that effect last night in Master Beardbush the barber's 55
    shop. But how will this sort? Who shall accuse him?
Gerardine. Refer that to me, I say, be that my care; all shall

---

44. I play] *Dyce;* he plaies *Q*.   49. paritor] *Q (Parritor);* crier *Dyce*.

---

40. *affect*] love, wish to obtain (*OED* n. 3 1a).

42. *crier*] officer in a common law court of justice who makes announcements, summons the jury and witnesses, etc. (*OED* n. 1b).

43. *Placket*] A convenient folded opening in a woman's skirt or underskirt allowing her to put on and fasten her clothes, but especially as offering a man the opportunity for sexual activity by putting his hand inside (hence, in extended use) the vagina (*OED* n. 1 2). As a name for a paritor, it suggests untrustworthiness.

paritor] apparitor; a summoning officer of an ecclesiastical court (*OED* n. obs.)

45. *proctor*] (1) professional solicitor or attorney in a court of canon or (formerly) civil law (*OED* n.1 4); (2) agent, proxy (*OED* n.1 1a).

47. *nine days*] proverbial, 'A wonder lasts but nine days' (Tilley W728). Comedian Will Kemp danced a morris from London to Norwich over nine days, publicising the feat in the pamphlet *Kemp's Nine Days' Wonder* (1600).

49. *paritor*] Dyce emended to 'crier' in keeping with 41–2 of Gerardine's speech. However, Dryfat may simply be befuddled by legal terms, providing a good laugh for Inns of Court men in the audience.

50. *upon ... summoned*] 'According to canon law the spiritual courts took cognisance of all things that touched the sacraments of the church, especially marriage' (Dillon).

56. *sort*] come to effect (*OED* v. 6c).

end in merriment, and no disgrace touch either of their reputations.

Dryfat. [*Shaking hands*] Then take both word and hand, 'tis done. Club, Mistress Purge's prentice, shall be the summoner.

Gerardine. Oh, my most precious Dryfat, may none of thy daughters prove vessels with foul bungholes, or none of thy sons hogsheads, but all true and honourable Dryfats like thyself.

Dryfat. Well, Master Gerardine, I hope to see you a Familist before I die.

Gerardine. That's most likely, for I hold most of their principles already: I never rail nor calumniate any man but in love and charity; I never cozen any man for any ill will I bear him, but in love and charity to myself; I never make my neighbour a cuckold for any hate or malice I bear him, but in love and charity to his wife.

Dryfat. And may those principles fructify in your weak members. I'll be gone, and with most quick dexterity provide you a crier. Tomorrow at my house, said you, they should appear?

Gerardine. Be that the time, most honoured Dryfat. But be this known to none, most loved sir, save Club, or to some other whom your judgement shall select as a fit person for our project.

---

60. SD] *this edn; not in Q.*   62. summoner] *Q (Sumner);* crier *Dyce.*

58–9. *no ... reputations*] See 54–6 of this scene; barbers' shops were prime sources of gossip, as, for example, Cutbeard in Jonson's *Epicene.*

62. *summoner*] petty officer who cites and warns persons to appear in court (*OED* n. 1). Dyce emended to 'crier', but retaining 'summoner' is in keeping with Dryfat's confusion and excitement over his roles.

64. *bungholes*] (1) holes at which barrels are filled (Schmidt, 1.153), playing on 'dryvat'; (2) sexual orifices, vaginas, cautioning against Dryfat's daughters proving promiscuous or becoming prostitutes.

65. *hogsheads*] large casks which hold liquid measures such as beer, juxtaposed to 'dryvats' in the sense of containers that hold dry material.

67. *Familist*] (1) member of the Family of Love; (2) family man, i.e., father.

75. *fructify*] prosper, cause to bear fruit (*OED* v. 2). Compare 3.2.17n.

Dryfat. Thus, enough time. Out of sight —   *Exit.*
Gerardine. Maria, thou art mine! Earth's affection and nature's
   glory! Woman, of what an excellency if her thoughts and   85
   acts were squared and levelled with the first celsitude of
   her creation!
T'enjoy a creature whose dishevelled locks,
Like gems against the repercussive sun,
Gives light and splendour — whose star-like eyes   90
Attract more gazer-loves to see them move
Than the Tartarians' god, when first Egeon's hill

---

83. time. Out] *this edn;* time out *Q.*   sight —] *this edn;* sight. *Q.*   84. affection] *Q* (affecton*)*; perfection *Dyce.*   90. splendour — whose] *this edn;* splendor.whose *Q.*   91. gazer-loves] *Dillon;* gazar loues *Q;* gazers' love *Bullen.*   92. Tartarians'] *Q;* Titanian *Dyce.*

---

83. *enough ... sight* —] No need to think about preparations since we can do this easily by tomorrow. The audience completes the old proverb 'Out of sight [out of mind]' (Tilley S438).

84–7. *Earth's ... creation!*] 'rhythmically reminiscent of [Shakespeare], *Ham.* [2.2.259–67]': 'this goodly frame, the earth ... this most excellent canopy ... What a piece of work is a man ... in action how like an angel, in apprehension how like a god' (Shepherd). See also Cathcart, *Marston*, 109.

84. *affection*] fondness, love (*OED* n.1 2a obs.). Gerardine views Maria as the superlative love-object, the darling of the earth. Dyce's reading is defensible in terms of the Familist notion of seeking perfect love by uniting with God and joining his family. On Familist ideas of spiritual and earthly perfection, see Loewenstein, 178; and Smith, ch. 4, passim.

86. *squared*] adjusted, regulated (Schmidt, 2.1108). Compare 3.3.5n. *celsitude*] eminence (*OED* n. 1a).

86–7. *first ... creation*] woman's perfection before the Fall, comparing Maria to Eve.

89. *repercussive*] reflected (*OED* 2 obs). 'Maria's hair gives out the light as jewels reflect the sun' (Dillon).

92. *Tartarians' god*] Tartarus, son of Gaia (Earth) and Aither (Sky), father of Typhon by Gaia. Tartarus was also the name for the deepest region of the underworld. In Ovid, Pluto is called 'Tartarus' when he comes to monitor Mount Aetna ('Egeon's hill'), which shakes with earthquakes (*Met.* 5.346–58).

Egeon's] Aegaeon, or Briareus, was one of three hundred-armed, fifty-headed giants who helped Zeus vanquish the Titans, as recounted in Hesiod's *Theogony*. 'Briareus' fate was often included in ... the fate of the fire-breathing Typhoeus, who ... is commonly conceived to have been put under Aetna (*Met.* 5.346–58)' (Dillon).

Egeon's hill] Mount Aetna, in Italy.

'A mounts in triumph; a skin more pure and soft
Than is the silkworm bed; tooth more white
Than new-fallen snow or shining ivory —   95
Is happiness sought by the gods themselves.
Celestial Venus, born without a mother,
Be thou propitious! Thee do I implore,
Not vulgar Venus, heaven's scorn and Mars his whore.
                                              Exit.

ACT 4 SCENE 3

Enter MISTRESS GLISTER *and* MARIA.

Maria. Good aunt, quiet yourself. Ground not upon dreams; you know they are ever contrary.

Mistress Glister. Minion, minion, coin no excuses. I grant dreams are deceitful, but a true judgement grounded

---

94. silkworm bed] *Q;* silk-worm's bed *Dyce.* tooth] *this edn;* to the *Q;* teeth *Dyce.* 98. propitious!] *Dyce;* probitious *Q.* thee do I] *Bullen;* thee and I *Q.*

Act 4 Scene 3] *Dyce (SCENE III); not in Q.*

---

94. *silkworm bed*] silkworm's bed.
97. *Celestial Venus*] Not the sexy Aphrodite of Plato's *Symposium*, but the heavenly Aphrodite (Urania), who represented love of virtue and philosophy. Gerardine invokes the heavenly Venus, idealising his relationship with Maria.
   born ... mother] Venus risen from the sea in full form (as a woman). Invokes the myth of Venus's birth told by Hesiod in his *Theogony* (173–206), which links the goddess to the male sex life. After the Titan Cronos severed his father Uranus's genitals and threw them into the sea, Venus rose from the foam that had gathered on the surface. The Greek 'Aphrodite' means foam-born.
98. *propitious*] gracious, disposed to be favourable.
99. *vulgar Venus*] Ficino's Venus Pandemos, goddess of sensual love. Venus was trapped in a net by her husband Vulcan while making love with Mars.

1. *ground*] rely upon, especially in argument (*OED* v. 4a obs.).
3. *Minion*] term of affection, from French *mignon*, sweetheart (*OED* n.1 3a obs.).

upon knowledge never fails. What? Have not I observed the rising and falling of the blood, the coming and going of the countenance, your qualms, your unlacings, your longings, most evident tokens, besides a more certain sign than all these, too. You know't, I need not speak it. Nay, I am as skilful in that point as my husband. I can tell you Aristotle speaks English enough to tell me these secrets. Body of me, so narrowly looked to, and yet fly out? Well, I see maids will ha't. In spite of laws or locks that restrain 'em, they will open, do men what they can.

Maria. I see my fault appears; simplicity
Hath no evasion. 'Tis bootless to deny,
Where guilty blood, cited by touch of shame,
Runs through my veins, and leaves my conscience' stain
Even in my face. Forbear, I do beseech you,

---

13. ha't. In spite] *this edn;* ha' te, in spite *Q;* ha't in spite *Dyce.* 18. conscience' stain] *Dyce;* conscience stain *Q.*

5–8. *Have ... tokens*] symptoms of pregnancy.

6. *rising ... blood*] fluctuations in body temperature.

6–7. *coming ... countenance*] alternate flushing and paling of the complexion.

7. *qualms*] feelings of nausea (*OED* n.3 2).

8–9. *a more ... these*] Mistress Glister alludes to Maria's cessation of monthly periods as the most direct evidence of her pregnancy.

11–12. *Aristotle ... secrets*] Renaissance writers cited Aristotle on copious matters, but not usually on pregnancy; see e.g., Marc Antonio Zimara, *The Problems of Aristotle with Other Philosophers* (1595). Mistress Glister probably names Aristotle so as to give authority to what she is saying. For popular understandings of such women's 'secrets', see *The Birth of Mankind*, published in multiple editions between 1540 and 1654 (*The Birth of Mankind: Otherwise Named, The Woman's Book*, ed. Elaine Hobby [Farnham: Ashgate, 2009]).

12. *Body ... me*] a mild oath (*OED* body P3).
narrowly ... to] closely guarded.

12–13. *fly out*] escape (*OED* fly v.1 9c).

13. *maids ... ha't*] young women will have sex.

14. *they ... open*] open their bodies, figured as doors that men try to keep shut with 'locks' (13).

16. *bootless*] useless (*OED* adj. 3).

17. *cited*] (1) prompted, evoked (*OED* cite v. 1c); (2) in a legal sense, called to appear before a court of law (*OED* adj. 1).

To publish my defame. What I have done 20
You shall not answer. I must bear mine own.
Mistress Glister. Bear your own? Ay, marry, there it goes —
what must you bear?
Maria. My sins, forsooth.
Mistress Glister. Your sins, forsooth. Confess to me, and go 25
not about the bush. You have been doing, that's flat; you
have caught a clap, that's round; and answer me roundly
to the point, or else I'll square. Come, whose act is't? I
cannot devise, unless it be my husband's, for none else
had access to thee. I am sure time has turned his bald 30
side to thee, and I do but wonder how thou tookst opportunity. Speak, tell me.
Maria. Now, good aunt, press me not, let time reveal
What you suspect, for never shall my tongue
Confess an act that tends unto my wrong. 35

Enter GERARDINE *like a porter.*

Mistress Glister. Will you not bolt? I must ha't out on you, and
will.
Gerardine. By your leave, mistress —
Mistress Glister. Passion of my heart, what art thou?
Gerardine. No ghost, forsooth, though I appear in white. 40
Mistress Glister. No, but a saucy knave, I perceive by your
manner.

---

20. *publish ... defame*] make public my disgrace.
21–3. *bear ... bear?*] puns on 'bear', meaning: (1) carry the blame (*OED* v. 7c); (2) endure the 'shame' (17) of an illegitimate pregnancy (*OED* v. 15a–c); (3) give birth to a child (*OED* v. 43a).
25–6. *go ... bush*] tell your mind freely without circumlocution, inverting the proverb 'To beat (go) about the bush' (Tilley B742).
26. *doing*] copulating.
27. *clap*] (1) gonorrhoea (*OED* n.2 a); (2) sudden mishap (*OED* n. 6 fig. obs.).
round] (1) of assertion: incontrovertible; (2) anticipating Maria's pregnant belly.
roundly] directly (*OED* adj. 4a obs.).
28. *square*] quarrel; compare Shakespeare, *MND* 2.1.28–30: 'now they never meet in grove or green ... / But they do square'.
30–2. *bald ... opportunity*] See 3.1.2n.
36. *bolt*] blurt out (*OED* v.2 5).
41. *saucy knave*] cheeky rascal.

Gerardine. None of that livery, neither. I am of the bearing
trade, forsooth, you may see by my smock — frock, I
would say. I am, if it please you, of the spick-and-span   45
new-set-up company of Porters. Here's my breastplate,
and besides our own arms we have the arms of the City
to help us in our burdens — *ecce signum!* Here's the cross
and the sword of justice in good pewter, I can tell you,
which goes as current with us as better metal.   50
Mistress Glister. What's your name, sir?
Gerardine. Nicholas Nebulo. There's but a straw's breadth
between that and the arms. 'Tis in the back side of the

---

48. burdens — *ecce*] Dyce; burthens, *Ecce* Q.   *signum!*] Dyce; *siguum* Q.

44. *forsooth*] in truth, truly (*OED* adv.), a mild oath. On the early modern stage, the word is associated with a studied innocence and humility, to the extent that Jonson uses it as the mark of an affected speaker in his 'Private Entertainment at Highgate' (1604): 'You sip so like a forsooth of the city' (line 218). The phrases 'forsooth' and 'your worship' (55) are as much a part of Gerardine's low-status disguise as a porter as his 'frock' (44) and 'dirty startups' (60).

smock] (1) staple women's undergarment, 'loose, wide, long-sleeved and ankle-length', Ewing, 24–5, figures 38–9; (2) womankind, punning on 'bearing' (43) in the senses of 'carrying' and 'giving birth to'.

frock] long habit or mantle worn chiefly by men in this period (*OED* 2); compare Shakespeare, *Ham.* 3.4.165: 'a frock or livery'. The three porters in the woodcut that accompanies the ballad 'in commendation of the ... company of the Porters' wear frocks of this kind (figure 2).

45. *spick-and-span*] proverbial: 'spick-and-span-new' (Dent S748).
46. *new-set-up*] recently established.
company ... Porters] See above 1.3.107–8n.
breastplate] See the ballad in commendation of the Company of Porters (1605): 'marks of admittance / Made out of tin, they bear / About their necks in ribbons' (cited in Maxwell, 'Date', 199).

47–8. *besides ... ecce signum!*] Lat., 'Behold the sign!' (proverbial, Tilley S443). Gerardine shows his coat of arms: 'the porters ... use [the arms] of the City of London, whence their authority arises' (Hazlitt, cited in Maxwell, 'Date', 198).

52. *Nicholas Nebulo*] (1) Gerardine is veiled by his disguise (Lat., *nebulosus*, foggy); (2) a 'precise parallel with the character of Nicholas Nifle in the Cambridge comedy, *Club Law*, the first names of both characters referencing the surname of Hendrik Niclaes, Familism's founder' (Cathcart, '*Club Law*', 67).

53. *back side ... cross*] (1) the bottom or 'base' part of the shield bearing the coat of arms (*OED* base n.1 5), here divided by a 'cross' into four quarters; (2) obvious pun, anticipating Gerardine being 'bummed' at 4.3.81–3.

cross here, and well known in the City for an ancient
name, and an honest, an't like your worship.   55
Maria. You are none of the twelve, are you?
Gerardine. No, forsooth, but one of the twenty-four —
Mistress Glister. Orders of knaves. I thought so. Sirrah, you're
a rascal, to come thus bluntly into my house with your
dirty startups. Get you without doors like a filthy fellow   60
as you are, a place more fit for you.
Gerardine. Oh, good words, mistress. I may be warden of my
company for aught you know, and for my bluntness, we
have a clause in our charter to warrant that for as we bear,
so likewise we may be borne with, and have free egress   65
and regress where our business lies.
Mistress Glister. And what's your business here?
Gerardine. I have a letter, an't please you, to master doctor.
Mistress Glister. From whence?
Gerardine. That I cannot show your worship, but I had it of   70
Curtal the carrier, whose lawful deputy I am.

[GERARDINE *bows obsequiously.*]

---

56. SH] *Q* (*Mar.*); MIS. G *Dyce.*

---

56. *twelve*] The number of livery companies of London, known as the Great Twelve.

57. *twenty-four*] The number of 'brethren' or junior members in the City Corporation of London, which comprised the mayor, aldermen and brethren, sometimes known as the 'Four and Twenty' (Moore Smith, xxvi–xxvii; *OED* brother n. 6b).

58. *Orders ... knaves*] 'Awdeley in his *Fraternity of Vagabonds* (1595) reckons up twenty-five orders of knaves; Harman in his *Caveat for Cursitors* (1567) gives the number at twenty-three' (Bullen).

60. *startups*] (1) boots made of rough leather worn, as here, by working men or clowns (Linthicum, 258–9); (2) upstarts (*OED* n. 2 obs.).

62. *warden*] member of a governing body or a guild, especially in the livery companies of the City of London (*OED* n. 5).

64. *charter*] constitution of a livery company (*OED* n. 1c).

70. *That ... worship*] because, as Mistress Glister finds out at 96–7, the letter purports to come from the wet nurse of Glister's bastard. Dyce adds '*Taking the letter*' at 69, but the actor playing Gerardine may determine when (before 96) he hands over the incriminating letter.

71. *Curtal*] a horse with its tail cut short or docked (*OED* n. 1, 2a); Gerardine chooses a name with overtones of abasement, suitable to the menial occupations of a carrier (4.2.24n) and porter.

SC 3]   THE FAMILY OF LOVE   163

Mistress Glister. Leave your scraping, sirrah. Fie, how rank the
    knave smells of grease and taps-droppings.

           GERARDINE *coughs and spits.*

Mistress Glister. What, are you rheumatic, too, with a vengeance?
Gerardine. Yes, indeed, mistress. Though I be but a poor   75
    man, I have a spice of the gentleman in me; master doctor
    could smell it quickly, because he's a gentleman himself.
    I must to the diet, and that is tobacco at the alehouse; I
    use n'other physic for it.
Mistress Glister. Did ever such a peasant defile my floor, or   80
    breathe so near me! — I'faith, sirrah, you would be
    bummed for your roguery if you were well served.
Gerardine. I am bummed well enough already, mistress. Look
    here else: [*Offering his bum to Mistress Glister*] sir-rever-
    ence in your worship, master doctor's lips are not made   85
    of better stuff.
Mistress Glister. What an impudent rogue is this! — Sirrah be
    gone, I say, I would be rid o'you!
Gerardine. Be rid o'me? I shall gallop, then. You mistake me,
    forsooth; I am a foot post. I do not use to ride.   90

71.1. SD] *this edn; not in* Q. 73.1. SD] Q *(Ger.* Coughes and spitts *in left margin)*. 84. SD] *this edn; not in* Q. 90. foot post] *Dyce;* footpost Q.

---

72. *scraping*] bobbing in obsequious bows, drawing the leg back noisily (*OED* scrape v. 8a obs.); compare *1st Pt. Return from Parnassus* (1600), Prol. 2: 'That scraping leg, that dopping curtsy', *The Three Parnassus Plays*, ed. J. B. Leishman (London: Nicholson and Watson, 1949).
73. *taps-droppings*] ale; Barry's coinage.
74. *rheumatic*] full of phlegm; specifically, in light of 'humorous' (83), afflicted by a flow or flux (of humours) (*OED* rheum n.1 1a, obs.).
78. *diet*] See 1.3.4n.
82. *bummed*] 1) beaten, especially as a punishment (*OED* v.3 obs., citing this usage); (2) padded out to give a rounded appearance to (*OED* v. 4 obs.).
84. SD] 'Gerardine ... offers his buttocks for Mistress Glister to kiss' (Cleary).
84–5. *sir-reverence*] (1) with apologies to; a corruption of 'save your reverence' (*OED* 1b obs.); (2) catch-phrase uttered when one comes upon a lump of human excrement (*OED* 2a).
88. *o'you!*] of you!
89. *Be ... gallop*] if you want to ride me in sex, I'm off.
90. *foot post*] person employed to deliver messages or letters on foot (*OED* n.1).
    I ... ride] I am not accustomed to ride (*OED* use v. 20c regional).

Mistress Glister. I think the rascal be humorous or drunk. Well,
    I will read the letter and send him packing, or else he will
    spew or do worse before me. Fie on him, I think he will
    infect me with some filthy disease.
Gerardine. [*Aside*] Or else I lose mine aim.   95
Mistress Glister. What's here? [*Reads*] 'Your poor nurse
    Thomasine Tweedles' — for my life, now shall I find out
    my husband's knavery I have so long suspected.
Gerardine. [*Aside*] She begins to nibble; 'twill take, i'faith.
    [*To Maria*] Mistress,   100
    I see some discontentment in your looks.
    Care ill befits so delicate a spirit.
    Be frolic, wench, for he that is so near thee
    Has been much nearer.
Maria. That accent sounds sweet music — 'tis my love!   105
    That tongue breathes life into my lifeless spirits.
    Gerardine? Oh rapture, why thus disguised?

---

95. SD] *Dyce; not in Q.*   96. SD] *Dyce; not in Q.*   97. Tweedles] *Dyce;* Sweedlesse *Qq.*   99. SD] *Dyce; not in Q.*   99–100. SD] *this edn; not in Q.*   106. lifeless] *Dyce;* liueles *Q.*

---

91. *humorous*] (1) fractious, bad-tempered (*OED* 3a 3b); (2) literally moist; possible effluvia associated with Gerardine as Nicholas Nebulo are sweat, saliva, catarrh, vomit, and excrement (*OED* 2). Paster's point ('Humor', 58–9) that in the Renaissance, 'humoral textualization tend[ed] to reproduce – and thus to biologize – prevailing narratives of social difference' (as in Shakespeare's portrayal of Christopher Sly as a 'sodden, lethargic tinker') illuminates Gerardine's impersonation of a boorish porter.

95. *mine aim*] Gerardine's wish to make Mistress Glister mad with jealousy (Dillon).

97. *Thomasine*] may invoke Thomasine Breame, one of a network of London prostitutes targeted by the governors of Bridewell prison in the late 1570s. Ian W. Archer classes her among women 'who rented themselves out as private mistresses forming long-term liaisons, although often residing within a brothel' (*The Pursuit of Stability: Social Relations in Elizabethan London* [Cambridge: Cambridge University Press, 1991], 213, 38n). Middleton's *Michaelmas Term* (1604, pub. 1607) features the wife of a woollen draper, Thomasine Quomodo.

Tweedles] Barry developed this name from the piper 'Timothy Tweedle' in Marston's *JDE*. Johnson's *Dictionary* offers the following gloss on the variant 'twidle': 'To touch lightly. A low word' (Johnson, 1755, *LEME*). The verb implies both musical and sexual fingering.

103. *frolic*] merry.

104. *much nearer*] i.e., when they made love.

Gerardine. No more, be mute. Thus must I vary forms
   To bring our cares to end. Her jealousy
   Ensues this drift, which, if it take true scope,   110
   Love's joy comes next. Be fearless in that hope.
Mistress Glister. 'Tis so. Rats-bane! I ha't, it racks on, it tor-
   ments me! Here 'tis: — *Woe worth the time that ever I gave*
   suck to a child that came in at the window, God knows how
   — villainous lecher! — *Yet if thou did but see how like the*   115
   pert little red-headed knave is to his father — damnable
   doctor! A bastard in the country, and another towards
   here. I am out of doubt this is his work. [*To Maria*] You
   are an arrant strumpet. — Incest, fornication, abomina-
   tion in my own house! Intolerable. Oh, for long nails to   120
   scratch out his eyes!
Gerardine. Or the breeches to fight with him.

---

109. end. Her] *this edn;* end her *Q;* end: her *Dyce.*   111. next. Be] *this edn;* next be *Q.*   112. ha't, it] *Dillon;* hate, it *Q.*   113. 'tis: — *Woe*] *this edn;* 'tis: [*reads*] *Woe Dyce.*   116. the pert little] *Dyce;* the little *Q.*   118. SD] *this edn;* not in *Q.*

---

110. *ensues*] follows from.
   drift] plot, design (*OED* 5, obs.).
113. Woe worth] May a curse be on (*OED* worth v.1 P2.a. arch.).
114. child ... window] common euphemism for bastard (Bullen).
115–16. how like ... father] how much he resembles Glister in looks and nature: on the implications of the child's red hair, see below, 5.1.13n.
116. knave] (1) boy (*OED* 1 obs.); (2) wag, rascal (*OED* 3b arch.).
117. towards] on the way, alluding to Maria's pregnancy.
118. *I ... doubt*] I have no doubt.
119. *arrant*] downright (*OED* adj. 3a).
122. breeches] (1) marker of growth from a male child wearing a shift to an age, usually around 6 years old, when he was assumed to be toilet-trained, and was then 'breeched', or rewarded with adult clothing; (2) courage, mastery: 'to wear the breeches' was to assume the authority of the husband (*OED* breech n. 2a obs). See Natalie Zemon Davis, 'Woman on Top: Symbolic Sexual Inversion and Political Disorder in Early Modern Europe', in B. Babcock (ed.), *The Reversible World: Symbolic Inversion in Arts and Society* (Ithaca, NY: Cornell University Press, 1978), 148–83.

Mistress Glister. Out of my sight, quean, thou shalt to
   Bridewell! — Oh, I shall be mad with rage!
Gerardine. Then you shall go to Bedlam.   125
Mistress Glister. Hence, you slave.
Gerardine. I must have a penny, you must pay me for my
   pains.
Mistress Glister. The devil pay thee!
Gerardine. Oh, that's the doctor; but he wants his horns.   130
Mistress Glister. But I'll furnish him ere long, if I live.
Gerardine. [*Aside*] It works as I would wish. — Farewell,
      Maria,
   This storm once past, fair weather ever after.   *Exit.*
Mistress Glister. Was ever woman so moved! But you shall be
   talked withal, and for mine old fornicator, he shall ha't   135
   as hot as coals, i'faith. Here's stuff, indeed! Come, minx,
   come, there's law for you both. Have I found your
   knavery? If I wink at this, let me be stone-blind, or stoned
   to death. Bear this, and bear all.   *Exeunt.*

---

132. SD] *Dyce; not in Q.*   133. SD] *Dyce; Exeunt Q.*

---

123. *quean*] whore (*OED* n. 1).
124. *Bridewell*] 'a workhouse, a prison and a place where whipping and hard labour as a means of "correction" were administered', especially for sexual transgressors; Martin Ingram, *Carnal Knowledge: Regulating Sex in England 1470–1600* (Cambridge: Cambridge University Press, 2017), 355.
125. *Bedlam*] familiar name of Bethlem Hospital, founded as a priory in 1247. Located near Bishopsgate, the building transitioned to an institution for those judged insane at the start of the fifteenth century. 'Bedlam' scenes feature in Dekker and Middleton's *Honest Whore, Pt. 1* (1604) and Dekker and Webster's *NHo!* (1607).
130. *wants*] lacks.
   his] i.e., the devil's.
131. *furnish him*] supply Glister with cuckolds' horns.
133.] See 2.4.41n.
135. *talked*] (1) scolded, reprimanded (*OED* talk v. 3a colloq.); (2) gossiped about (*OED* talk 3b).
   withal] in consequence of this matter (Schmidt, 2.1383, withal 1).
135–6. *he ... coals*] he'll receive the full force of my fury.
138. *stone blind*] (1) completely blind; (2) sexually unaware (Shepherd).
138–9. *stoned ... death*] play on the sex–death nexus, 'stone' meaning 'testicle' (Williams, *Dictionary*, stone 3.1322).
139. *Bear ... all*] If I tolerate this outrage, I'll have to tolerate anything.

ACT 4 SCENE 4

Enter LIPSALVE *and* GUDGEON [*with* SHRIMP *and* PERIWINKLE].

Lipsalve. Our hopes are crossed. Sure there's some providence
Which countermands libidinous appetites,
For what we most intend is counterchecked
By strange and unexpected accidents;
For, by disguise procuring full access, 5
Nay, ready to have feared th'expected prize,
The candle out, steps 'twixt my hopes and me
Some pleasant groin, possessed and full enjoyed
That sweet for which our vigilant eyes have watched,
And in one moment frustrates all our hopes. 10
Gudgeon. Upon my life, we are bewitched. The greasy rascal that first seized Mistress Purge, by the last reflection of the light appeared to my sight not much unlike her husband.

Act 4 Scene 4] *Dyce (SCENE IV); not in Q.* 0.1–2. SD] *this edn;* Enter Lypsalue and Gudgin. *Q.* 6. feared] *Q (*feard*);* seized *Dyce.* 8. pleasant] *Q;* peasant *Dyce.* groin] *Q (*Groine*);* groom *Dyce.*

---

2. *countermands*] obstructs.
3. *counterchecked*] stopped by counteraction (*OED* v. 2).
5. *full access*] i.e., to the Familist meeting.
6. *feared*] inspired with fear, terrified (*OED* fear v. 1a), as a rapist might treat his victim. Following Dyce, Dillon explains 'feard' as a compositorial error for 'seiz'd' (4.4.6n). However, Q's reading, together with Lipsalve's metaphor of Mistress Purge as booty or 'prize' (6), makes clear his naked aggression. See Introduction, 22–3.
th'expected prize] Mistress Purge.
8. *pleasant*] boisterous or excited from drinking alcohol (*OED* adj. 4b. obs., citing Raleigh, *Discovery Guiana*, 1596: 'Some of our captains caroused of his wine till they were reasonable pleasant').
groin] contemptuously, face, an obsolete usage (*OED* n.1). Dyce emended 'pleasant groin' to 'peasant groom', when Q means something like 'drunken prick'.

Lipsalve. The court's gall, the City's plague, and Europa's   15
sea-form be his perpetual crest, what e'er 'a was. To lose
Mistress Purge for lack of dexterity is a disgrace insalvable. The like opportunity will never present itself.
Gudgeon. 'Twas an egregious grief, I must confess, to see a
knave slip betwixt us both and take occasion by the   20
foretop, but since these projects have had so star-crossed
events, let's lay some plot how to revenge our late disgrace on the doctor by making him a cuckold.

Enter PURGE.

Lipsalve. Agreed, but what melancholy sir with acrostic arms
now comes from the Family?   25
Gudgeon. Purge, the pothecary. I prithee, let's step aside and
hear the issue of this discontent.

[*They step aside with the pages.*]

Purge. Oh, the misery of married men's estate!
Lipsalve. [*Aside*] 'A begins very pitifully.
Purge. Oh, women, what are many of you?   30
Lipsalve. [*Aside*] Why, disease to bachelors and plagues to
married men.

---

21. star-crossed] *Dyce;* star crosse *Q.*   24. acrostic] *Dyce;* a crostick *Q.*
27.1. SD] *Dillon;* They retire with the two pages. *Dyce.*   29. SD] *Dyce; not in Q.*   31. SD] *Dyce; not in Q.*   31. disease] *Q;* disease[s] *Dyce.*

15–16. *The court's ... crest*] While adultery is a 'gall' or annoyance at court, it reaches epidemic proportions in the City, not least through the predatory approaches to citizen wives made by courtiers such as Lipsalve.

Europa's sea-form] The broad-backed bull sent or inhabited by Zeus, who fell in love with Europa after sighting her playing on the beach. Enticed by the animal's mildness to climb on its back, Europa was borne across the sea to Crete, where Zeus made love to her. Modified by 'perpetual crest' (16), 'sea-form' signifies the (bull's) horns, from 'form' meaning 'bench' (*OED* form n. 17).

17–18. *insalvable*] impossible to remedy (*OED* salve v.1 3a fig.).

20–1. *occasion ... foretop*] akin to grasping opportunity by the forelock. See notes to 3.1.2 and 4.3.31–2.

21. *star-crossed*] obstructed by the heavens. Compare Shakespeare, *R&J* Prol. 6: 'A pair of star-crossed lovers'.

24. *acrostic*] crossed, folded across (*OED* adj.2).

28. *estate*] (1) lot, situation; (2) condition of existence (*OED* n. 1b).

31. *disease*] i.e., bringers of venereal disease.

plagues] disasters.

SC 4] THE FAMILY OF LOVE 169

Purge. O marriage, the rage of all our miseries! My wife is a dissembling strumpet.

Gudgeon. [*Aside*] So is many a man's besides yours, and what of that? 35

Purge. I would have a law that all such which pray little should instantly be married, for then would they pray continually, if it were but to be rid of their wives.

Lipsalve. [*Aside*] This is a charitable request, and surely would pass the lower house. 40

Purge. Surely, if affliction can bring a man to heaven, I cannot see how any married man can be damned. I have made myself a plain cuckold.

[*Gudgeon.*] [*Aside*] A pile on ye, want you? Had you not been so manable, here are some would have saved you that labour. 45

Purge. What shall I do in this extremity? Had I but witness of the fact, I would make her answer it before authority. This is my wedding ring. 'Tis it, I know it by the posy. This I took from her finger in the dark, and she was therewith very well pleased. Were not this, trow, a sufficient testimony? She knows not that it was myself got so near her. I will take counsel. Well, little know bachelors 50

---

35. SD] *Dyce; not in Q.* 40. SD] *Dyce; not in Q.* 45. SH] *Dyce; not in Q.* 45. SD] *Dyce; not in Q.* 45. want you?] *Q;* won't you! *Dyce.* 50. 'Tis it] *this edn;* Tis hit *Q.*

---

34. *dissembling strumpet*] hypocritical, lying whore.

41. *lower house*] the House of Commons, which in 1604 was drawing up a code of ecclesiastical law (Shepherd).

44. *plain*] (1) complete (*OED* adj.1 obs.); (2) clear.

45. *pile*] (1) haemorrhoid; (2) heraldic design of two diagonal lines meeting in a downward point like a V, hence horns (Shepherd).

want you?] So you want to preserve your family as a gentleman's estate, and look where that got you – cuckold's horns!

46. *manable*] old enough to marry and seduce women (*OED* adj. citing this usage); (2) manlike, 'able-to-be-a-man' (Dillon).

51. *posy*] emblem, inscription (*OED* n. 1).

51–2. *she ... pleased*] she was very pleased by my doing so.

52. *trow*] don't you think? (direct address to the audience). Compare 2.1.12–19, 3.2.105–6.

53. *testimony*] evidence of Mistress Purge's adulterous inclinations.

the miseries they undergo when they prostrate themselves 55
to women.

[Lipsalve and Gudgeon come forward.]

Lipsalve. Oh, most true, Master Purge, little knows a man
what elements 'a is to pass when 'a puts his head under
a woman's girdle. Your passion, Master Purge, is overheard and, plain tale to tell, we were eyewitnesses of your 60
wife's treachery, and if need be will be ready to depose
as much.
Purge. What, Master Lipsalve and Master Gudgeon, are you
disguised testimonies?
    Nay then, Revenge, look big; elf and fairy 65
    Help to revenge the wrongèd pothecary!
Gudgeon. Why, now 'a speaks like himself, get me a paritor
for her straight.
Lipsalve. Conceal the ring, my little Purge; let not thy wife
know thou hast it until she comes to her trial. 70

Enter DRYFAT *and* GERARDINE *[disguised as a paritor].*

56.1. SD] *Dillon; not in* Q.   65. Nay ... big] *verse in Dyce; prose in* Q.   70.1.
SD] *Dyce (subst); Enter Drifat and Gerardine.* Q.

55–6. *prostrate ... women*] (1) submit to women's wills, by marrying; (2) lewdly, assume a face-down position for sexual (or anal) intercourse.

58–9. *puts ... girdle*] subjects himself to a woman's control (*OED* girdle n.1 1c). Compare Barry, *Ram Alley* 3.4.62: 'Creep under my mistress' farthingale'.

58. *elements*] liquids and smells emitted from women's sexual organs. Compare Barry, *Ram Alley* 3.4.65–6: 'Stir not, whate'er you hear, / See, or smell'.

pass] go or travel into (*OED* v. 9b).

59. *passion*] passionate outburst (*OED* n. 6c 6d obs.).

60. *plain ... tell*] to speak frankly.

61. *depose*] testify, esp. give evidence under oath in a court of law (*OED* v. 5a).

64. *disguised*] concealed.
testimonies] witnesses.

65. *big*] See 3.1.111n.

elf ... fairy] supernatural beings, invoked here for their malevolent powers.

68. *straight*] immediately.

Purge. Your advices are very pithy; therefore, in private let me
   disclose my intent.
Gudgeon. Off, boys!

   [*Purge, Lipsalve, and Gudgeon move to one side of
                       the stage.*]

[*Shrimp.*] What dost thou think of thy master? Is 'a not a rare
   gull?   75
Periwinkle. I think 'a will swallow and pocket more disgraces
   than large cozening-lawyer fees in a Michaelmas term.
   Thy master, my honest Shrimp, comes not much short
   of a fool too, but that 'a is a courtier.
Shrimp. Draw somewhat near, and overhear their conference!   80

   [*They go and eavesdrop upon their masters.*]

Gerardine. This shape of the crier must Club tomorrow
   assume. Are you fitted for Poppin the proctor?

73.1–2. SD] *Dillon; not in* Q.   74. SH *Shrimp*] *Dyce; misplaced in* Q *following*
67.   77. large cozening-lawyer] *this edn;* large cousenst Lawyer *Q;* large-
conscienced lawyer *Dyce.*   78. *Shrimp*] *Dyce;* Periwincle *Q.*   80.1. SD] *this
edn; not in* Q.   82. Poppin] *Qu (*Popin*); Exigent Qc.*

---

   73. *Off boys!*] Temporarily there are three separate groups onstage.
   76. *swallow*] tolerate, digest. Sustains the bird image of Shrimp's 'gull'
(75), highlighting Gudgeon's 'oral appetitiveness' (Paster, 'Purgation', 194).
   77. *than ... fees*] than the huge fees charged by a trickster lawyer.
   large] (1) great in size, more than a small quantity of (*OED* adj. 2 obs.);
(2) extravagant (*OED* adj. 1. Scottish).
   cozening-lawyer] See Middleton, *Michaelmas Term*, 2.3.485–6: 'Admire
me, all you students at Inns of Cozenage'. Dyce emended Q's 'large cousenst' to 'large-conscienced', assuming (as does Dillon) that the 'u' in 'cousenst' was a turned 'n'. But a compositor's eye-skipping to 'honest' could
explain why the word was set with a terminal 'st'.
   Michaelmas term] period of court sessions beginning 1 October, after the
summer recess. As the first term of the legal year, Michaelmas was assumed to
be especially busy. Compare Michaelmas Term's anticipation of the riches he
will reap by 'this silver harvest, Law', Middleton, *Michaelmas Term*, Ind. 10.
   82. *Poppin*] (1) English regional usage for 'puppet', fitting Dryfat's impersonation of a proctor (*OED* n. obs.); (2) echoes the surname of Sir John
Popham, the Lord Chief Justice, who died in June 1607. He had a reputation
as being both severe and scrupulously fair (*ODNB*). On Wiggins's theory
that the correction of 'Poppin' to 'Exigent' in some copies of Q is evidence
of censorship, see Introduction, 6–7; (3) person who goes somewhere ('pops
in') quickly or unexpectedly, esp. for a short time (*OED* pop v. 3a), perhaps
alluding to Dryfat's infiltration of a Familist meeting in 3.2.

Dryfat. Excellent, and have spent some study in the mystical cases of venery. I can describe how often a man may lie with another man's wife, before 'a come to the white sheet. 85

Gerardine. How long is that?

Dryfat. Why, till 'a be taken tardy — how long all womenkind may by the statute profess and swear they are maids.

Gerardine. And how long is that? 90

Dryfat. Why, till their bellies be so big that it cannot be no longer concealed. But come forward towards Glister's.

Lipsalve. [*To Purge*] It must be so. Let the summoner tickle her, you shall bring in these allegations, and let us alone to swear them. [*Advancing with Purge and Gudgeon*] 95 Who's this? Master Dryfat? Opportunely met, sir; and whither so fast? The news, the news?

Dryfat. Faith, gentlemen, I think to relate for news what I hear of Doctor Glister would come stale to your hearings.

Lipsalve. Oh, the getting of his niece with child? Tut, that's 100 apparently known to all the company. — [*To Gerardine*] But in the name of Jupiter, what art thou? Or from whence camest thou?

Gerardine. Why, sir, I come from compassing the corners of the land. 105

---

88. tardy — how] *this edn;* tardy: — how *Dyce;* tardy. / How *Q.*   93. SD] *this edn; not in Q.*   95. SD] *Dyce; Lipsalve, Purge, and Gudgeon move to greet Dryfat and Gerardine Dillon; not in Q.*   101. SD] *this edn; not in Q.*

---

84. *venery*] indulgence of sexual desire (*OED* n.2 1).

85–6. *white sheet*] worn in public as penance for fornication or adultery. See G. R. Quaife, *Wanton Wenches and Wayward Wives: Peasants and Illicit Sex in Early Seventeenth-Century England* (London: Croom Helm, 1979), 92–5.

88. *taken tardy*] detected (*OED* tardy adj. 2a obs.).

89. *by ... statute*] strictly, by fixed rule (*OED* statute n. P1 obs.).

91. *it*] i.e., the women's pregnancies.

93. *tickle*] (1) incite, provoke (*OED* 7a, 7b); (2) chastise (*OED* 6b. iron.); (3) gratify. Compare Chaucer's Summoner, who is 'lecherous as a sparrow' ('Gen. Prol.', 626).

102–6. *in ... Jupiter ... Pluto*] Compare Barry, *Ram Alley* 4.2.134: 'By Dis'; conventional mockery of oaths (Shepherd).

102. *Jupiter*] king of the classical gods.

104–5.] Compare Job 1.7: 'Then the Lord said unto Satan, "Whence commest thou?" And Satan answered the Lord ... "From compassing the earth to and fro, and from walking in it."'

Gudgeon. Of what trade, in the name of Pluto?
Gerardine. Of the devil's trade, for I live as he does, by the sins of the people. In brief, sir, I am Placket, the paritor.
Lipsalve. As the devil would, we have, my noble paritor, instant employment for thee. A grey groat is to be purchased without sneaking, my little summoner. Where's thy *quorum nomina*, my honest Placket? 110
Gerardine. Sir, according to the old ballad,
    My quorum nomina *ready have I,*
    With my pen and ink-horn hanging by. 115
Her name, sir, her name?
Gudgeon. Is't no more but so?
Purge. I have most right to her name. Her name, Master Placket, is my wife, Mistress Purge. Sir, to what place dost thou belong? 120
Gerardine. To the commissioners, which sit tomorrow at Master Dryfat's upon the crimes of Doctor Glister and others.
Lipsalve. Sits there a commission, Dryfat? Now for the love of lechery let's have Mistress Purge summoned thither. 125

114–15.] *verse as in Dyce; prose in* Q.   124. SH] *printed in full* Q.

106. *Pluto*] king of the classical underworld.

108. *sins ... people*] Compare the character of an apparitor, Overbury, 235–6: 'There went but a pair of shears between him and the pursuivant of hell, for they both delight in sin, grow richer by it, and are by justice appointed to punish it.'

110–11. *A ... summoner*] Here's a chance to earn some change without stealing on the sly, as you summoners do. A groat was a silver coin worth fourpence; a 'grey groat' means a trivial sum (*OED* grey adj. C1c (a)). Compare Marlowe, *JM* 4.2.115: 'I'll not leave him worth a grey groat'. See also below, 165n.

112. quorum nomina] list of names (Lat.); legal tag.

114–15.] Cited from the ballad 'The Paritor and the Devil'; see J.W. Ebsworth, *The Roxburgh Ballads*, vol. 9 (Hertford: Ballad Society of S. Austin, 1895), xxxvii.

115. pen] allusion to male genitals; 'pen' = penis.
 ink-horn] small portable vessel (originally made of a horn) for holding writing ink (*OED*).

119–20. *Sir ... belong?*] What is your role in this business?

121. *commissioners*] (1) magistrates, Justices of the Peace; (2) ecclesiastical officials (deacons etc.) who judge sexual crimes.

174   THE FAMILY OF LOVE   [ACT 4

Gerardine. She makes my *quorum nomina* reasonable full. My grant, sir, and she shall appear there upon a crime of concupiscence. Is not that your meaning?
Purge. Yes, my honest paritor, here's thy fee.

Enter CLUB *and* MISTRESS PURGE.

Gudgeon. And see how happily it succeeds; Mistress Purge is new come from the Family. Let us step aside whilst Placket the paritor gives her a summons.   130
Lipsalve. Content. — To her, Placket. But see for the bribery of twelvepence you strike her not out of your *quorum nomina.*
Gerardine. Fear not, sir.   135

[*Lipsalve, Gudgeon, Purge, and Dryfat move aside.*]

Mistress Purge. Forward apace, Club.
Gerardine. Your name I take to be Mistress Purge, fair gentlewoman.
Mistress Purge. I am Mistress Purge, Purge's wife, the pothecary. What of that?   140
Dryfat. [*Aside*] Now you shall see him tickle her with a *quorum nomina.*
Gerardine. I cite you by virtue of my *quorum nomina* to make your personal appearance by eight of the clock in the morrow morning before certain commissioners at Master Dryfat's house to answer to an accusation of a crime of concupiscence!   145
Mistress Purge. To answer a crime of concupiscence? What's that, I pray?

---

133. SH] *printed in full* Q.   135.1. SD] *Dillon;* LIPSALVE, GUDGEON, PURGE, *and* DRYFAT *retire. Dyce.*   141. SD] *Dyce; not in* Q.

126–7. *My ... there*] Give me my fee, if you want to see her appear in court. Q's 'and' may result from a compositor correcting 'an' in the sense of 'if'.
127. *grant*] a gift of money (*OED* n.1 3a).
concupiscence] sensual appetite, lust (*OED* n. 2a).
133–4. *bribery ... twelvepence*] See Chaucer, 'Friar's Tale', 1598–9: 'pay anon ... / Twelf pens to me, and I wol thee acquite'.
134. *twelvepence*] a shilling (*OED* n. obs.). James I issued a new coin worth this amount in November 1604 (Shepherd).

SC 4]   THE FAMILY OF LOVE   175

Gerardine. Why, 'tis to answer a venereal crime, for having   150
    carnal copulation with others beside your husband.
Mistress Purge. What are you, I pray?
Gerardine. By name, Placket; by trade, a paritor.
Mistress Purge. And must I answer, say you, to a venereal
    crime? I tell thee, Placket the paritor, I am able to answer   155
    thee, or any man else in any venereal crime they'll put
    me to. And so tell your commissioners!
Gerardine. If you fail your appearance, the penalty must fall
    heavy.
Mistress Purge. If it fall never so heavy, I am able to bear it.   160
    — And so, set forward, Club.
                            Exeunt CLUB *and* MISTRESS PURGE.
Lipsalve. [*Coming forward*] Excellent, i'faith! — After your
    wife, Purge.
                                                    [*Exit* PURGE]
    [*To Gerardine*] Read, Placket, thy *quorum nomina*, my
    noble groat-monger.   165
Gerardine. Silence! The first that marcheth in this fair rank is
    Thrum the feltmaker, for getting his maid with child and
    sending his prentice to Bridewell for the fact; Whip the
    beadle, for letting a punk escape for a night's lodging,

161.1. SD] *Q; Exit with* CLUB *Dyce.*   162. SD] *Dillon; not in Q.*   163.1.
SD] *this edn; following 165 Dyce; not in Q.*   164. SD] *this edn; not in Q.*
167. Thrum] *Dyce; Thum Q.*

---

150. *venereal*] relating to sexual desire or intercourse (*OED* adj. 1);
derived from 'Venus'.

155. *answer*] (1) reply to (*OED* v. 1c); (2) make a rejoinder to a superior
(*OED* v. 4); (3) fulfil desires expressed by (*OED* v. 5a).

158. *fail ... appearance*] fail to appear as summoned.

160. *If ... it*] alluding to a woman bearing a man in sexual intercourse.

165. *groat-monger*] alludes to summoners' reputation for taking bribes,
famously exemplified by Chaucer's Summoner. Compare 'bribe of ten
groats', 170.

167. *Thrum*] (1) loose end of a thread (*OED* n.2); compare Shakespeare,
MND 5.1.275: 'Cut thread and thrum'; (2) contemptuous name for a person
(*OED* 6); compare Jonson, *Alch.* 1.1.15–17: 'the good / Honest, plain, livery-
three-pound-thrum that kept / Your master's Worship's house ... in the
Friars'.

169. *beadle*] parish constable who administered physical punishment
(*OED* n. 4a).

for] for the price of.

176   THE FAMILY OF LOVE   [ACT 4

    and bribe of ten groats; Bat the bellman, for lying with a 170
wench in a tailor's stall at midnight when 'a should be
performing his office.
Gudgeon. [*Snatching list from Gerardine*] And Tipple the
tapster, for deflowering a virgin in his cellar; Doctor
Glister; his wife; Maria; Mistress Purge. These be the 175
complete number.
Lipsalve. Now dissolve, and each to his occasion till tomorrow morning.   [*Exeunt severally.*]

---

   173. SD] *this edn; not in Q.*   178. SD] *Dyce; not in Q.*

---

  170. *bellman*] night watchman (*OED* n. 1a)
  171. *stall*] covered stand for the sale of wares (*OED* n.1 6a).
  172. *his office*] ringing his bell on the hour.
  173. SH] Q has no indentation at the insertion of '*Gud.*' as speech heading. Gudgeon may read over Gerardine's shoulder, as if wondering why it's taking so long to get to the main case (as far as he is concerned).
  174. *tapster*] man or woman who draws beer etc. for customers in an alehouse (*OED* n).

Act 5

ACT 5 SCENE 1

Enter DOCTOR GLISTER *and* MISTRESS GLISTER.

Mistress Glister. This was your colour to keep her close, but what cloak ha' you for hers and your own shame? What, your own niece, your brother's daughter, besides your bastard in the country?

Glister. Wife, range not too far, I would advise you. Come 5 home in time! Vex me not beyond sufferance. The two-edged sword of thy tongue hath drawn blood o'my patience! I say thou art all this while in an error.

Mistress Glister. No, thou hast been all this while in an urinal; thou hast gone out of thy compass in women's waters. 10 You're a conjurer, forsooth, and can rouse your spirits into circles. Ah, you old fornicator, that ever I saw that

---

Act 5 Scene 1] *Q (ACTVS QVINTUS./ Actus quintus Scena Prima)*. 7–8. o'my patience!] *this edn*; o'my? patience *Q*; o' me. Patience *Dyce*.

---

1. *colour ... close*] trick to keep Maria confined.
5. *range*] roam (*OED* v.1 1a).
5–6. *Come ... time!*] Come to your senses!
6–7. *two-edged ... tongue*] (1) compare Revelation 1.16: 'out of his mouth went a sharp two-edged sword'; (2) proverbial: 'The tongue is not steel yet it cuts' (Tilley T405). No matter what Glister says, he will incriminate himself further in the eyes of his wife.
9. *urinal*] beaker for the inspection of urine by physicians.
10. *out ... compass*] beyond the bounds of moderation (*OED* n.1 2 obs.), a compass being an instrument of navigation for measuring nautical position.
waters] urine, which doctors routinely inspected as a means of diagnosis (*OED* water n. 17a).
11–12. *rouse ... circles*] When raising spirits magicians either protected themselves within a magic circle or confined the spirit to one; compare *Club Law*, 2.4.814–15: 'learned men, that conjure the devil into a circle'.
11. *spirits*] (1) sexual excitement (Dillon); (2) penis (Williams, *Dictionary*, 3.1286–8, citing this line); (3) semen (Williams, *Dictionary*, 3.1286). Compare Shakespeare, *R&J* 2.1.24: 'To raise a spirit in his mistress' circle'.
12. *circles*] vulvas (Williams, *Dictionary*, 1.244).

178   THE FAMILY OF LOVE   [ACT 5

red beard of thine! Now could I rail against thy complexion. I think in my conscience the traces and caparison of
Venus's coach are made o'red hairs, which may be a true   15
emblem that no flaxen stuff or tanned white leather draws
love like 'em. I think thou manuredst thy chin with the
droppings of eggs and muscadine before it bristled. A
shame take thee and thy loadstone! But 'tis no matter.
Master Placket the paritor has cited you, and you shall   20
answer it.
Glister. Oh, the raging jealousy of a woman! Do you hear,
wife, I will show myself a man of sense, and answer you

---

13. *red beard*] Red beards were fashionable in England in the early seventeenth century, although the colour was linked with licentiousness and,
through association with Judas's 'reddish-yellow hair', with treachery and
craftiness (Linthicum, 42). Compare Barry, *Ram Alley* 1.2.5: 'a red [beard]
... is most in fashion'. On the use of prosthetic beards by boy companies,
see Will Fisher, 'The Renaissance Beard: Masculinity in Early Modern
England', *RQ* 54 (2001), 163–5.
  14. *traces*] pair of leather straps by which the draught-animal's collar is
attached to the crossbar that draws the coach (*OED* n.2).
  caparison] cloth over a horse's back, often gaily ornamented (*OED* n.).
  15. *Venus's coach*] traditionally pictured as drawn by doves or swallows in
the air.
  16. *emblem*] allegorical picture, labelled with a motto or title to show its
significance, usually accompanied by explanatory verses. Famous English
emblem books were produced by Geoffrey Whitney (*Choice of Emblems*,
1586), Henry Peacham (*Minerva Britanna*, 1612) and George Wither (*A
Collection of Emblems*, 1635).
  flaxen stuff] rope or cord made from flax.
  stuff] material (*OED* n.1).
  tanned] of animal skin or hide: converted into leather by steeping in an
infusion of an astringent bark, like that of the oak, the natural tannins of
which have a preservative effect (*OED* 1a).
  draws] (1) pulls behind; (2) attracts.
  18. *droppings*] (1) liquid dregs, drips; (2) in view of 'manuredst' in 17, the
sense of 'animal dung' is also present (*OED* n. 6).
  eggs ... muscadine] joke about using egg yolks to promote hair growth and
virility, here from drips left on the chin after drinking a mixture of eggs and
muscadine (a sweetish wine made from muscat grapes), reputedly an aph-
rodisiac (Williams, *Dictionary*, 1.433–4). Catherine of Medici introduced the
use of egg yolk to enhance hair growth; see Ralph M. Trüeb, *Female Alopecia:
Guide to Successful Management* (Berlin: Springer, 2013), 4.
  19. *loadstone*] (1) something that attracts, here Glister's red beard
(Bullen); (2) penis.

with silence, or like a man of wisdom, speak in brief. I
say you are a scold, and beware the cucking stool! 25
Mistress Glister. I say you are a ninnyhammer, and beware the
cuckoo; for as sure as I have ware, I'll traffic with the
next merchant venturer

[*Glister goes aside, but overhears.*]

— and in good time, here comes gallants of the right
trade. 30

Enter LIPSALVE *and* GUDGEON.

Lipsalve. All alone, Mistress Glister? Meditating who shall be
your next child's father?
Gudgeon. Indeed, methinks that should be one end of her
thought, an't be but to cry quittance with her husband,
of whose abuse the town rings. 35
Glister. [*Aside*] Flax and fire, flax and fire, here are fellows
come in the nick to light their matches at my tinder.

28.1. SD] *this edn; not in* Q.   29. comes] Q; come *Dyce.*   36. SD] *Dyce; not in* Q.

---

25. *scold*] woman of ribald, abusive speech (*OED* 1a 1b).
   cucking-stool!] stool or chair suspended at the end of a pole which, with the offender strapped into it, was dunked into a river or muddy pond as a punishment (*OED* n.). See Boose, figures 1–4, '[the cucking stool] seems to have originated as a dung cart and ... retained its association with excrement through such designs as the privy-stool model (Fig. 2)' (185).
   26. *ninnyhammer*] blockhead, braggart (*OED*).
   27. *cuckoo*] The cuckoo's song was a warning to married men to beware lest they be made cuckolds. Compare Shakespeare, *MWW* 2.1.113–14: 'Take heed ere summer comes, or cuckoo / Birds do sing'.
   ware] genitals as commodities (Williams, *Dictionary*, 3.1501–2), with a play on 'beware' (26) and 'ware'.
   28. *merchant venturer*] one who undertakes or shares in a commercial venture, especially by sending goods or ships beyond the seas (*OED* n.).
   34. *an't*] if it (Schmidt, 1.37)
   cry quittance] get even with (*OED* quittance P2).
   36. *Flax and fire*] The incendiary nature of flax was used as a metaphor for youthful desire. See the proverb, 'Keep flax from fire and youth from gaming' (Tilley F351).
   37. *nick*] (1) opportune juncture (*OED* n.1 11a); (2) vagina or clitoris (Williams, *Dictionary*, 2.947); (3) possibly an allusion to the devil, known familiarly as 'Old Nick' (*OED* Nick n.2)
   matches] penises (Williams, *Dictionary*, tinderbox 3.1394–5).
   tinder] any substance that readily takes fire from a spark and burns (*OED* n. a); by extension, Mistress Glister's vagina.

Lipsalve. He tells you true, Mistress Glister, the doctor hath made you ordinary in our ordinaries, satires whet their tooths and steep rods in piss, epigrams lie in poetry's pickle, and we shall have rhyme out of all reason against you.

Gudgeon. Ere long he will take up his station at a stationer's, where we shall see him do penance in a sheet, at least.

Mistress Glister. Oh, I am nettled! My patience is so provoked that I must doff my modesty. What shall I do? If ye be honest gentlemen, counsel me in my revenge. Teach me what to do; make my case your own.

Lipsalve. Why, you are in the common road of revenge; take which hand you will, you cannot go out o'your way. 'Tis as soon taken as time by his forepart.

---

39. *ordinaries*] inns or taverns where meals were provided at a fixed price (*OED* n. 12c).

39–40. *satires ... tooths*] compare Barry, *Ram Alley* Prol. 2: 'The satire's tooth and waspish sting'. On 'comical satire' as pioneered by Jonson in the early 1600s, see Ostovich, 11–13.

40. *steep ... piss*] prepare punishment; the soaking makes the whipping administered by the rods of satire more painful (Shepherd).

rods] in classical times satires were called 'rods' or 'whips'. The title of Joseph Hall's *Virgidemiarum* (1597) means 'a harvest of rods', i.e., a severe beating.

piss] urine, used as bleach and as astringent by laundresses and barber-surgeons; hence 'pickle' (41).

epigrams] short poems marked by compression and polish following the Roman poet Martial in being satirical, often scandalous, and featuring prominent figures of the day. Jonson published his *Epigrams* in 1616, but wrote many at least 10–15 years before.

lie] (1) recline; (2) punning on 'lye', or stale urine (Schmidt, 1.185); (3) speak falsely.

41. *rhyme ... reason*] proverbial: 'neither rhyme nor reason' (Tilley R98).

43. *stationer's*] bookshop (*OED* n.1). For a comparable stationer joke, see Barry, *Ram Alley* 1.3.59–62.

44. *do ... sheet*] (1) see 4.4.85–6n.; (2) punning on a 'sheet' of paper on which Glister might see his head or his predicament put into a broadside ballad and sold at a printer's shop.

48. *case*] (1) pun on 'cause'; (2) slang for vagina; compare Shakespeare, *MWW* (F) 4.1.54–5: 'Vengeance of Jenny's case! ... never name her ... if she be a whore!' See Bly, 63: 'The female case hovers in early modern parlance, threateningly open and, from a satirical point of view, unclosable.'

50. *hand*] fork of the road.

go out o'] lose.

SC I]   THE FAMILY OF LOVE   181

Gudgeon. Faith, since he has struck with the sword, strike you
    with the scabbard. In plain terms, cuckold him. You may
    as easily do it as lie down o'your bed.
Glister. [*Aside*] This gear cottons, i'faith.   55
Mistress Glister. I apprehend you, gentlemen. Lord, how
    much better are two heads than one, to make one large
    head!
Lipsalve. You say true, Mistress Glister, there's help required
    in grafting, and how happily we come to tender our   60
    service. Let our pretence be to take physic of the doctor,
    and that he may with as much ease minister to us as we
    to you, we'll take a lodging in his house.
Gudgeon. How say you to this? Is the colour good? Does't like
    you?   65
Mistress Glister. Passing well; the colour is so good that you
    shall wear my favour out o'the same piece.
Lipsalve. Excellent, excellent. Now shall we be revenged for
    the whipping. Mistress Glister, let me be your first man!
Gudgeon. Nay, soft sir; I plied her as soon as you.   70
Glister. [*Aside*] I should have an oar in her boat too, by right!

---

55. SD] *Dyce; not in* Q.   64. Does't] *Dyce; do'st* Q.   71. SD] *Dyce; spoke by following 71* Q.

---

52. *sword*] penis. Glister has notionally 'struck with the sword' by getting Maria pregnant.
53. *scabbard*] vagina, from *scabbard* as a *case* (48) for the *sword* (52) (Williams, *Dictionary*, 3.1199–200, citing this line).
55. *gear cottons*] plan succeeds. See 3.1.128n.
57–8. *to make ... head!*] to give Glister horns (Dillon).
60. *grafting*] (1) cuckoldry; (2) adulterous sex (Williams, *Dictionary*, graft 2.614–16, citing this usage).
    happily] opportunely.
    tender] proffer.
64–5. *Does't ... you?*] Do you like it?
66. *passing*] surpassingly.
67. *wear ... piece*] enjoy my sexual favours too; combines a cloth joke with the idea of being sexually possessed, as in the phrase 'to win and wear' (a woman as one's wife). Compare Shakespeare, *MAdo* 5.1.82: 'Win me and wear me!'
70. *plied*] (1) solicited for sexual favours (*OED* ply v.2 5a obs.); (2) assailed sexually, part of the metaphor of Mistress Glister as a sailing vessel in 70–1 (*OED* ply v.2 4a 6 obs).

Lipsalve. How ill-advised were you to marry one with a red beard!

Mistress Glister. Oh, Master Lipsalve, I am not the first that has fallen under that ensign; there's no complexion more attractive in this time for women than gold and red beards. Such men are all liver. 75

Gudgeon. Ay, but small heart, and less honesty.

Lipsalve. Yes, they are honest too, in some kind, for they'll beg before they'll steal. 80

Gudgeon. That's true, for, for one that holds up his hand at the sessions, you shall have ten come into the bawdy court.

Glister. [*Aside*] Was ever beard so backbitten? This were enough to make red beards turn medley, and dash 'em 85 clean out of countenance, but I hope like mine they fear no colours. An you were ten courtiers, I'll front you. I

---

78. Ay] *Dyce;* J *Q.*   84. SD] *Dyce; not in Q.*   87. An] *this edn; and Q.*

---

75. *ensign*] battle flag (*OED* n.1).
76. *gold*] yellow, blonde (*OED* n.1 5). 'Gold' hair was subject to the same opprobrium as red: both were associated with licentiousness (Linthicum, 42).
77. *all liver*] (1) sexually vigorous; (2) physically courageous (see Barry, *Ram Alley* 1.2.5n).
78. *small heart*] lacking in courage. As well as being associated with lust, the liver was regarded as the seat of cowardice (*OED* liver n. 4a).
honesty] chastity.
79. *honest*] honourable, decent (*OED* 1b 1c).
80. *beg*] i.e., for sex.
81–3. *for one ... court*] for one man who swears the customary oath at the sitting of the common law courts (that tried offences such as theft), there will be ten people tried at the 'bawdy court' (managed by the Church, which handled sexual transgressions as well as religious offences).
84. *backbitten*] slandered.
85. *medley*] variegated, hence greyed.
85–6. *dash ... countenance*] (1) knock the wearers of red beards completely off balance; (2) pull the beards right off their faces.
86–7. *fear ... colours*] (1) are afraid of no opponent, from 'colours' as military flag (*OED* colour n.1 20a, P7); proverbial, 'to fear no colours' (Tilley C520); (2) quibble on 'cholers'.
87. *An*] if.
front] strike, kick or drive back (*OED* v.2).

must give you physic with a pox; well, if I pepper you
not, call me Doctor Doddipoll. — [*Aloud*] Master
Lipsalve and Master Gudgeon, you are heartily welcome. 90
I am very glad to see you well.
Lipsalve. Oh, master doctor, your salutation is very suspicious!
Glister. Why, Master Lipsalve?
Lipsalve. It can scarce be hearty, for physicians are rather glad
    to see men ill than well. 95
Glister. Not so, sir, you must distinguish of men, though this
    I know; virtue is not the end of all science, which com-
    monly keeps the professor poor; some study quaestuary
    and gainful arts, and everyone would thrive in's calling.
    But i'faith, gentlemen, what wind drives you hither? 100
Gudgeon. The wind colic, master doctor, or some such disease.
Glister. But not the stone colic?
Lipsalve. Oh, no, sir, we have no obstructions in those parts;
    we are loose enough there.
Glister. If you were troubled with that, my wife can tell you 105
    of an excellent remedy.

---

89. SD] *this edn; [Comes forward] Cleary; not in Q.*   101. wind colic] *Dyce
(subst);* wind Collect *Q.*   102. stone colic] *Dyce (subst);* Stone Collect *Q.*

---

88. *pepper*] (1) beat or bombard with shots, from the biting qualities of
pepper (*OED* v. 3 7a); (2) infect with venereal disease, triggered by 'pox'
(*OED* v. 5b obs).
    89. *Doctor Doddipoll*] proverbially, a thick-headed person (Tilley D429).
An anonymous comedy *The Wisdom of Doctor Dodypoll* was published in 1600
(*BD* 4.1227).
    97. *end*] point, purpose (*OED* n. 12).
    science] knowledge (*OED* n. 1a).
    98. *professor*] practitioner, expert.
    quaestuary] moneymaking, from Lat. *quaestus*, gain (*OED* n. obs.).
    99. *gainful*] lucrative.
    everyone ... calling] a profit-oriented twist to the proverb 'Everyone must
walk (labour) in his own calling' (Tilley C23).
    calling] vocation, occupation (*OED* n. 9b).
    101. *wind colic*] flatulence. Compare the proverb, 'It is an ill wind that
blows no man good' (Tilley W421).
    102. *stone-colic*] kidney stones or venereal disease, from 'stone' meaning
a testicle (Partridge, 250). If Doctor Glister suggests ironically that these
gallants are sick with lust, then the gallants, assuming he means gallstones,
smile to assure Glister that they do not suffer from that infirmity.
    105–6.] i.e., Mistress Glister would be willing to sleep with the gallants.

184 THE FAMILY OF LOVE [ACT 5

Gudgeon. We need it not, we need it not; but indeed, master
doctor, for some private infirmities, which our waters
shall make known to you, we desire to take some physic
of you for a few days, and to that end we would take a   110
lodging in your house during the time.

Lipsalve. Shall we entreat your favour?

Glister. No entreaty, gentlemen, you shall command me to
search the very profundity of my skill for you. — Have
them in, wife, and show them their lodging! — I will think   115
upon another receipt, and follow you immediately.

Gudgeon. And, i'faith, we shall requite your pains to the full.

                    Exeunt LIPSALVE, GUDGEON,
                    [*and*] MISTRESS GLISTER.

Glister. To the fool, you mean. I know you ha' the horn of
plenty for me, which you would derive unto me from the
liberality of your bawdies, not your minds. Here are lords   120
that, having learned the OPQ of courtship, travel up and
down among citizens' wives to show their learning and
bringing up, as if the City were not already a good proficient in the court hornbook. Yes, I warrant they have

---

124. warrant they] *Q;* warrant, they *Dyce.*

---

117. *we ... full*] ironic; the gallants will repay Glister by cuckolding him.
118. *fool*] punning on 'full' in 117.
118–19. *horn ... plenty*] (1) abundance; literal translation of the Latin *cornucopia,* a goat's horn overflowing with flowers, fruits and corn (*OED* cornucopia n. a); (2) horns of a cuckold (*OED* horn n. 7a).
119. *derive*] (1) bestow (*OED* 4a obs.); (2) divide by branching, with a recherché pun on the forked horns of a cuckold (*OED* 3b).
120. *bawdies*] (1) bodies; (2) obscene doings, an obvious pun.
121. *OPQ ... courtship*] not merely the rudiments but the advanced tenets of gallantry; see 5.3.393–4: 'ABC of better manners'; (1) echoes the proverb 'to remember one's P's and Q's' (Tilley P1); (2) pun on 'pee' = urine; compare Shakespeare, *TwN* 2.5.78–9: 'thus makes she her great P's'; (3) pun on French *queue,* a term from heraldry meaning the forked or double tail of a beast (*OED* queue n. 3); (4) pun on 'tail' in the sense of sexual organ (Williams, *Dictionary,* queue 3.1128); (5) a modification of 'ABC' in the sense of a spelling book or primer, born out in 'hornbook' (124).
123. *bringing up*] upbringing.
124. *hornbook*] (1) primer; a leaf or paper containing the alphabet, some elements of spelling, and the Lord's Prayer. It was protected by a thin plate of transparent horn and mounted on wood (*OED*); (2) pun on cuckoldry, as cuckolds were fancifully said to wear horns on their forehead (see 118–19n).
they] male citizens.

heads as capable as other men; ay, and some of them can 125
wisely say with the philosopher that in knowing all they
know nothing. Well, because I am of the livery, and pay
scot and lot amongst you, do but observe how I'll fetch
over my gallants for your sakes. They say I am of the right
hair, and indeed they may stand to't, and hold the posi- 130
tion good, saving with my wife. Soft, are they not at *pro*
and *contra* already? I know they are hotspurs, and I must
have an eye to the main. They have been whipped already
for lechery, and yet the pride of the flesh pricks 'em.

---

125. *capable*] capable of receiving 'horns' (Dillon).
125-7. *some ... know nothing*] (1) the maxim attributed to Democritus, 'Do not strive to know all things lest you become ignorant of all things' (Shepherd); (2) aphorism derived from Plato's account of the trial and death of Socrates, where the latter is represented as ventriloquising God: 'He, O men, is wisest, who, like Socrates, knows his wisdom is in truth worth nothing'; *Great Dialogues of Plato*, trans. W.H.D. Rouse (New York: New American Library, 1956), 427f. (Dillon); (3) Glister alleges that citizens such as Purge, whom he has cuckolded, although aware of their wives' infidelity, 'wink at small faults' (2.1.22-3) or pretend to 'know nothing' in order to maintain a commercial or social advantage.
127. *livery*] (1) citizenry; (2) College of Physicians and Surgeons; (3) figuratively, 'of the livery of the company of Fornicators', punning on 'liver' as bodily organ and seat of the passions (Dillon).
128. *scot ... lot*] municipal tax (*OED* scot n.2 2a).
128-9. *fetch over*] succeed in delivering (a blow to); get the better of (*OED* fetch v.).
you ... your] direct address to the audience.
129-30. *right hair*] i.e., red hair, traditionally a sign of craftiness.
130. *stand to't*] (1) stick to their opinion; (2) sexual pun, see 3.4.55n.
131. *Soft*] hush.
131-2. *at* pro ... contra] (1) engaging in heady debate (Lat., 'for and against'); (2) euphemistically, having sexual intercourse, with a pun on *con*, French, 'cunt' (Williams, *Dictionary*, 1.289-90).
132. *hotspurs*] (1) impetuous men, whose spurs are hot with constant riding; (2) lusty fornicators (Williams, *Dictionary*, 2.693-4, citing this usage); (3) Hotspur, the familiar name of Sir Henry Percy, son of the Earl of Northumberland (*OED* hotspur n. 1), a character in Shakespeare, *1H4*.
133. *main*] target.

Well, I must in, I have given them such a pill 135
Shall take 'em down, for lust must have his fill. *Exit.*

ACT 5 SCENE 2

Enter MARIA *above.*

Maria. Now nature's pencil and the hand of time
Gives life and limb to generation's act;
My shame and guilt in wordless notes appear
The argument of scorn. Oh, now I stand
The theme and comment to each liberal tongue, 5
Whilst hope breeds comfort and fear threats my wrong.
O Gerardine, how oft thy lively figure,
Deadly impressed in my yielding temper,

135–6.] *verse as in* Dyce; *prose in* Q.   135. I have] Q; I've *Dyce.*

Act 5 Scene 2] *Dyce (SCENE II); not in* Q.   2. Gives] Q; Give *Dyce.*   8. Deadly] Q; Deeply *Dyce.*

---

135. *such a pill*] the laxative pill which produces the extreme diarrhoea from which the gallants are suffering in 5.3.

136. *take 'em down*] (1) deflate their pride; (2) reduce their erection (Partridge, 200).

1. *nature's pencil*] Gerardine's phallus. In Jean de Meun's continuation of *The Romance of the Rose* (De Lorris, 91.1–64), Genius exhorts humankind to use the instruments of procreation with which Nature has equipped them, such as 'a tablet and a style' (91.36), i.e., stylus = pencil.

2. *life ... act*] (1) growing baby produced by sexual act initiating next generation; (2) definite form; a visibly pregnant Maria may feel her child kicking in her womb.

3. *wordless notes*] physical signs.

4. *argument*] (1) subject (or object) (*OED* n. 6); (2) that which prompts.

5. *liberal*] (1) loose, wanton; (2) gossiping.

6. *threats ... wrong*] threatens harm.

7. *lively*] (1) lifelike (*OED* adj. 4a); (2) vivid, intense (*OED* adj. 3b). *figure*] image.

8. *Deadly*] (1) dangerously; (2) grievously (*OED* adj. 2); potentially, mortally (*OED* 1); (3) resembling death, death-like (*OED* 7a 7c). Balancing 'lively' in line 7, the word crystallises Maria's anxiety about the public opprobrium with which unmarried mothers were regarded, and their harsh treatment by society. There are undertones of Gerardine's possible betrayal, and Maria's consequent suicide.

impressed] a strongly physical verb, evoking the metaphor of Maria's body as a tablet inscribed by Gerardine's phallus. Compare Shakespeare, *Oth.* 4.2.70–1: 'Was this fair paper, this most goodly book, / Made to write "whore" upon?'

SC 2]   THE FAMILY OF LOVE   187

    Assures me thou art mine; how fancy paints
    Thy true proportion in my troubled sleep,   10
    Because sole subject of my daily thoughts;
    Oh, if thy vows prove feigned, and thou unjust,
    I say and swear, in men there is no trust.

        Enter GERARDINE [*as himself*].

Gerardine. Thus have I passed the round and court of guard,
    Without the word; either conceit is strong,   15
    Or else the body where true love's confined
    Walks as a spirit, and doth force his way
    Through greatest dangers, frightful to those eyes
    That wait to intercept him. — [*Looking up*] Maria!
    How like to Cynthia in her silver orb   20
    She seems to me, attended by love's lamp,
    Whose mutual influence and soul's sympathy
    Doth show heaven's model in mortality.
Maria. [*Looking down*] Gerardine?
    Aurora, now the blushing sun approaches,   25
    Darts not more comfort to this universe
    Than thou to me. Most acceptably come!

13.1. SD] *this edn; Enter Gerardine. Q.* 19. SD] *this edn; not in Q.* 24. SD] *this edn; not in Q.* 25. sun approaches] *Dyce*; Sons aproache *Q.* 26. Darts] *Dyce (subst);* D'art *Q.*

---

  9. *fancy*] imagination.
  10. *proportion*] form, shape (*OED* n. 5 obs.).
  14. *round*] (1) watch or patrol responsible for making a circuit of a military zone or town, implicitly Glister (*OED* n.1 23b); (2) the circuit thus made (*OED* 23a).
  15. *word*] watchword (Bullen) or password.
  conceit] (1) thought (*OED* n. 1a); (2) intellectual faculty for conceiving something (*OED* 2a obs).
  19–23.] Gerardine seems to be admiring the picture of Maria, not catching her attention. He talks about her in the third person.
  20. *Cynthia*] surname of Diana, the Roman moon goddess. The comparison is apt, as Cynthia watched over women in labour.
  21. *love's lamp*] the glow or light of love, made visible in and by the moon.
  23. *mortality*] mortals collectively (*OED* n. 1b).
  25–7. *Aurora ... me*] Dawn (like Maria), signalling the approach of the sun (Gerardine), can't offer more comfort to the world than Gerardine to Maria.

          The art of number cannot count the hours
          Thou hast been absent.
Gerardine.   Infinity of love
    Holds no proportion with arithmetic.   30
    Think not, Maria, but my heart retains
    A deep impression of such thoughts as these.
    I have been forging of a mirthful plot
    To celebrate our wished conjunction,
    Which, now digested, come to summon thee   35
    To be an actress in the comedy.
Maria. How? Where? When? Speak! Mine ears are quick to
          hear —
    I stand on thorns already to be there.
Gerardine. At Dryfat's house, the merchant, there's our
          scene,
    Whose sequel, if I fail not in intent,   40
    Shall answer our desires, and each content.
    But when saw'st thou Lipsalve and Gudgeon, our two
          gallants?
Maria. They are here in the house, so handled by mine uncle
    that they are the pitifullest patients that ever you beheld. 45
Gerardine. No matter, he serves them in their kind; they were
    infamous in the court and now are grown as notorious in

41–2. content. / But ... thou] *Dyce;* content: But when saw'st / thou *Q.*

---

  29. *Infinity ... love*] I (Gerardine) love you (Maria) more than I can count; arithmetic lacks numbers to quantify my love. Gerardine juxtaposes the finite numbers of arithmetic to 'Infinity' in 29. Compare Dekker, *Blurt* 5.2.3–5: 'Thou art welcome a thousand degrees beyond the reach of arithmetic'.
  34. *conjunction*] (1) sexual and marital union (*OED* n. 2a 2b. obs.); (2) planetary alignment (*OED* 3); (3) mixture of elements in alchemy (*OED* 2d). The word captures Gerardine's sense of the couple's love as sublime.
  36. *actress*] (1) female performer on the stage (*OED* 2a, citing this usage); (2) female agent or doer (*OED* 1). See Tomlinson, 'Jacobean'.
  37. *quick*] eager, excited; alive, alluding to Maria's pregnancy; see 1.2.126n.
  38. *stand ... thorns*] proverbial (Tilley T239). Maria is painfully eager to go ahead with Gerardine's plans.
  39. *scene*] stage. Compare Shakespeare, *R&J* Prol. 2: 'In fair Verona, where we lay our scene'.
  46. *he ... kind*] he treats them in their own fashion, i.e., appropriately (*OED* kind n. 6b). Gerardine thinks the base punishment of diarrhoea is deserved by the rakes.

SC 3]   THE FAMILY OF LOVE   189

the City. They may happily prove particles in our sport
and fit subjects for laughter.
Time calls me hence; adieu, prepare to meet.   50
Maria. I shall outstrip the nimblest in my feet.   *Exeunt.*

ACT 5 SCENE 3

Enter DRYFAT [*disguised as a proctor*]
and CLUB [*as a crier*].

Dryfat. Come, Club, come, there's a merry fray towards. We
    shall see the death of melancholy, wherein thou and I
    must call a grand jury of jests together, and pass upon
    them with the club-law.
Club. Now as I am Oy the crier and yet but a young Club, I   5
    have not yet practised that law. You have a whole dryvat
    on't. I pray you instruct me.
Dryfat. Why, 'tis a law enacted by the common council of
    statute caps to qualify the rage of the time, to follow, to

---

50–1.] *verse in Dyce; prose in Q.*

Act 5 Scene 3] *Dyce; Act.5.Scæna ultima.* Q.   0.1–2. SD] *Dyce; Enter Dryfat and Club.* Q.   5. Oy] O Q.

51.] This evokes Atalanta, the Arcadian maiden who challenged her many suitors to a race in order to free herself from their importunities.

3. *grand ... jests*] pre-trial jury conducting a mock trial. A 'grand jury' was a jury of accusation, consisting of from 12 to 23 'good and lawful men of a county' who were returned by the sheriff to every session of the peace and of the assizes, to receive and inquire into indictments before these were submitted to a trial jury (*OED* grand jury n. 2b).

pass upon] (1) pronounce sentence on (*OED* pass v. 29); (2) dupe (*OED* v. 43c obs., but gives first usage as 1673).

4. *club-law*] enforcement of obedience with the club; physical force as contrasted with argument (*OED* 1); *Club Law* (1600) ends with a trial scene (Shepherd).

5. *Oy the crier*] alias derived from a crier's call.

8. *common council*] administrative body of an incorporated town or city, made up of citizens rather than representatives of the nobility (*OED* council n. 10).

8–9. *common ... caps*] trade corporation, imagined as that of the capmakers; here, metonymically, citizens who wore such caps. A statute of 1571 ordered citizens to wear knitted woollen caps on Sundays and holidays for the benefit of the cappers' trade (Linthicum, 227).

9. *qualify*] regulate (*OED* v. 13).

call back, and sometimes to encounter gentlemen when they run in arrearages. I tell thee, there's no averment against our book-cases. 'Tis the law called make-peace: it makes them even when they are at odds; it shows 'em a flat case as plain as a packstaff, that is, knocks 'em down without circumstance.

Club. Ay, marry, I like that law well, 'tis studied with the turning of a hand. There's no quiddits nor pedlar's French in't; there needs no book for th'exposition o'th' terms. 'Tis as easily learned as the felling of wood and getting of children; all is but laying on load the downright blow.

Dryfat. Ay, and by the way of exhortation it prints this moral sentence on their costards, in capital letters: 'Agree, for the law is costly.'

Club. Good, good. But all this while, there's no doctor thought on. We must have one to arbitrate.

---

11. *arrearages*] the state of being behind in payment of what is due (*OED* n.1a).

11–12. *averment ... book-cases*] arguing against our legal precedents (*OED* book-case n.2).

13. *them ... 'em*] gentlemen or other opponents of the 'common council of statute caps' (8–9).

even] reconciled; also sets up contrast with 'odds' (12).

at odds] (1) in conflict; (2) in financial distress.

14. *flat*] definite, absolute (*OED* adj. 6a).

as ... packstaff] proverbial; as clear as the unadorned staff on which a pedlar carried his pack (Tilley P322).

15. *without circumstance*] unceremoniously (*OED* n. 7a).

17. *turning ... hand*] preparing to slap someone or deliver a blow.

quiddits] niceties of argument (= quiddities, *OED* n. rare). Compare Barry, *Ram Alley* 5.2.34: 'What trick, what quiddit, what vagary is this?'

17–18. *pedlar's French*] gibberish, thieves' cant (Shepherd). Examples on stage appear in Middleton and Dekker's *The Roaring Girl* (1611) and Brome's *A Jovial Crew* (1641).

18–19. *th'exposition ... terms*] the explanation of hard words.

20. *getting*] begetting, conceiving.

laying ... load] dealing heavy blows, as part of Club's spontaneous reaction to persons involved in events (*OED* load n. 7a. 'to lay on load', obs.).

23. *sentence*] saying.

costards ... capital] pun on heads of bodies ('costards') and heads of objects (columns, initial letters of words).

25. *doctor*] someone proficient in the knowledge of the law (*OED* n. 5b).

Dryfat. Why, Master Gerardine, man, has his name for the purpose; he shall be called Doctor Stickler. *Lupus est in fabula.* Here he comes!

Enter GERARDINE.

Gerardine. How now, lads, does our conceit cotton? Ha' you summoned your wits from wool-gathering? Are you fraught with matter for this merriment? 30
Dryfat. Full, full, we are in labour, man, and we shall die without midwifery.
Club. We are ravished with delight like the wench that was got with child against her stomach. — Oh, but if we could wrest this smock law, now in hand, to our club-law, it were excellent! 35
Dryfat. Easily, easily, all shall be called the club-law.
Gerardine. As how? 40
Dryfat. Why, thus: Club is the crier, I am Poppin the proctor, and you Stickler the doctor. He calls them to appear, I must be of their counsel, and you must atone them, put

41. Poppin] *Qu* (Poppin); Exigent *Qc*.

28. *Stickler*] (1) umpire or moderator, originally in wrestling matches; (2) more generally, someone who intercedes between disputants; a mediator (*OED* n.1). The modern sense of 'a person who insists that something should be done in a prescribed way' (*OED* 3b) post-dates *FoL*.

28–9. *Lupus ... fabula*] Talk of the devil! (Lat., 'the wolf in the fable'), Terence, *Brothers* 4.1.541. Adapted as the proverb, 'Speak of the Devil and he will appear' (Tilley D294).

30. *cotton*] proceed. Compare 3.1.128, 5.1.55.

31. *wits ... wool-gathering*] Proverbially, 'his wits go a wool gathering' (Tilley, W582).

32. *fraught*] heavily loaded; sets up Dryfat's pun on 'labour' (33).

33. *in labour*] (1) hard at work; (2) in the process of giving birth.

34. *midwifery*] the assistance of a midwife.

36. *stomach*] inclination (Schmidt, 2.1126, n. 3).

37. *smock-law*] women's affairs (*OED* smock n. 1c). Metonym encompassing the accusing of Mistress Purge with adultery and Glister with fornication and incest. Compare Barry, *Ram Alley* 4.1.86: 'smock fees'.

now ... hand] i.e., their impersonation of legal officers to prosecute sexual offenders.

42. *them*] the accused, Mistress Purge and Glister, and the plaintiff, Purge.

43. *of ... counsel*] legal representative or attorney for the accused, Glister and Mistress Purge (*OED* counsel n. 6 obs.).

atone] reconcile (Bullen).

'em together. We may know their cases, and be in their elements (mark you me), but they cannot be in ours. Tut, none knows our secrets; we can speak fustian above their understanding, and make asses' ears attentive. I'll play Ambidexter, tell 'em 'tis a plain case and put 'em down with the club law; so that, as Club said well enow, our knavery is as near allied as felling of wood and getting of children. 45

50

Gerardine. Excellent, excellent. [*Hears sound.*] By this they are at hand. Let's bear these things like ourselves. I'll withdraw and put on my habiliments and then enter for the doctor. 55
Dryfat. Do so, they come, they come!

Exit [GERARDINE].

Enter DOCTOR GLISTER *and* PURGE.

Welcome Master Doctor Glister and Master Purge. There's a commission to be sat upon this day to open a passage for imprisoned truth, concerning acts yet *in tenebris*. 60
Glister. True. I am brought hither by the malice of my wife.
Purge. And I have a just appeal against my wife.

---

52. SD] *this edn; not in* Q.   56.1. SD] *Dyce; in right margin opp. 55* Q. 56.2. SD] *Dyce; following 48* Q.

---

44. *cases ... elements*] bawdy innuendo.

46. *fustian*] bombastic rhetoric, used by Dryfat in this scene to impress listeners with his legal discourse.

47. *asses' ears*] alluding to King Midas, to whom Apollo gave ass's ears after Midas chose Pan as the winner in a musical contest between Pan and Apollo.

48. *Ambidexter*] (1) in law, one who takes bribes from both sides, a double-dealer (*OED* n. 2 3); medieval Lat., 'right-handed on both sides' (*OED* adj. 1); (2) Vice character in Thomas Preston, *Cambises* (1569), mentioned in Barry, *Ram Alley* 4.4.79: 'You, Sir Ambo-dexter'.

49. *as ... enow*] as Club rightly said just now (*OED* enow adv. Scottish, elision for 'even now', but gives first usage as 1816), referring to lines 19–20. Compare 'E'en', at 266, below.

54. *habiliments*] clothing, disguise (*OED* n. 1).

58. *commission*] judicial investigation (*OED* n. 2).

59–60. *in tenebris*] Lat., in the dark.

Glister. Master Poppin (so I think you are called), I understand you have the law at your fingers' ends.
Dryfat. I can box cases, and scold and scratch it out amongst them. 65
Glister. Indeed, fame reports you to be a good trumpeter of causes. I must retain you, sir, to sound mine.
Dryfat. My sackbut shall do it most pathetically. Tell me in brief the nature of your case. 70
Glister. Faith, sir, a scandalous letter devised to wrong my reputation, about a bastard in the country which should be mine.
Dryfat. About a bastard in the country which should be yours? Hum. 'Tis very like you, then, it should seem. 75
Glister. Oh, no sir, understand me: only fathered upon me.
Dryfat. Only fathered upon you, *cum nemini obtrudi potest.* I understand you and like you well, too: you do not flatter yourself in your own case, no. 'Tis not good. Well, what more? 80
Glister. And about my niece, got with child in my own house.
Dryfat. Byrlady, burdens of some weight, which you make light of — you deny?
Glister. What else, sir? I have reason.
Dryfat. I know it well, I take you for no beast. Believe me, 85 master doctor, denial and reason are two main grounds; stand upon them and you cannot err. — Your case, Master Purge?

---

63. Poppin] *Qu; Exigent Qc.*

63. *so ... called*] Glister has not yet been introduced to Dryfat as Poppin.
65. *box*] (1) fight (Cleary); (2) lodge a document in a court of law (*OED* v.1 4, but gives first usage as 1868).
69. *sackbut*] (1) proto-trombone with a slide for altering the pitch, triggered by 'trumpeter' in 67 (*OED* n. 1a); (2) pun on 'butt of sack' (Shepherd).
pathetically] affectingly (*OED* pathetic adv. 1b. obs.).
72-4. *should ... be*] is alleged to be ... should be, when considered in the right light. Dryfat deliberately misunderstands Glister.
75. *'Tis ... you*] It looks a lot like you.
76. *fathered ... me*] assumed to be my child.
77. cum nemini obtrudi potest] 'since they can't foist [him] on anyone else', paraphrasing Terence, *Woman of Andros*, 1.5.250 (*ea quoniam nemini obtrudi potest*). Dryfat quotes Latin 'to confuse Glister as well as underline how an imaginary baby is being palmed off on him' (Dillon).
86. *grounds*] foundations (*OED* n. 5a).

Purge. First take your fee, Master Poppin, that you may have the more feeling, and urge it home when you come to't. [*Gives money.*] Mine is a discovery of my wife's iniquity at the Family of Love. 90

Dryfat. Otherwise called the house of venery, where they hunger and thirst for it.

Purge. True, sir, you have heard of the Hole in the Wall, where they assemble together in the daytime, like so many bees under a hive. 95

Dryfat. Come home *crura thymo plena*, and lodge among hornets, is't not so?

Purge. I cannot tell, sir, but for my part, I am much noted as I go. 100

Dryfat. No doubt of that, sir; your wife can furnish you with notes out of her quotations.

Club. Ay, and give him a two-tagged point to tie 'em together.

Dryfat. But how came you to detect her? 105

Purge. Why thus, sir: getting the word, I dogged her to the

---

89. Poppin] *Qu; Exigent Qc.*   91. SD] *Dyce; not in Q.*

---

90. *home*] to the very heart of the matter (*OED* adv. 4a).

93. *house of venery*] brothel. Compare Marston, *Dutch C.* 1.1.173: 'house of salvation'. 'House of Love' was another name for the Family of Love.

95. *Hole in the Wall*] (1) traditional name for a pub (Cleary), the daytime meeting place of the Family in Barry's play; (2) bawdy innuendo; compare Shakespeare, *MND* 5.1.199: 'I kiss the wall's hole'.

98. crura thymo plena] (1) Lat., 'thighs laden with thyme' [pollen from the herb], adapted from Virgil, *Georgics*, 4.181; (2) in connection with 'hornets' (see next note), the phrase implies, obscenely, cunts full of other men's semen, via the proximity of thighs to sexual organs. The Familists so described are implicitly women (in Latin, bees are grammatically feminine). Compare Dekker and Webster, *WHo!* 2.1.141–3: 'see what golden-winged bee from Hybla, flies humming, with *Crura thymo plena*, which he will empty in the hive of your bosom'.

99. *hornets*] (1) aggressive large wasps, implying husbands hostile to Familism. Virgil lists the hornet as an enemy of the bee in *Georgics*, 4.245; (2) pun on Purge's cuckold horns.

100. *noted*] commented upon, gossiped about.

103. *quotations*] (1) reference (usually in margin) to a passage of text by page, chapter, etc. (*OED* n. 2a obs.); (2) notes of what passed at the meeting.

104. *two-tagged*] (1) having two metal tags; (2) double-dealing (Cleary).

point] (1) argument, idea (*OED* n. 10a), to tie up Mistress Purge's notes (88); (2) component of early modern clothing, see 2.3.81n.

106. *dogged*] followed.

SC 3]   THE FAMILY OF LOVE   195

    Family, where closing with her I whispered so pleasing a
    tale in her ear that I got from her her wedding ring, and
    here 'tis.
Dryfat. Well, out of that ring we will wring matter that shall   110
    carry meat i'th' mouth. But what witness or proof can
    you produce to make good your wife's iniquity and your
    own cuckoldry?
Purge. Master Lipsalve and Master Gudgeon, who were her
    companions at that same time.   115
Dryfat. Very good. Are they cited in the *quorum nomina*?
Club. They will be here, sir.
Glister. If they be, they will bewray all.
Dryfat. So much the better. 'Twill savour well for Master
    Purge.   120
Purge. You understand my case now?
Glister. And mine too, sir?
Dryfat. I do, I do, they are as different as a doctor and a
    dunce, a man and a beast. Here's the compendium.
    Yours, master doctor, stands upon the negative, and   125
    yours, Master Purge, upon the affirmative. *Pauca sapienti*,
    I ha't, I ha't.
Purge. Mine is very current, sir, I can show you good guilt.
Dryfat. Ay, marry, there spoke an angel; gilt's current indeed.
    Let me feel't, let me feel't.   130

---

107. *closing*] meeting, coming into close contact (*OED* close v. 10a).

111. *carry ... mouth*] have serious consequences, triggered by 'dogged' in 106. Proverbial; see Tilley M816: 'He carries meat in his mouth.'

112. *make good*] prove.

118. *bewray*] (1) reveal (*OED*,v. 7 obs.); (2) pun on 'beray' = defile, spatter with excrement (*OED* be'ray v. 1a).

119. *savour*] (1) taste piquant (*OED* v. 2b obs.); (2) stink (*OED* v. 3b obs.); (3) be redolent of, esp. something bad (*OED* v. 4a).

124. *compendium*] summary, more of Dryfat's 'fustian' (46).

126. pauca sapienti] Lat. 'Few (words are necessary for) the wise'; compare Barry, *Ram Alley* 2.2.53. Another legal tag common to *FoL* and *Ram Alley*, giving evidence of Barry's authorship (Taylor, Mulholland, and Jackson, 232).

128. *guilt*] i.e., Mistress Purge's guilt in respect of the charge of adultery.

129. *angel*] See above, 1.2.149n.

gilt] Dryfat opts to misunderstand Purge's 'guilt' (128) in the sense of money.

Purge. I mean my wife's guilt.

Glister. Master Poppin, you shall have innocence to speak for me!

Dryfat. Tut, innocence is a fool, I care not for's company; I can speak enough without him. 135

Glister. Then I hope you will be as good to us as the five-finger at maw.

Dryfat. No, rather as Hercules, to lip-labour 'em with the club-law. Tut, let me alone.

Enter MISTRESS GLISTER, MISTRESS PURGE, *and* MARIA.

Mistress Glister. Oh, are you here, sir? I have brought you a full barn to glut your greedy appetite. If you have any maw, feed here till you choke again. Now shall I see the whole carcass of your knavery ripped up. If thou hast any grace, now will thy red beard turn white upon't. 140

Mistress Purge. Oh, how have I been tossed from post to pillar 145

---

141. appetite. If] *this edn;* appetite if *Q.*

---

132. *innocence*] freedom from cunning; ignorance, silliness (*OED* n. 3).

136. *five-finger*] five of trumps (*OED* n. 3). See Chapman, *May Day*, 5.1.189–91: 'my game stood ... upon my last two tricks, when I made sure of the set, and yet lost it, having the varlet and the five finger to make two tricks'.

137. *maw*] trick-taking card game played in Ireland and Scotland, in which the highest trump is the five (formerly known as the *five-finger*) (*OED* n. 4 1a hist.).

138–9. *Hercules ... club-law*] The Greek hero was always depicted with his club, illustrating his strength.

138. *lip-labour*] (1) bamboozle with legal rhetoric (*OED* n. a); (2) pun on Hercules' twelve labours.

141. *full barn*] pun on Maria's pregnant womb, containing a 'bairn' or 'child' (*OED*).

142. *maw*] figuratively, appetite (*OED* n. 4 obs.), chiming with 'maw' at 137.

144. *now ... upon't*] Glister's red beard, an emblem of lechery, should turn white in humiliation and penance.

upon't] in response to his crime and the corresponding shame he should feel.

145. *post ... pillar*] proverbial: Tilley P328, citing *Liberality and Prodigality*, 'tossed / Like a tennis ball, from pillar to post'.

          In this libidinous world! The yoke I bear
          Is so uneven, as if an innocent lamb
          And a mad hare-brained ox should draw together.
          But I must have patience. There's no remedy.
Dryfat. There's some difference between these two tempers.   150
Glister. [*Aside*] I would give a hundred pounds my wife had
          so gentle a spirit.
Purge. [*Aside*] My wife must needs be gentle, for she can bear
          double.

          Re-enter GERARDINE [*disguised as a doctor of law*].

Dryfat. Here comes master doctor. Now rig up your vessels,   155
          every one to his tackling.
Gerardine. Good day to all at once, and peace amongst you.
          Fie, how I sweat; I think Vulcan ne'er toiled at his anvil,
          as I have done, and all to make maid's water to slake
          Cupid's fire, and to turn his shafts from the featherbed   160
          to the bedpost, from the heart to the heel. — Come,
          Master Poppin, shall we to this gear?

---

151. SD] *Dyce; not in Q.*   153. SD] *Dyce; not in Q.*   154.1. SD] *this edn;*
Enter Gerardine. Q; disguised as a doctor Dyce.

146–8. *yoke ... together*] Puritans believed that marriage was an equal partnership, likening it to a burden borne equally by two oxen yoked together.

147. *uneven*] pronounced disyllabically, un-e'en.

innocent] pronounced disyllabically, inn-'cent.

151–2. *I ... spirit*] Compare *Club Law*, 1.4.14–15: 'I had as leve as an 100l. my wife were of as good constitution.' Glister uses 'gentle' (152) in the sense of 'meek', while at 153 Purge puns on 'gentle' as meaning 'sexually receptive'.

153–4. *bear double*] support two men on top of her: her lover and her husband.

156. *every ... tackling*] hold to your guns; maintain your assumed roles (*OED* n. 3).

tackling] rigging of a ship; sustains the metaphor of 'vessels' (133).

158. *Vulcan*] blacksmith of the Roman gods and husband of Venus.

159. *maid's water*] (1) young woman's urine (5.1.10n); (2) a virgin's tears (*OED* water n. 17d).

159–60. *slake ... fire*] Fire and water were seen as antagonistic, hence Gerardine pictures virginal tears (and urine) as quenching the fires of lust.

160–1. *turn ... heel*] Gerardine posits the force of virginity deflecting Cupid's arrows from the luxurious 'featherbed' to the impenetrable 'bedpost', making the lover turn heel and leave.

Dryfat. Reverend doctor, we have stayed your coming. — Crier, cry silence!

[*Club*] *cries* ['*Oyez, oyez, oyez*'].

Master doctor, I have heard in general terms the tales of Master Doctor Glister and Master Purge, which have in mutual manner jumped into the quagmire of my mind, out of which quagmire (by your enforcement, and mine own duty), I pluck them up by the ears, and thus in naked appearance I present them. 165

170

Gerardine. Ad rem, ad rem, Master Poppin. Leave your allegories, your metaphors, and circumlocutions, and to the point.

Dryfat. Then, briefly, thus: I have compared their tales; how short they will come of their wives I know not. And first for Mistress Purge. — Crier, call Mistress Purge. 175

Club. Rebecca Purge, wife to Peter Purge, pothecary, appear upon thy purgation, upon pain of excommunication.

Mistress Purge. Here I am. Oh, time's impiety!
Hither I come from out the harmless fold
To have my good name eaten up by wolves.
See how they grin! Well, the weak must to the wall, 180

164.1. SD] *this edn; He cries.* Q; *Club.* Silence! *Dyce.*

---

163. *stayed ... coming*] waited for your arrival. See 1.3.123n.

164.1. SD '*Oyez*'] Middle or Law French, 'Hear ye!'; traditionally uttered by public crier or court official to gain attention. I owe this emendation to Helen Ostovich.

169. *pluck ... ears*] (1) exert complete control over, by artful speech (*OED* ear n.1 P1c (a) obs.); (2) keep captive, figuratively, by incessant talk (*OED* P1c (b)); (3) put at variance (*OED* P1(c) d).

naked] having no defence (*OED* adj. 6a).

171. Ad rem] Lat., 'to the point' (Dillon).

174–5. *tales ... wives*] (1) to what extent they will differ from their wives' stories; (2) obscene innuendo, punning on 'tails' meaning 'penises' (Partridge, 255, 257).

178. *purgation*] action of clearing oneself from an accusation of crime or guilt (*OED* 1, arch.). Compare Shakespeare, *AYL* 5.4.42–3: 'let him put me to my purgation'.

180. *fold*] (1) enclosure, esp. a sheep's pen (*OED* n.2 1a); (2) in a spiritual sense, as in 'the fold of Christ' (*OED* 1b).

182. *weak ... wall*] proverbial, see Tilley W185: 'The weakest goes to the wall'. Compare Shakespeare, *R&J* 1.1.14–15: 'women, being the weaker vessels, are ever thrust to the wall'.

I must bear wrong, but shame shall them befall.
Gerardine. Who is her accuser?
Dryfat. Her own husband, upon the late discovery of a crew   185
of narrow-ruffed, strait-laced, yet loose-bodied dames,
with a rout of omnium gatherums, assembled by the title
of the Family of Love, which, master doctor, if they be
not punished and suppressed by our club-law, each man's
copyhold will become freehold, specialities will turn to   190
generalities; and so from unity to parity, from parity to
plurality, and from plurality to universality. Their wives,
the only ornaments of their houses and of all their wares,

---

186. narrow-ruffed] *Qc (*narrow Ruste*);* narrow Rusty *Qu.*

---

186. *narrow-ruffed*] As opposed to a wide ruff which, with the assistance of starch, 'would stand up by itself', 'narrow-ruffed' implies small ruffs made with a minimum of lace, in keeping with the hypocritical image of pious modesty that Dryfat ascribes to women Familists. See Ewing, 31.
    strait-laced ... loose-bodied] wearing bodices that are tight-fitting; figuratively, over-scrupulous and prudish in behaviour and moral judgement (*OED* strait-laced adj. 1a 2d); yet in contrast, wearing a loose-fitting dress, thus physically unrestricted and figuratively wanton (*OED* loose adj. C3.d).
    dames] mistresses of households; implicitly, married women.
187. *rout*] (1) disreputable group; (2) in a specific legal sense, an assembly of three or more people that has gathered with the intention of committing an unlawful act, and has taken steps towards its execution (*OED* n. 4 hist.).
    omnium gatherums] miscellaneous people (*OED* n. 1), 'anyones and everyones', mock-Latin.
190. *copyhold ... freehold*] Dryfat contemplates a shift from patriarchal ownership of wives as 'copyhold', analogous to land held at the will of the lord of the manor (*OED* n. 1a), to wives becoming 'freehold', or sexually independent, analogous to land held by a tenant for life.
190–1. *specialities ... generalities*] men's exclusive sexual ownership of their wives ceding place to wives as generally available to all.
191. *unity*] husband and wife as one entity.
191–2. *parity ... universality*] from equality between marital partners, to the wife having many sexual partners, to a state of total promiscuity, anticipating the anarchy in 'common' (195).
192. *Their*] refers to husbands of female Familists, such as Master Purge.
192–5. *Their ... common*] Their wives will be sexually available to all men, making them 'common' women, or whores. See Marsh, *FLES*, 209: 'As early as 1580, the author of *An apology* had been aware that the Family's members were reputed to "lie with one another's wife, desiring to have all men's goods in common".'
192–4. *wives ... movables*] Compare Overbury, 220–1: 'A Good Wife is a man's best movable'.

goods, and chattels the chief movables, will be made common. 195

Purge. Most voluble and eloquent proctor.

Gerardine. Byrlady, these enormities must and shall be redressed; otherwise I see their charter will be infringed, and their ancient staff of government the club (from whence we derive our law of castigation), this club, I say 200 (they seeming nothing less than men by their forepart) will be turned upon their own heads. Speak, Rebecca Purge, art thou one of this Family? Hast thou ever known the body of any man there, or elsewhere, concupiscentically?

Mistress Purge. No, master doctor, those are but devices of the 205 wicked to trap the innocent, but I thank my spirit I have fear before my eyes, which my husband sees not because something hangs in's light.

Purge. That's my horns! She flouts me to my face, and I will not endure it — I shall carry her mark to my grave. Master 210 doctor, she has given me that, that Aesculapius, were he now extant, could not heal, nor *edax rerum* take away!

Gerardine. Produce your witness, Master Purge, and blow not your own horn.

Purge. Master Lipsalve and Master Gudgeon, let them be 215 called.

Club. Laurence Lipsalve and Gregory Gudgeon, late of *hic et ubique*, in the county of *nusquam*, gentlemen, come into

---

194. chattels] *Dyce (subst);* Chattell *Q.*

198. *their charter*] Glister's and Purge's right to rule over their wives as patriarchs.

200-2. *this club ... heads*] Glister and Purge will be beaten with their own (phallic) clubs, which will morph into cuckolds' horns. The focus shifts from the apocalyptic promiscuity of women envisaged by Dryfat to the specific plight of the two husbands on stage.

201. *forepart*] codpiece, used emblematically.

204. *concupiscentally*] lustfully.

210. *mark*] sign of infamy (*OED* n.1 12c, 12d).

211. *Aesculapius*] legendary Greek physician, later made the Greek god of medicine.

212. edax rerum] Lat. '(tempus) edax rerum' (time) the devourer of (all) things (Ovid, *Met.* 15.234).

217–18. hic ... ubique] Lat., here and everywhere.

218. nusquam] Lat., nowhere.

SC 3]   THE FAMILY OF LOVE   201

    the court and give your evidence, upon pain of that which
    shall ensue.   220

                Enter LIPSALVE *and* GUDGEON.

Glister. Here they come, in pain I warrant them. How works
    your physic, gallants? Do you go well to the ground? Now
    'cuckold the doctor'? Wife, who's your 'first man' now?
    Now 'strike with the scabbard!' Ha, ha, ha!
Gudgeon. A villainous doctor.   225
Lipsalve. Mountebank, you're a rascal, and we will cast about
    to be revenged.
Dryfat. Cast about this way, and bewray what you can con-
    cerning Mistress Purge, who stands here upon her purga-
    tion, either to prove mundified or contaminated,   230
    according to the tenor piece of your principal evidence.
    — First, give 'em the book.
Club. Come, lay your hands upon the book. You shall speak
    and aver no more, nor wade no farther into the cream-
    pots of this woman's crime than the naked truth and the   235
    cart-rope of your conscience shall conduct you, so help
    you the contents. Kiss the book.
Lipsalve. Alas, we are not in case to answer largely, but if
    you will have our evidence in brief, I think I kissed her

223. 'cuckold ... doctor'?] *this edn;* now ... Doctor? *Q.*

---

    222. *physic*] purge, laxative (Dillon).
    Do ... ground?] are you overthrown? (*OED* n. 8b).
    222–4. *Now ... scabbard!*] Compare Gudgeon at 5.1.52–3: 'strike you with the scabbard'.
    223. *Wife ... now?*] See Lipsalve at 5.1.69: 'let me be your first man!'
    226. *cast*] (1) scheme (*OED* v. 43a); (2) vomit (*OED* 25a).
    230. *mundified*] cleansed (*OED* adj.).
    231. *tenor*] the substance of something written or spoken; in legal use, implying the actual wording of a document (*OED* n.1 1a).
    232. *book*] probably a Bible.
    234–5. *cream-pots*] vessels for holding milk while the cream is forming (*OED* cream n. C1(c) b).
    236. *cart-rope*] sneering reference to the cart in which criminals were carried to execution or for public exposure.
    237. *Kiss ... book*] instruction to witness in court to kiss the Bible, rather than reading an oath, given the numbers in early modern England who could not read or write.
    238. *in case*] in a position (*OED* case n.1 5a).
    largely] at length.

at the Family some three times: once at coming, once at 240
going, and once in the midst; otherwise never knew her
dishonestly.
Purge. Ay, mark that middle kiss, master doctor!
Gudgeon. And for my part, I have been more mortified by her
than ever I was provoked. 245
Gerardine. How say you to this, Master Purge? Your witness
is weak, and sir-reverence on't, without sounder proof
they may depart to the close-stool whence they came, and
you to your pothecary's shop.
Purge. No, master doctor, I have another bolt to shoot that 250
shall strike her dead. She shall not have a word to say.
Dryfat. Answer me to this, Mistress Purge, where's your
wedding ring?
Mistress Purge. My wedding ring? Why, what should I do with
unnecessary things about me when the poor begs at my 255
gate ready to starve? Is it not better, as I learned last
lecture, to send my substance before me, where I may
find it, than to leave it behind me, where I must forgo it?
Yes, verily, wherefore, to put you out of doubt, I have
given that ring to charitable uses! 260
Dryfat. Nay, now she falters. My client can show that ring,
got from her at the Family, when these two courtlings
had at the same time beleaguered her fort.
Gerardine. This alters the case clean. — What starting hole
ha' you now, Mistress Purge? 265

---

247. on't] *Dyce;* on *Q.*   262. courtlings] *Dyce;* Courtling *Q.*

---

250. *bolt*] arrow (Schmidt, 1.127).
254–60. *My ... uses!*] Compare Mistress Purge's deflection of Dryfat's question with the more conventional treatment of the ring motif by Dekker and Webster, *NHo!* 1.3.91–125.
259. *verily*] truly. A Puritan-inspired word.
260. *ring*] with overtone of vagina (Williams, *Dictionary*, 3.1159). Compare 295 of this scene.
263. *fort*] (1) vagina; (2) sustains the military language used in this scene: see 50, 269 and 271; (3) pun on 'for it'.
264. *starting hole*] (1) hole in which a hunted animal takes refuge (*OED* n. 1); (2) loophole; compare Middleton, *Phoenix*, 2.154–6: 'an old crafty client, who ... has more tricks and starting holes than the dizzy pates of fifteen attorneys'.

Mistress Purge. E'en the sanctuary of a safe conscience. Now truly, truly, however he came by that ring, by my sisterhood, I gave it to the relief of the distressed Geneva.

Purge. How? To the relief of the distressed Geneva? — Justice, master doctor! I may now decline *victus victa victum*; one word more shall overthrow her. I myself was a Familist that day, who, more jealous than zealous in devotion, thrust in amongst the rest (as I had most right), on purpose to sound her, to find out the knavery. Short tale to make, I got her ring, and here it is! Let her deny it if she can, and what more I discovered, *non est nunc narrandi locus*.

Mistress Purge. Husband, I see you are hoodwinked in the right use of feeling and knowledge — as if I knew you not then, as well as the child knows his own father. Look in the posy of my ring: does it not tell you that we two are one flesh? And hath not fellow-feeling taught us to know one another as well by night as by day? Husband, husband, will you do as the blind jade, break your neck down a hill because you see it not? Ha' you no light of

---

266. *E'en*] even.
268. *relief ... Geneva*] The siege of Geneva by Charles Emmanuel of Savoy lasted from December 1602 to July 1603. The allusion gives phrasal evidence for the attribution of the play to Barry, as 'relief for the distressed Geneva' appears also in his *Ram Alley* 5.3.285.
270. *decline*] recite in order the cases of a noun.
I ... victum] I can now proclaim, 'she is conquered' (Lat.), glancing at Julius Caesar's famous boast at his Pontic triumph, '*veni, vidi, vici*' ('I came, I saw, I conquered'). To 'decline' is to recite in order the cases of a Latin word; here, the adjective derived from *vincere*, to defeat. Compare Marston, *Dutch C.* 1.1.151: '*O justus justa justum!*'
274. *sound*] See above, 2.3.62n.
276–7. non est nunc narrandi locus] Lat., now is not the place for telling, minimally altered from Terence, *Woman of Andros*, 2.1.354.
278. *hoodwinked*] blinded (*OED*).
279–80. *as if ... father*] Compare Falstaff's claim to have recognised Prince Hal during the Gadshill robbery; see Shakespeare, *1H4* 2.4.244: 'I knew ye as well as he that made ye.' Mistress Purge adapts the proverb, 'it is a wise child that knows his own father' (Tilley C309).
281. *posy*] emblem (*OED* n. 1b obs.).
284. *jade*] contemptuous name for a horse (*OED* n.1 1a); also, a sexually promiscuous woman (see 2.2.4–6n).

nature in that flesh of yours? Now, as true as I live, master
doctor, I had a secret operation, and I knew him then to
be my husband e'en by very instinct.

Purge. Impudence, dost not blush? Art not ashamed to lie so
abominable? 290

Mistress Purge. No, husband, rather be you ashamed of your
own weakness, for, for my part, I neither fear nor shame
what man can do unto me.

Gerardine. Master Purge, I see you have spent your pith.
Therefore best make a full point at the ring, and attend 295
our pleasure. — Master Poppin, proceed to the rest.

Dryfat. Crier, call Doctor Glister!

Club. Doctor Glister, alias suppositor, doctor of physic,
appear upon thy purgation, upon the belly pain that may
ensue therein. 300

Glister. Here, master doctor.

Gerardine. Who is his accuser?

Dryfat. His clamorous wife, who seems to enforce a separation about a bastard in the country which should be his,
only fathered upon him. 305

Gerardine. What proof of that?

Mistress Glister. Proof unanswerable, master doctor: the
nurse's letter. Let it be read, but first observe his countenance. It may be his blushing will bewray his guilt.

Gerardine. Now by this light, I thought it had, indeed, but I 310
see 'tis but the reflection of his beard. — Read the letter,
master Poppin.

---

290. abominable] *Q* (abhominable).   295. Poppin] *Dyce;* Exigent *Q*.

287. *operation*] revelation.
287-8. *I ... then ... instinct*] Compare Shakespeare, *1H4* 2.4.248-9: 'I was now a coward on instinct.'
288. *very*] mere.
294. *pith*] vigour, might (*OED* n 5a).
295. *full ... ring*] alludes to the sport of 'running at the ring', in which the tilter aimed to thrust his lance through a suspended ring; compare 'set it a-tilt', 2.3.6n and below, 388.
 ring] (1) circlet of metal hung from a post which mounted riders tried to carry off on the point of a lance (*OED* n.1 4a); (2) pun on 'ring' meaning 'vagina'.
298. alias suppositer] also known as, *alias* (Lat.), 'otherwise', *suppositer* (Lat.), 'standing for' (*OED*).
304. *should be*] is alleged to be.

SC 3]   THE FAMILY OF LOVE   205

[*Dryfat.*] [*Reading*] *After my hearty commendations remembered unto your worshipful doctorship, trusting in God that you are as well as I was at the making hereof, thanks be to him therefore. The cause of my writing unto you at this time is to let you understand that your little son is turned a ragged colt, a very stripling, for being now stripped of all his clothing, his backside wants a tail-piece, commends itself to your fatherly consideration. Woe worth the time that ever I gave suck to a child that came in at the window, God knows how! Yet if you did but see how like the pert little red-headed knave is to his father, and how like a cock sparrow he mouses and touses my little Bess already, you would take him for your own, and pay me my hire. I write not of the want of one thing, for I want all things, wherefore take some speedy order or else as naked as he came from the mother will I send him to the father. From Pissing Alley, the 22 of —— Your poor nurse* Thomasine Tweedles   315 320 325

Glister. Master doctor, truth needs not the foil of rhetoric. I will only in *monosyllaba* answer for myself, as sometimes a wise man did: such and such things are laid to my charge, which I deny. You may think of me what you please, but I am as innocent in this as the child newborn.   330

Gerardine. Why, there's partly a confession: the child, we know, is innocent, and not newborn, neither, for it should seem by the letter he is able to call his dad 'knave'.   335

313. Poppin] *Dyce;* Exigent? *Q.*   314. SH] *Dyce;* Club. *Qq.*   314. SD] *Dyce; not in Q.*   329. Pissing Alley] *this edn;* Pis. *Q.*   329. 22.] *this edn;* xxii *Q.*

---

318. stripling] youth, one passing from boyhood to early manhood.

319. tail-piece, commends] covering for the behind; an auditor understands, 'tail-piece, [and] commends'.

323. cock sparrow] male sparrow, symbol of lechery.

mouses ... touses] toys with in a sexual way (*OED* mouse v. 2b; *OED* touse v. 3 fig.). Compare *R&J* 4.4.11: 'Ay, you have been a mouse-hunt in your time'.

325. hire] salary.

326. speedy order] immediate action.

328. Pissing Alley] 'Two passages in Old London enjoyed this appellation: one running from Friday St to Bread St, the other from the Strand into Holywell St' (Sugden, 252). Sugden believes this usage refers to the first locale.

331. monosyllaba] Lat., words of one syllable.

206   THE FAMILY OF LOVE   [ACT 5

Glister. You take me wrong. [*To Dryfat*] Master proctor?
Dryfat. Under correction, thus much can I say for my client's
  justification: indeed he hath travelled well in the beating   340
  of pulses, and hath been much conversant in women's
  jordans, but he had ever a care to raise his patient, being
  before cast down. His charitable disposition hath been
  such to poor folk that he never took above fourpence for
  the casting of a water, which good custom was so well   345
  known among all his patients that if sixpence were at any
  time offered him, they might be bold to ask and have
  twopence again. He hath been so skilful and painful
  withal in the cure of the green sickness, that, of my
  knowledge, he hath risen at all hours in the night to   350
  pleasure maids that have had it. And for that foul-
  mouthed disease termed by a fine phrase — a pox on't,
  what d'ye call't? Oh, the grincomes — at that he hath
  played his doctor's prize, and writes *nil ultra* to all mountebanks, so that neither the wise woman in Pissing Alley,   355

---

339. SD] *this edn; not in Q.*   339. Master proctor] *Q (master Proctor);* master doctor *Dyce.*   355–6. mountebanks] *Dyce; Bountibanckes Q.*

338–40.] Q raises the question of whether Glister speaks emotionally to Gerardine as judge in 338, requiring Dyce's emendation, or whether, after curtly rebuking Gerardine, Glister appeals to his lawyer for support. Dryfat's 'Under correction' expresses customary courtesy to the court's authority, but far from defending Glister from the charge of fathering a bastard, his 'justification' (340) further implicates him in sexual relations with his patients.

  342. *jordans*] (1) chamber-pots; cf. Shakespeare, *1H4* 2.1.18–19: 'they will allow us ne'er a jordan, and then we leak in your chimney'; (2) vessels used by physicians and alchemists for the diagnosis of urine.

  345. *casting*] diagnosing.
  348. *painful*] painstaking (*OED* adj. 4b).
  349. *green sickness*] disease affecting pubescent girls characterised by greenish discoloration of the skin, believed in this period to be cured by sexual intercourse (Williams, *Dictionary*, 2.621–4).
  of] to.
  350. *risen*] (1) got out of bed; (2) got an erection.
  351–3. *foul-mouthed ... grincomes*] disease referred to by lewd slang. 'Pox' and 'grincomes' are both euphemisms for syphilis.
  354–5. *played ... mountebanks*] made an expert effort and gone further than any mountebank can in treating the condition. 'Play a prize' was an expression derived from fencing.
  354. *nil ultra*] Lat., 'nothing beyond'.

nor she in Do Little Lane, are more famous for good
deeds than he. Then, master doctor, out of these presumptions, besides his flat denial (a more infallible
ground), you may gather his innocence, and let him have
his purgation.   360
Gerardine. No, Master Poppin, it is not so to be foisted off.
Mistress Glister. Nay, master doctor, what say you to his own
niece that looks big upon him, an arrow that sticks for the
upshot against all comers, which by his restraint of her
from Master Gerardine, an honest gentleman that loved   365
her, and upon that colour, from the sight and intercourse
of other men, must by all presumptions be his own act.
Gerardine. Oh, monstrous! This is a foul blot in your tables,
indeed.
Glister. Wife, thou hast no shame nor womanhood in thee!   370
Thy conscience knows me.
Mistress Glister. True of thy flesh — who knows not that? Thy

---

356. that neither] *this edn;* that the *Q.*   362. Poppin] *Qu; Exigent Qc.*

---

356. *Do Little Lane*] Described by John Stow as 'a place not inhabited by artificers, or open shopkeepers, but serving for a near passage from Knightrider's Street to Carter Lane'; https://mapoflondon.uvic.ca/DOLI1.htm (accessed 20 April 2021).

361. *it ... off*] you can't palm off the matter like that. 'Foisted' is a term derived from the game of dicing, where it meant literally to palm (a 'flat' or false die) in order to use it when needed (*OED* foist v.1 1a obs. 3c); also, to cheat by this means.

363. *big*] 'cocky', punning on Maria's big-bellied state (*OED* adj. 10); see 3.1.181n.

363–4. *that ... comers*] that conclusively demolishes any pretence Glister might make of innocence. 'Upshot' meant a closing shot, a term from archery (*OED* n. 1 obs.).

366. *upon ... colour*] i.e., for the ulterior motive of having sex with Maria.

367. *must ... act*] (Maria's pregnancy) must by all inferences be Glister's own doing.

presumptions] (1) beliefs based on available evidence (*OED* n. 3a); (2) legal term; suppositions that the court allows or requires to be made (*OED* n. 3b).

368. *foul blot*] (1) stain of ink; (2) moral stain.

tables] writing tablet.

371. *knows me*] knows that I'm innocent of incest with my niece.

372. *True ... flesh*] Faithful to your sensual impulses (*OED* flesh n. 11).

beard speaks for thee. Ay, ay, thou liest by me like a stone,
but abroad th'art like a stone-horse, you old limb-lifter!
Dryfat. Cease your clamour, and attend my speech. Most   375
worshipful, reverend, and judicial doctor, for the quickening of your memory I will give you a breviate of all that
hath been spoken: Master Doctor Glister hath a cradleful
and a bellyful (you see) thrust upon him, and Master
Purge a head fool. — [*To Glister*] Your wife is an angry   380
honeyless wasp, whose sting I hope you need not fear
— [*To Purge*] and yours carries honey in her mouth, but
her sting makes your forehead swell. — [*To Glister*] Your
wife makes you deaf with the shrill treble of her tongue,
— [*To Purge*] and yours makes you horn mad with the   385
tenor of her tale. In fine, master doctor's refuge is his
conscience, and Master Purge runs at his wife's ring.
Gerardine. Summa totalis, a good audit ha' you made, Master
Poppin. Now attend my arbitrament. For you gallants,
though you have incurred the danger of the law by using   390
counterfeit keys and putting your hands into the wrong
pocket, yet, because I see you punished and purged

---

375. limb-lifter!] *Dyce;* Timelifter *Q.* 381. head fool] *Q (*head foole*);* headful *Dyce.* 387. tale] *Dyce;* Taile *Q.* 390. Poppin] *Qu;* Exigent *Qc.* arbitrament] *this edn;* Arbitterment *Q.*

---

374. *stone-horse*] uncastrated horse, stallion, i.e., libertine.

limb-lifter!] (1) fornicator (*OED* limb n.1 C2 obs.); (2) a fool who toys with his time; see Florio (1598), *LEME: Arzigogalo*, a lifter, an underprop, a fond toyish fellow; (3) a man absolutely not to be trusted; see Florio (1598), *LEME: Levantino*, a shifter, a limlifter, a pilferer. Compare Gosson, *School of Abuse* (1579), 16: 'Better might they [players] say themselves to be ... perfect limb-lifters, for teaching the tricks of every strumpet'.

377. *breviate*] short account (*OED* n. 1a).

380. *head fool*] pun on 'headful', i.e., Purge's cuckold's horns.

381. *honeyless*] (1) unattractive; (2) infertile; (3) incapable of experiencing sexual pleasure, frigid; compare above 98n.

382. *honey ... mouth*] sweet words of innocence.

386. *tale*] pun on 'tail' as 'pudend' (Dillon).

In fine] In sum (*OED* fine n. P1b).

387. *runs ... ring*] (1) tilting metaphor, compare 259n; (2) asserts sexual ownership of his wife.

388. *summa totalis*] (Lat.) the sum total.

389. *arbitrament*] Q's 'Ar*bitter*ment' suggests a painful edge to Gerardine's judgement.

already, my advice is that you learn the ABC of better
manners; go back and tell how you have been used in the
City, and being thus scoured keep yourselves clean, and   395
the bed undefiled. — For you, Master Purge, because I
see your evidence insufficient, and indeed too weak to
soil your wife's uprightness, and seeing jealousy and
unkindness hath only made her a stranger in your land
of Ham, my counsel is that you re-advance your stand-   400
ard, give her new press money!

Purge. You may enjoin me, sir, but ——

Gerardine. 'But' not at me, man; I will enjoin you, and conjoin
you, and briefly thus: you have your ring that has made
this combustion and uproar; that keep still, wear it, and   405
here by my edict be it proclaimed to all that are jealous,
to wear their wives' ring still on their fingers as best for
their security, and the only charm against cuckoldry.

Purge. Then, wife, at master doctor's enjoinment, so thou wilt
promise me to come no more at the Family, I receive thee   410
into the lists of my favour.

Mistress Purge. Truly, husband, my love must be free still to
God's creatures; yea, nevertheless preserving you still as
the head of my body, I will do as the spirit shall enable
me.   415

Gerardine. Go to, thou hast a good wife, and there an end.
— Upon you, master doctor, being solicited by so

---

404. 'But' not] *this edn;* But not *Q.*   408. wives' ring] *Q* (wiues Ring); wives' ring[s] *Dyce.*   410. enjoinment] *Dyce;* enioyntment *Q.*   417. there an] *Q;* there'[s] an *Dyce.*

---

393. *ABC*] An Elizabethan detractor claimed that Familists treated the Bible as 'but an ABC to Christianity', cited in Marsh, *FLES,* 33.

399–400. *land ... Ham*] (1) biblical place of peace and fertility (1 Chronicles 4.40); (2) loins.

401. *press money!*] money paid to soldier on joining up, with bawdy play on 'press', linking with 'stand/ard' (Shepherd).

407. *wear ... fingers*] compare Middleton and Rowley, *Chang.* 1.2.27: 'I would wear my ring on my own finger.'

411. *lists*] (1) catalogues (*OED* list n.6 a); (2) punning on 'inclinations' (*OED* list n.4 2).

412–13. *my ... creatures*] See Introduction, 58.

414–15. *as ... me*] as the spirit (of God in me) permits or invites me to do.

210   THE FAMILY OF LOVE   [ACT 5

apparent proof, I can do no less than pronounce a severe
sentence — and yet, i'faith, the reverence of your calling
and profession doth somewhat check my austerity. What   420
if master Gerardine, by my persuasion, would yet be
induced to take your niece and father the child, would
you launch with a thousand pound, besides her father's
portion?
Glister. Master doctor, I would, were it but to redeem her lost 425
good name.
Gerardine. Then, foreknowing what would happen, I thought
good in Master Gerardine's name to have this bond
ready, which if you seal to, he shall take her with all faults.
Glister. That will I instantly. [*He seals the bond.*] So, this is 430
done, which together with my niece do I deliver by these
presents to the use of Master Gerardine.
Gerardine. He thanks you heartily, and lets you know

           [*Gerardine, Dryfat, and Club*] *discover themselves.*

That Indian mines and Tagus' glittering ore
To this bequest were unto me but poor.   435
Glister. What? Gerardine, Dryfat, and Club!
Dryfat and Club. The very same. You are welcome to our
club-law!
Gerardine. Cease admiration here. What doubt remains
I'll satisfy at full. Now join with me,   440
For approbation of our Family.

---

431. SD] Dillon (*subst*); — *Q*.   434.1. SD] *Dyce; They discouer themselues.*
Q in margin beside 385–6.   438. You are] *Dyce;* your are *Q*.

---

420. *check*] restrain, mitigate.
423. *launch*] generously gift (*OED* v. 3c, citing this line).
thousand pound] an exorbitant amount. Compare Middleton, *Mad World*, 5.2.308: 'I spice the bottom with a thousand mark.'
434. *Tagus'*] river in Lusitania.
441. *Family*] (1) Gerardine, Maria and their unborn child; (2) the 'family' of actors who have performed the play; (3) the play the audience have watched.

Epilogue

Gentles, whose favour have o'erspread this place
And shed the real influence of grace
On harmless mirth, we thank you; for our hope
Attracts such vigour and unmeasured scope
From the reflecting splendour of your eyes   5
That, grace presumed, fear in oblivion dies.
Your judgement, as it is the touch and trier
Of good from bad, so from your hearts comes fire
That gives both ardour to the wit refined,
And sweetness to th'incense of each willing mind.   10
Oh, may that fire ne'er die, nor let your favours
Depart from us. Give countenance to their labours,
Proposed a sacrifice, which may no less
Their strong desires than our true zeals express.

[Exeunt omnes.]

FINIS

Epilogue] *Q* (*EPILOGVS*). 1. favour have] *Q;* favour[s] have *Dyce.* 10. sweetness to] *Dyce (subst);* sweetnesse th'Incense *Q.* 14.1. SD] *Dyce; not in Q.*

1–14.] The speaker is probably Gerardine (Bullen).
1. *Gentles*] Gentlemen (in the audience).
7–10.] These lines evoke the relationship between spectators, actors, and play, suggesting a compact of judgement, appreciation, and good will that binds together all those present in the theatre.
7. *touch*] touchstone.
trier] (1) discriminator; (2) juror (*OED* n. 1).
9. *ardour*] warmth, intensity.
10. *sweetness ... th'incense*] Combined with 'fire' (8) and 'ardour' (9), this phrase likens the projected applause of the educated playgoer ('wit refined', 9) to a religious ritual, the theatre being the new church of smart gentlemen, another Family of Love.
12. *Give countenance*] Continue to favour and approve of this company of actors by helping to maintain them (*OED* n.1 8a).
12–14. *their ... our*] The personal pronouns suggest the collaborative nature of theatre, in which support by patrons, by attending and appreciating the play, enables the actors, producers, and playwrights to give their best in return.
14. *strong desires*] perhaps the desires of the shareholders for financial success and continuation of the company.

APPENDIX 1
Marginal annotations in *The Familie of Love*

The title page of STC: 17879a (Huntington Library, KD292) is inscribed by at least four separate hands, from different time periods (figure 3). John Philip Kemble has left his trademark 'Collated / & / Perfect.', followed by the initials 'J.P.K. 1798', in the top right-hand corner. There are two separate handwritten attributions, to 'Middleton' and 'By Thomas Middleton'. The words 'First Edition' appear above the printer's device, possibly in the same hand as 'By Thomas Middleton'. Beneath, and to the right of the play title and name of the theatre company, is written the phrase 'Sorry Comedy'; the Jacobethan hand resembles that of the first ascription to Middleton. Within the text, there are handwritten annotations on six leaves: C2, C3r, D4, E2v, F, and Fv. The annotations are described below, listed as they occur by signature.

(C2) In the last line of Maria's second speech in verse, the final printed word is 'society'. A hand using ink resembling the signature J.[ohn] [P].hilip K.[emble] on the title page has written over the letters 'oc' with the letters 'at', giving the word 'satiety'. The annotation anticipates Dyce's emendation (see collation, 2.4.37n). This annotation is visible in the online STC quarto.

(C3r) On C3v a speech assigned to '*Nun.*' is preceded by the printed stage direction, '*Enter Viall*'. Halfway down C3r, to the right of the word 'feates' that terminates Doctor Glister's speech, a Jacobethan hand has written, 'Enter Viall', supplying a stage direction that makes sense of the speech heading '*Nun.*' (for '*Nuntius*') in the following speech. The annotation supplies a missing stage direction.

Following Glister's next speech ending 'the conceit tickles me', on the same line as '*Enter Gudgin*', justified left, the same hand has written '*Exit both*'. At the start of this speech, Glister has instructed Lipsalve, 'Walke you into that roome.' The word '*both*' refers to Vial, Doctor Glister's servant, and to Lipsalve; after ushering Gudgeon into Glister's room, Vial leads Lipsalve offstage. The annotation supplies a missing stage direction.

(D4) In Gerardine's verse lines that conclude the scene, there is a typesetting error. The word 'our' in the phrase 'our cruell foe' is printed (in some copies of Q) 'nor'. In *FoL* STC17879a, a hand using ink resembling the signature J.[ohn] P.[hilip] K.[emble] has written over the first two letters of 'nor' with the letters 'ou', to give the correct pronoun 'our'. This correction is visible in the online STC quarto.

(E2v) Four lines up from the bottom, a speech heading is missing from the lines of dialogue beginning 'Then shall we prove to be honest Gulls'. The lines are clearly spoken by Gudgeon, in alternating dialogue with Lipsalve. The word '*Gudg*' is written in ink on the left of the dialogue. The correcting hand supplies the missing speech heading.

(F) To the right of the stage direction '*Enter Mayster Purge*', there is a faint annotation that reads '*And ever he was there*'. Beneath the printed stage direction, the heading to Mistress Purge's speech is printed erroneously as '*Ma.Pur.*' The Jacobethan hand has emended the first part of the speech heading to '*Mi.*' Aligned with the last line of dialogue on this page ('Enter in peace', spoken '*Within*') the same hand has written, to the right of the signature letter 'F', slanting slightly upwards, '*Let in*'. The printed phrase '*Let in*' occurs at 3.2.91.1, at the point where Dryfat, Mistress Purge and her link carrier Club, having delivered the correct password, are admitted to the Familist meeting. The hand comments on the stage action and supplies a missing stage direction.

(Fv) Following the final piece of dialogue, 'Enter, and welcome', the hand has written again, '*Let in*'.

APPENDIX 2
'Marstonian?' features of *The Family of Love* identified by Charles Cathcart

Charles Cathcart in *Marston, Rivalry, Rapprochement, and Jonson* (2008) pays sustained attention to *FoL*'s Prologue and Epilogue, drawing on Mary Bly's argument for the 'singularly interactive' composition habits of playwrights for the King's Revels Children (*Marston*, 92). He identifies as a common feature of the Prologue and Epilogue to *FoL*, *Ram Alley*, and Mason's *The Turk* the 'decidedly casual mention of the author … through the use of a pronoun lacking any referent' (*Marston*, 94). Use of the 'unadorned "he"', Cathcart maintains, typifies Marston's own practice, thus linking the 'interactive' writing practices of the King's Revels playwrights with 'a deep and widely shared familiarity with Marston's playtexts' (*Marston*, 93, 94). While I strongly agree with the latter assertion, neither the bare use of 'his' nor the adjective 'slight' in *FoL*'s Prologue (line 3) form compelling evidence for what Cathcart terms Marston's 'contributory authorship' of *FoL* (*Marston*, 94). Nor is Cathcart's reading of the Prologue's first line, 'If, for opinion hath not blazed his fame', as referring to Marston's struggle against critical hostility more convincing than Taylor et al.'s interpretation of the line as signifying the unknown status of the author.

While I reject the claim for Marston's part-authorship of *FoL*, there are parallels between Marston's drama and *FoL* that Cathcart misses. The name 'Gudgeon', used by Cocledemoy as an alias in his gulling of Mulligrub (*Dutch C.* 2.1.210–11), reappears as the name of one of the fatuous gallants in *FoL*, while the surname 'Thomasine Tweedles' (4.3.97) is borrowed from *Jack Drum's Entertainment* (1600, pub. 1601), the first act of which features the piper 'Timothy Tweedle'. Crispinella's citing of 'the famous "long word, *Honorificabilitudinitatibus*"' (*Dutch C.* 5.2.24) might have inspired Barry's 'paraperopandemical' (3.3.77). Phrasal echoes between *FoL* and *The Dutch Courtesan*, such as Lipsalve's advice to Maria, 'Joy not too much, extremes are perilous' (3.3.305–6), echoing Beatrice's warning to Freevill, 'Nothing extreme lives long' (2.1.50), are persuasively accounted for by the proximity in dates of the two texts. The commentary to this edition notes many more parallels between *FoL* and contemporary literature.

APPENDIX 3
Representations of the Family of Love in *Basilicon Doron* and *The Displaying of an Horrible Sect*

King James I, *Basilicon Doron. Or His Majesty's Instructions to his Dearest Son, Henry the Prince* (1603), 'To the Reader', A3–A5v.

[In this new preface King James I identifies two points of misinterpretation arising from the publication of *Basilicon Doron* in 1599: the first concerns his sincerity in the Protestant religion; the second that 'the malicious sort of men' have construed some passages as indicating that he nurtures 'a vindictive resolution against England' for the sake of his mother's 'quarrel', i.e., on behalf of the Catholic Mary Stuart, executed for treason under Elizabeth I in 1587. His remarks about Familists are an attempt to clarify his criticism of Puritans.]

The first calumny ... is grounded upon the sharp and bitter words that therein [i.e., in *Basilicon Doron*] are used in the description of the humours of Puritans and rash-heady preachers, that think it their honour to contend with kings, and perturb whole kingdoms ... if there were no more to be   5
looked into but the very method and order of the book, it will sufficiently clear me of that first and grievousest imputation, in the point of religion, since in the first part, where religion is only treated of, I speak so plainly. And what in other parts I speak of Puritans, it is only of their moral faults, in that part   10
where I speak of policy, declaring when they condemn the law and sovereign authority what exemplar punishment they deserve

First then, as to the name of Puritans, I am not ignorant that the style thereof doth properly belong only to that   15

---

9. *exemplar*] serving as a deterrent to others (*OED* n. 2 obs.).
11. *style*] title, proper name (*OED* n. 18a 18b obs.).

vile sect amongst the Anabaptists called the Family of Love, because they think themselves only pure, and in a manner, without sin, the only true Church, and only worthy to be participant of the sacraments ... Of this special sect I principally mean when I speak of Puritans: diverse of them, as Browne, Penry, and others, having at sundry times come in Scotland to sow their popple amongst us ... and partly, indeed, I give this style to such brainsick and heady preachers, their disciples and followers, as refusing to be called of that sect, yet participates too much with their humours, in maintaining the above-mentioned errors; not only agreeing with the general rule of all Anabaptists in the contempt of the civil magistrate, and in leaning to their own dreams and revelations, but particularly with this sect, in accounting all men profane that swears not to all their fantasies; in making for every particular question of the policy of the Church as great commotion as if the article of the Trinity were called in controversy; in making the scriptures to be ruled by their conscience, and not their conscience by the scripture, and he that denies the least jot of their grounds, *sit tibi tanquam ethnicus et publicanus*; not worthy to enjoy the benefit of breathing, much less to participate with

---

16. *Browne*] Robert Browne (1550?–1633), one of the first English separatists. See Barry, *Ram Alley* 1.2.123–6: 'Panderism! Why, 'tis grown a liberal science / Or a new sect, and the good professors / Will, like the Brownist, frequent gravel pits shortly / For they use woods and obscure holes already.'
    16. *Penry*] John Penry (1562/3–1593), Welsh religious controversialist, pursued by the authorities for treasonous activities, finally executed in 1593. '[T]he conviction that Penry was Martin Marprelate lay behind his condemnation' (*ODNB*).
    16. *in*] into (*OED* adv. 1a).
    17. *popple*] weeds of the corncockle or poppy.
    21. *Anabaptists*] dissenting Puritan sect who disapproved of infant baptism. They believed in holding property in common, including wives, but their experiment in Münster in the early 1530s failed in less than a year. Jonson parodied their zealous quest for money in *The Alchemist* (1610).
    27. sit tibi tanquam ethnicus et publicanus] (Lat.), let him be unto thee as a heathen man, and a publican (Matthew 18.17). 'Publican' here means a person cut off from the Church or excommunicated (*OED* n.1 2).
    33. *in ... sect*] in calling Familists Puritans.
    35. *son*] heir to the throne, Henry, Prince of Wales (1594–1612), addressee of *Basilicon Doron*. His unexpected death in 1612 precipitated a national outbreak of mourning.

them of the sacraments; and before that any of their grounds
be impugned, let king, people, law and all be tread under foot.
Such holy wars are to be preferred unto an ungodly peace: no,
in such cases, Christian princes are not only to be resisted ...   40
but not to be prayed for ... Judge then, Christian reader, if I
wrong this sort of people in giving them the style of that sect,
whose errors they imitate ... It is only of this kind of men that
in this book I write so sharply, and whom I wish my son to
punish, in case they refuse to obey the law, and will not cease   45
to stir up a rebellion.

From J.[ohn] R.[ogers], *The Displaying of an Horrible Sect of Gross and Wicked Heretics, naming themselves the Family of Love*, 1578 (1579 edn), H3v–I2v.

[*Displaying* is one of several hostile attacks on Hendrik Niclaes published in England in the 1570s by zealous Protestant clerics. Rogers extracts statements from depositions made before a Surrey magistrate, William More, on 28 May 1561 by two ex-members of a religious group based in the village of Wonersh, near Guildford. What follows are selections from 53 enumerated points that Rogers represents as constituting the 'confession' of the two Surrey dissenters.[1] Passages that Barry echoes in *The Family of Love* are noted by line number in the commentary.]

A confession made by two of the Family of Love before a worthy and worshipful Justice of Peace, the 28 May 1561, touching the errors taught amongst them at their assemblies, and also their behaviours.

1. First, they be generally all unlearned, saving that some of   5
   them can read English, and that not very perfectly, and
   of them that can so read they have chosen bishops, elders,
   and deacons.
3. When any person shall be received into their congregation, they cause all their brethren to assemble, and the   10
   bishop or elder doth declare unto the new elected brother
   that if he will be content that all his goods shall be in
   common amongst the rest of all his brethren, he shall be
   received, whereunto he answering 'yea', then he is admitted with a kiss, viz., all the company, both men and   15
   women, kiss him, one after another.

5. They are called together ever in the night time, and commonly to such houses as be far from neighbours. One of them doth always warn another, and when they come to the house of meeting, they knock at the door, saying, 'here is a brother in Christ', or 'a sister in Christ'.
6. When they be all together before their bishop, or elder, or deacon will read the scripture unto them, he saith these words: 'All ye that are but weak and not come to perfection, withdraw yourselves a while, and pray, that you may be made worthy thereof'. Whereupon those weaklings do repair into another place, and be not partakers of the doctrine that then shall be taught, but afterwards, as the bishop, elder, or deacon seeth them frame themselves, they shall be received to hear the doctrine.
10. In the beginning of Queen Mary's time, they would not come to the church, thinking it damnable so to do. But within a year after, they were changed from that opinion, openly declaring unto their brethren that they were all bound to come unto the church, and to do outwardly there all such things as the law required then at their hands, upon pain of damnation, although inwardly they did profess the contrary.
11. They cannot abide any of their sect to pray but those that be new-received brethren, whom they call weaklings, thinking it a great fault to the rest, whom they affirm to be perfect, to pray unto God as though they were importunate troublers and vexers of him, having no need to do so.
12. They scorn all those that say, 'Good lord, have mercy upon us miserable sinners', saying, they that so say declare themselves never to amend, but still to be miserable sinners, whereas we do live perfectly and sin not.
14. They may not say, 'God save' anything. For they affirm that all things are ruled by nature and not directed by God.
15. They did prohibit bearing of weapons, but at ... length, perceiving themselves to be noted and marked for the same, they have allowed the bearing of staves.

---

50. *demandant*] questioner.

17. They may answer to every demandant (not being of their sect) in such sort as they think best shall please him. For they say they are bound to deal truly with no man in word or deed that is not of their congregation, alleging that he is no neighbour, and that therefore they may abuse him at their pleasure.
19. If any of their sect do die, the wife or husband that overliveth must marry again with one of their congregation, or else the offence is great. The marriage is made by the brethren, who bring them together sometime that dwell above a hundred miles asunder: as for example, Thomas Chaundler of Wonersh, in the county of Surrey, had his wife fetched out of the Isle of Ely by two of the congregation, the man and the woman being utter strangers before they came together to be married.
20. They do divorce ... themselves asunder if they cannot agree, before certain of the congregation, as the said Chaundler and his wife did, upon a misliking, after they had been one year married together.
22. They hold that he which is one of their congregation is either as perfect as Christ, or else a very devil.
23. They hold it is lawful to do whatsoever the higher powers command to be done, though it be against the commandment of God.
24. They deny that Christ is equal with God the father in his godhead, upon this place of scripture: 'My father is greater than I'.
25. It is odious for them to say, 'God the son', for they deny him to be God.
26. They deny the Trinity.
27. They hold that no man should be baptised before he be of the age of 30 years.
28. They hold that every man ought first to be in an error before he can come to the knowledge of the truth.
30. They hold that heaven and hell are present in this world amongst us, and that there is none other.

---

55. *overliveth*] survives her or his spouse.
60–1. *fetched ... of*] sought for and conducted back from (*OED* fetch v. 1a).
74–5. *'My father ... I'*] John 14.28.

APPENDICES

31. They hold that they are bound to give alms to none other persons but to those of their sect, and if they do, they give their alms to the devil.
33. They hold that they should so provide that, if any perish, all should perish, so that every one of them should relieve   95
him with his goods that decayeth.
40. They hold that there ought to be no Sabbath day, but that all should be like, and for that they allege, 'The son of man is Lord over the Sabbath day'.
43. They hold that there was a world before Adam's time, as   100
there is now.
44. They hold that they ought to keep silence amongst themselves, that the liberty they have in the Lord may not be espied of others.
45. They hold that no man should be put to death for his   105
opinion, therefore they condemn Master Cranmer and Master Ridley for burning Joan of Kent.
48. They brag very much of their own sincere lives, justifying themselves, saying, 'Mark, how purely we live'.

ENDNOTE

1 For discussion of the manuscript depositions, held in the Folger Shakespeare Library, see Marsh, *FLES*, 33–4, 66–7; Marsh, 'Heresy', 71, 80–1, 64n; Martin, 56, 8n. For commentary on *Displaying* in the context of Barry's play, see Loewenstein, 176, 178–81.

---

100. *Master Cranmer*] Archbishop Thomas Cranmer, one of the three 'Oxford martyrs' burned at the stake for heresy on 21 March 1556.
100. *Master Ridley*] Nicholas Ridley, an Anglican bishop, burned at the stake for heresy with fellow bishop Hugh Latimer on 16 October 1555.
101. *Joan ... Kent*] Joan Bocher (d. 2 May 1550), also known as Joan of Kent, an English Anabaptist burned at the stake for heresy in Smithfield during the Protestant reign of King Edward VI.

Index

Alberti, Leon Battista 30–1
Anabaptism 13, 42, 216, 220
angels 1.2.149
Apollo 76, 153, 192
Archer, Edward 19
ardour, Epilogue 9
Armin, Robert
  Tarleton's News out of Purgatory
  25
Aristotle 159, 4.3.11
arms across 1.2.4
a-tilt 2.3.6
authorship, collaborative 20,
  52n91

Baker, Richard 11
Bald, R.C. 24, 53nn113–14
Barksted, William 55n144
barriers 30, 3.3.27
Barry, Lording 1
  attribution of *FoL* to 19–23
  biography of 9–13, 50nn51–3
  critical attitudes to 49–50n50
  The Family of Love (*FoL*)
    'Actorum Nomina' 3, 61–2
    authorship of 19–23
    choice of title 18–19
    conclusion of 45–7
    critical response to 33–4
    date of composition 14–18
    emendations to text 6–8
    genre of 34–9
    language and style 39–43
    marginal annotations in 8–9,
      212–13
    marriage and sexuality in 43–5
    'Marstonian' features of 214
    printing of 1–6
    Sig. Av of 1608 Quarto 4
    sources and intertexts 23–9
    staging and stagecraft 10,
      29–33, 50n67
    title page 58

'To the Reader' 2–3, 8, 15,
  59–60
Ram Alley
  and *commedia dell'arte* 27
  expressions in common with
    FoL 65, 119, 145, 154,
    170, 172, 178, 190–2,
    195, 203
  Familism in 19
  influences on text of 23
  parallels with *FoL* 21
  performances of 10
  Robert Browne in 216
  theatricality in 32
Barry, Nicholas 9
bass 1.3.179
bastards, euphemisms for 165
bawds 2.4.160, 4.1.35–41
bawdy court 5.1.82–3
beard, red 61, 5.1.13, 72–3,
  5.3.144
Beaumont, Francis
  Knight of the Burning Pestle 17,
    51n74, 55n148, 112, 144
Bedlam 4.3.125
Bell, Maureen 59
bellows-menders 4.1.19
Bennett, Edward 12
best companion 32, 1.2.84
bewray 39, 5.3.118, 228, 309
Blackfriars 10, 29, 49n34,
  55n138
Bly, Mary 2, 22, 41, 43, 56n167
Bocardo 52n92, 1.3.8
Boccaccio, Giovanni
  Decameron 23, 52n109
Bocher, Joan 220
bodices 97, 199
bodkin 1.3.148, 154
bonds 1.3.53
Book of Common Prayer 102, 114,
  117
Bowers, Fredson 20

221

* box 5.3.65
boy companies 85, 178
Bradock, Richard 2–3
Breame, Thomasine 164
breeches 103, 4.3.122
Brewer, Thomas 86
Bridewell 166, 175
brother 3.2.91
Browne, John 3
Browne, Robert 216
Brussels 34, 95
Bullen, Arthur H. 1, 8, 19
bungholes 4.2.64
burlesque 28
buxom 3.4.2

Calvert, Samuel 48n24
caps 5.3.9
carnal crudities 2.3.60
carnival misrule 44, 46
cartship 2.3.11
cast 39, 5.3.228
Cathcart, Charles 18, 22, 52n100, 214
censorship 6–7, 17–18, 48n24, 171
Chakravorty, Swapan 25
Chapman, George
  EHo! (with Jonson and Marston) 50n65
  Sir Giles Goosecap 50n65
chapmen 'To the Reader' 9
charges 4.1.64
Chaucer, Geoffrey 13, 52n96, 71–2, 139, 141, 172, 174–5
  in *FoL* 21–2, 24, 120
  'Friar's Tale' 24, 141, 174
chest, infiltrating a woman's room in a 23, 53n109
child that came in at the window 4.3.114
Children of the King's Revels 1–2, 13, 214
  age of 31
  foundation of 9–11
  at Whitefriars Playhouse 29
Children of the Queen's Revels 48n24
Children of the Whitefriars 29
* cincture 3.4.3

circle, vulva as 120, 5.1.12
citizen comedy 34, 43
city comedies 34–5
City (of London) 60, 4.3.54
  Corporation, 'To the Reader' 13
Cleary, Chris 1
close-stool 34, 47, 1.3.145, 3.3.17, 5.3.248
club, 'Names of the Characters' 7
Club Law (play) 26–8, 52n92, 54n131, 94, 134, 146, 161, 189, 197
Clubb, Louise 25–6, 53n118
club-law 38, 45–6, 5.3.4
clyster 39, 61, 140
codpiece 3.1.143, 200
colours 5.1.86–7
come 3.1.57–9
commedia dell'arte 27
commedia erudita 23, 26
common custom 79
'communialtie' 19, 51n80
condescension, mock 85
conjoinèd 40, 2.4.33
copyhold 38, 5.3.190
Corbin, Peter 32
Cornelius' tub 3.3.54–5
corner-cap 4.1.15
corps 40, 2.4.38
cosmetics 80
cottons 3.1.128, 5.1.55, 5.3.30
Cranmer, Thomas 220
creeping to 1.2.14
crew 37–8, 5.3.185
cucking-stool 5.1.25
cuckoldry 66, 69, 1.3.163, 3.2.55, 3.4.78, 4.2.37, 73, 3.3.78, 44, 5.1.53, 5.3.113, 223, 408
  see also horns
cuckoo 5.1.27
Cupid 66, 1.2.1, 113, 143, 4.2.11, 13, 5.3.160
Curtal 4.3.71
Cynthia 5.2.20

Dahl, Marcus 23
Day, John
  Humour Out of Breath 2
  Isle of Gulls 50n65

deadly 5.2.8
death-day 1.2.8
Dekker, Thomas 1, 19–21
Della Porta, Giambattista 25–6, 53–4n122
  La Furiosa 25–6, 53n117, 54n122
diarrhoea 138, 148, 186, 188
Dillon, Andrew 1–3, 5, 8, 24
Do Little Lane 34, 5.3.356
doings 2.3.81
good 2.1.5
Drayton, Michael 9, 49n34
dryvats 61, 156
Dutton, Richard 33
Dyce, Alexander 1, 3, 5–8, 19

Eberle, Gerald 20
Edward of London (ship) 12
Egeon 4.2.92
elders 33, 'Names of the Characters' 12
elements 4.4.58
Elizabeth I, Queen 13–14
Ellis, Havelock 1
Elysium 40, 2.4.35
emblem 5.1.16
* encumbrances 1.3.79
enlarge 1.1.32, 1.2.124
* enow 5.3.49
envy's tooth, Prologue 7
epigrams 70, 5.1.40
Europa 153, 4.4.15
Ewen, Cecil L'Estrange 10

Falstaff 44, 203
Familism
  in *FoL* 27, 31, 36–8, 46–7, 51n80, 55n160
  King James' attack on 10, 13
  plays about 14
  teachings of 13–14, 129, 157
  terms used for members 133
  writings of 42–3
Family of Love (sect) 10, 13–14, 18, 215–20
  other names for 194
  see also Familism
* far seen 2.4.152
fasting 1.1.41
firk 2.4.189

Fishmongers' Company 9, 12
flax 5.1.36
  flaxen stuff 5.1.16
footcloth 2.4.97
forsooth 1.3.10, 2.4.61, 4.3.24–5, 40, 44
fox fur 2.3.33–4
Fraser, Robert 10–11
Freebury-Jones, Darren xii, xxi, 22–3, 27, 52
freehold 38, 82, 5.3.190

Galen 4.1.105
gallery 1.1.31
gender, *FoL*'s representation of 26
general round, Prologue 2
Geneva, blockade of 17, 21, 5.3.268–9
genitals, female *see* vagina; vulva
gentility 1.3.37
George, David 25
gold 3.1.27, 5.1.76
great-breeched 1.1.7–8
green sickness 5.3.349
Greene, Robert 53n113
Greg, W.W. 3, 19
grey-eyed 2.1.1
grincomes 1.3.12, 5.3.353
groat-monger 4.4.165
groat, grey 4.4.110
groin 4.4.8
gudgeon, 'Names of the Characters' 6
  use of name in Marston 214

hair
  gold 5.1.76
  red 5.1.15
hairlaces 1.2.41
Helen of Troy 92
Helmes, John 3
Helms, Anne 3
Henry, Prince of Wales 215–16
herbals 4.1.110
Hercules 5.3.138
Hilton, Walter 43
Holborn Bridge 34, 4.2.121
Hole in the Wall (tavern) 31, 5.3.95
Holmes, David 54n125
hornbook 5.1.124

hornets 5.3.99
horns 66, 1.2.1, 2.1.6, 12,
    3.2.126–9, 169, 181,
    5.1.118, 194, 5.3.209,
    214, 208
hot-house 3.3.12
hotspurs 5.1.132
Huguenots 1.2.148
humorous 2.2.3, 3.4.24, 4.3.91
humours 34, 1.1.23
Hymen 3.1.182, 143

Ignatius, Saint 43
incest 25–6, 34, 41, 45, 4.3.119,
    191, 207
incomprehensible 3.1.12
Inns of Court 9, 29, 59, 2.4.3,
    155
intertextuality, seven types of 27
ivy 3.1.144

Jack of Dover, his Quest of Inquiry
    25
Jackson, MacDonald P. 13, 17,
    19–22, 35, 51n76
James I, King 9–10, 13–14, 17,
    54n122, 174
    Basilicon Doron 13–14, 215–17
jests 22–3, 3.1.55, 5.3.3
Jonson, Ben 22, 28–30
    Alch. 28, 34
    EHo! (with Chapman and
        Marston) 50n65
    Epicene 29, 34, 55n139, 59,
        156
    EMO 41, 61, 99–100
    and Inns of Court 101
    and masques 150
    *Private Entertainment of the King
        and Queen* 161
    Volp. 29, 38
jordans 5.3.342
judgement, Prologue 4

Kemble, John Philip 1, 212–13
Kemp's Nine Days' Wonder 24,
    155
* kiss behind 2.3.19
knaves 4.3.58
knowledge, carnal 4.1.62

lace 3.1.171
Lake, David 20
laxatives 25–6, 53n119, 97,
    3.3.40, 148, 186, 201
lectuary 2.3.57–8
lecturing, private 3.2.105
left-side 1.2.26
limb-lifter 6, 45, 5.3.374
link 3.2.0
lipsalve, 'Names of the Characters'
    5
Little Ease 17, 30, 114, 3.1.9
liver 2.3.97, 5.1.77
livery 5.1.127
Lollardy 42
loose-bodied 2.3.55, 121
Lopez, Jeremy 9
Lording, Alice 12
Lording, Anne 9
Love, Harold 23
lure 1.2.147
lute 32, 1.2.70.1, 84

Machin, Lewis
    Every Woman in Her Humour
        50n65
MacIntyre, Jean 30
malapropisms 102, 107, 134
Mantuanus, Baptista 2–3
Marlowe, Christopher 22, 40
    Dr Faust. 40
    Hero and Leander 40, 113, 123
Marsh, Christopher 13, 18, 20, 33
Marston, John 14, 18–19, 22–3
    Dutch C. 14, 18, 23, 32, 38,
        50n65, 51n76, 73, 214
    EHo! (with Chapman and
        Jonson) 50n65
    JDE 28, 164, 214
masques 67, 4.1.91
Massinger, Phillip
    Parliament of Love 53n119
maternity, performance of 44
maw 5.3.142
McKerrow, Ronald 3
Michaelmas 6, 147, 4.4.77
    Michaeltide 4.1.50
Middleton, Thomas
    attribution of *FoL* to 1–2, 7,
        19–22

INDEX

and Barry 10
Chang. (with Rowley) 53n119
Chaste Maid 36, 43
Fair Quarrel (with Rowley) 43
and Familism 14
Mad World 14, 50n65
No Wit, No Help 26, 53n122
Trick 49n41
Yorkshire Tragedy 2–3, 15
minikin 1.3.179
Miola, Robert 27–8
monstrum horrendum 3.1.60
More, William 217
movables 1.3.132–8, 5.3.194
Mulholland, Paul 13, 17, 19, 21, 35
mummeries 4.1.91
muscadine 5.1.18
music 32

neatest, 'To the Reader' 7
Neill, Michael 51n76
neo-Ovidianism 54n134
Niclaes, Hendrik 13, 19, 28, 40, 42, 104, 161, 217
Norfolk 4.1.4
Notting, Roger 11
now, 'To the Reader' 11

opportunity 2.5.58
Ordo Sacerdotis 42
organs 42, 3.2.25–8
overture 1.1.27

paints 1.3.6–9
pamphlet literature 24
pandemic 140
paraperopandemical 3.3.77
Paracelsus 4.1.105
paritor 4.2.43–4, 49
parody 17, 22, 31, 54n136
* pass upon 45, 5.3.3
pastiche 22, 27, 34
pearls 1.3.148
penis, euphemisms for 67, 88, 173, 179, 181, 186, 198
Penry, John 216
pepper 5.1.88
perfection 37, 2.4.68
Petronel Flashes 3.1.166

Phitonissa 3.4.5
Phoebus 1.2.97
    see also Apollo
Pissing Alley 34, 5.3.328, 355
Pluto 157, 4.4.106
pocky 3.3.77
Poole, Kristen 14, 20
Popham, Sir John 6, 18, 171
porters 1.3.108, 4.3.46
    London Company of 15–18
pothecary 45, 'Names of the Characters' 2
pox 3.3.51, 5.1.88, 5.3.352
prentice, 'Names of the Characters' 7–8
press money 5.3.401
pricks 1.1.25
prostitutes 74, 156, 164
    on carts 94
    compared to plays 59
    in *Dutch Court.* 73
    terms for 123, 140
    in Whitefriars 29
protestations 1.3.53
proud 2.3.92
puns 41–2
purging comfits 2.3.55
Puritanism 10, 13, 131–3, 3.3.79–80, 197, 215–16
    against drama 86

quick 1.2.126
quiddits 5.3.17
quiver 2.3.40
quotations 22, 27, 5.3.103

rack-rent 1.2.67
Raleigh, Sir Walter 12
restorative 3.1.162
revengeable 1.2.36
riding 1.2.103, 2.4.21, 3.1.150, 3.2.15
Ridley, Nicholas 220
ring
    riding the 2.4.21
    running at the 5.3.295
rogation 2.3.15
Rogers, John 27
    Displaying 27, 217–20
Roman New Comedy 38

ropture 3.1.111
rout 37–8, 5.3.187
Rowlands, Samuel 53n113
Rowley, William 43
  Birth of Merlin 44
  Chang. (with Middleton) 53n119
  Fair Quarrel (with Middleton) 43
ruffs 35, 2.3.51, 145, 5.3.186
Ruggle, George 26, 53n122, 54n131
rundlets 2.3.8
running heads 2.3.8–9

sables 2.3.33
Samson 33, 1.3.100, 103–5
satiety 40, 2.4.40, 212
satires 19, 34–5, 54n131, 5.1.39
Scarborough, Charles 12
Scarborough, Edward 12
Scarborough, Edmund 12
scatology 56n164
Scott, Jonathan 51n78, 55n149
Scott, Sarah 19
sect 2.4.31
sectarianism 35, 42
Sedge, Douglas 32
sequester 1.1.30
Shadwell, Thomas
  Squire of Alsatia 29
Shakespeare, William
  All's Well 44
  Cymbeline 24
  FoL as pastiche of 22
  making Italian sources chaste 56n172
  Merchant 33
  R&J 28
Shapiro, Michael 43
Shepherd, Simon 1, 21–2
Sherley, Sir Thomas 17
Silus, Titus 4.1.120–1
sir-reverence 39, 47, 4.3.84–5, 5.3.247
sister 3.2.91
Slater, Martin 32
smell-smock 2.3.82
spirits 5.1.11
Spufford, Margaret 39
squares 1.3.95

St John, William 11
standing 1.3.144
standing collars 35, 2.3.43
starry-spangled 1.2.88
startups, dirty 35, 162, 4.3.60
statutes 1.1.3
  statutes staple 1.3.86
Stickler 5.3.28
stone-horse 45, 5.3.374
stones 4.3.138–9, 5.1.102
Stubbes, Philip
  Anatomy of Abuses (Stubbes) 52n92
stuffed 1.3.21
suppository 61, 3.3.71
Swetnam the Woman Hater 61
Swinburne, Algernon 1, 33
syphilis 81, 139–40, 206

taps-droppings 34, 4.3.73
Tarlinskaja, Marina 23
Tartarus 4.2.92
Taylor, Gary 13, 17, 19, 21, 35
tenters 3.1.126
termers, 'To the Reader' 9
term-time 1.2.67
Thomas à Kempis 43
Thomasine Tweedles 41, 4.3.97, 214
thrum 4.4.167
tickles 1.3.113, 179, 2.4.145, 4.4.93
Tower of London 17
Trench, John 17, 30
trow 36–7, 4.4.52
twelvepence 4.4.134

upper stage 30, 33, 67, 69, 1.2.50, 116

vacation, long 2.3.17
vagina, euphemisms for 73, 81, 96, 120, 155–6, 179–81, 202
* vapour 4.1.25
vented, 'To the Reader' 8
Venus 153, 4.2.97.99, 175, 5.1.15, 197
vessel of ease 37, 2.4.143
Vittels, Christopher 13

vulva: as circle 120, 177; liquids
    and smells emitted from 170

wagship 2.3.9
wagtail 1.2.40
wainscot 3.2.112
Walter, Melissa 53n110
wanting worth, Prologue 9
Welshmen 1.3.42, 4.2.24
Werstine, Paul 48n16
whipping cheer 2.3.36
Whitefriars
    and Inner Temple 101
    as sanctuary 29
Whitefriars Playhouse 9–11
    Articles of Agreement 15, 32, 51n71
    FoL at 29–32
    great hall of 29, 54–5n138
    upper stage 75

Wiggins, Martin 6–7, 17, 19, 21, 54n131
Wilkins, George 15
Williams, Deanne 32
wind colic 5.1.101
window 1.2.70
windy 1.2.57
winnowing 1.2.59
Winwood, Ralph 48n24
wits, 'To the Reader' 13
wolves 2.5.51, 3.1.28
woodcock 2.4.119
Woodford, Thomas 49n44
wool-packs 1.3.82

Yaxley, John 54n131
yeomen 1.3.41

zeal 3.2.56

EU authorised representative for GPSR:
Easy Access System Europe, Mustamäe tee 50,
10621 Tallinn, Estonia
gpsr.requests@easproject.com